Counseling Families

Counseling Families

Play-Based Treatment

Edited by Eric J. Green, Jennifer N. Baggerly,
and Amie C. Myrick

ROWMAN & LITTLEFIELD
Lanham • Boulder • New York • London

Published by Rowman & Littlefield
A wholly owned subsidiary of The Rowman & Littlefield Publishing Group, Inc.
4501 Forbes Boulevard, Suite 200, Lanham, Maryland 20706
www.rowman.com

Unit A, Whitacre Mews, 26-34 Stannary Street, London SE11 4AB

British Library Cataloguing in Publication Information Available

Library of Congress Cataloging-in-Publication Data

Counseling families : play-based treatment / edited by Eric J. Green, Jennifer N. Baggerly, and Amie C. Myrick.
pages cm
Includes bibliographical references and index.
ISBN 978-1-4422-4404-7 (cloth : alk. paper) -- ISBN 978-1-4422-4415-3 (pbk. : alk. paper) -- ISBN 978-1-4422-4414-6 (electronic)
1. Family psychotherapy. 2. Play therapy. I. Green, Eric J., editor. II. Baggerly, Jennifer, editor. III. Myrick, Amie, editor.
RC488.5.C6788 2015
616.89'156--dc23
2015034949

™ The paper used in this publication meets the minimum requirements of American National Standard for Information Sciences—Permanence of Paper for Printed Library Materials, ANSI/NISO Z39.48-1992.

Printed in the United States of America

I dedicate this book to my grandmother, Edith, as well as my late grandfather, Pappy, for providing a safe home filled with music, food, and joy, which helped me understand, at a young age, what family is.

—Eric Green

I dedicate this book to my mother, Jean Louise Baggerly, for cultivating in me our family legacy of faith in God, which I proudly pass on to my daughter, Katelyn Jean.

—Jennifer Baggerly

To my family, who, every day, makes me proud to be a daughter, sister, niece, aunt, cousin, wife, and mother. I love you.

—Amie Myrick

Contents

III: Clinical Applications for Psychosocial and Developmental Issues

Foreword

Louise F. Guerney

I am honored to have been asked to write this foreword for this valuable book. I am really grateful that the editors included me in this work. It is especially meaningful because the editors are members of the new leadership in the profession of play therapy. I think it is valuable to have new leadership connecting with the "old" play therapy leadership. Such continuity is to be rewarded and nurtured. From our history comes the future.

As a truism goes, no young child has ever been known to appear alone at the door of a clinician seeking personal behavioral or psychological help. The implication of this truism is that some adult, in all probability a family member, has decided that the child is suffering from a problem that requires professional service. It is also presumed that, in small or major ways, a family member (generally a parent or parent surrogate) will in fact bring in the child and later become involved in any recommended intervention. Schools can be the exception because they can provide services within the school setting without the direct involvement of family members. Inevitably, all members are linked in both positive and negative ways.

Whether or not a clinician believes that family involvement is necessary to bring about desirable changes in a child's life, the contribution of family members to a child problem cannot be denied. As clinicians know, without a positive role in child intervention, parents can sabotage the clinician's efforts to help the child. Since clinicians must recognize the inevitability of the family as a system, they need to adopt a therapeutic approach that is designed to involve all relevant family members in a meaningful way. The method chosen, of course, must be compatible with their theoretical beliefs and intervention techniques. Only by doing so can they bring about desired changes in the entire family system.

For this book, the editors have selected five empirically validated methods that do just that: cognitive behavioral therapy, Theraplay®, Filial Therapy, Jungian therapy, and Adlerian. All of these provide a positive role for family members in play approaches with children. In Part II of the book, the editors have highlighted three specific clinical groups: divorced and blended families, autistic children, and traumatized children. The respective authors of these chapters describe how a family method can be utilized effectively to meet the needs of these specific groups.

The chapter "Play-Based Family Assessment and Treatment Planning," written by Koehler, Wilson, and Baggerly, completes this part of the book. The authors of this chapter provide clear descriptions of assessment instruments and techniques that would be appropriate for use with the populations in this section, as well as other types of child/family presentations encountered in clinical practice. Appropriate use of assessment instruments can be of great value to clinicians in treatment planning.

Over the years, for a variety of reasons, the particular family approaches professionals choose to use tend to vary according to their discipline. Linda Homeyer identifies, in a very comprehensive and insightful chapter on supervision, another truism—that it seems to be easier for family counselors to expand the scope of their child work to include family members than for family therapists to utilize methods that provide the child with a meaningful role in a family intervention. My supposition is that family mental health therapists are generally not educated in child therapy within their graduate programs. This book provides, methodically laid out by each of the authors, methods that should be compatible with the respective disciplined philosophies and practices of all mental health providers.

In the field of family counseling, as reflected in this book, there exist differences in the degree to which all family members serve as change agents. Typically, the counselor assigns family participants a therapeutic task. The execution of the therapy lies with the counselor.

Two of the methods described in this book, Theraplay and Filial Therapy, rely on family members (generally parents or parent surrogates) to execute the direct therapy with the child. The parents provide the services in play therapy with the child under the instruction and supervision of the professional therapist. The advantage to assigning a therapeutic role to the parents is that they become temporarily removed from the entanglements of the family dynamics. They learn new ways of relating to the child. They execute new concepts and perceptions of family relationships. To use a well-worn but appropriate expression, parents become part of the solution, instead of part of the problem.

My long-term bias toward parents as change agents shows here, but I am not apologizing. I acknowledge that parents as therapists are not for every case and every therapist, but for those seeking to broaden their clinical skills, they are relatively easy to learn and can be incorporated in whatever their professional orientation.

The editors have concluded the book with a section on professional development. The first chapter on supervision of family therapists, by Homeyer and Lyles, lays out some of the complexities for family therapists to include play for the children in a family model. The second chapter in this section is by Rosalind Heiko, who offers self-care recommendations for therapists themselves, since they are subject to burnout due to psychological and physical pressures.

The chapters in this section add a splendid touch by providing support for therapists wishing to use family approaches. Family counselors are called upon to perform many roles, which can be emotionally taxing. It is not uncommon that therapists experience some conflict, and perhaps even trauma at times, arising from their own family-of-origin life experiences when they work with families—this can be draining.

I would like to compliment the editors and the authors of all the chapters for a job well done. This book is a valuable contribution to anyone practicing or learning play therapy and/or family therapy.

Louise F. Guerney, PhD, RPT-S
Professor Emerita, The Pennsylvania State University
National Institute of Relationship Enhancement, Bethesda, MD
July 2015

Introduction

Eric Green, Amie Myrick, and Jennifer Baggerly

THE GARDEN OF ENCHANTMENTS[1]

Once upon a time, in faraway Persia, there lived a good king and queen who had three children. Unfortunately, the children were separated from their parents at birth by their evil aunts, who placed each of the newborn babies in a willow basket and floated them down a stream. As luck would have it, an old gardener and his wife who had no children of their own rescued the babies. Convinced that God had answered their prayers, they lovingly named the boys Farid and Firoz, and the girl, Farina. When the old gardener was on his deathbed, he told the children the story of how he had found them in little baskets in the stream. He also gave them three gold coins with the king's crest on them that he had found in the baskets. He told them that one day the coins would help them find true happiness.

One day, when the two brothers had gone hunting and Farina was alone at home, an old woman knocked at the garden gate. She admired the lovely, scented flowers, and the trees laden with delicious figs, plums, pomegranates, and apricots. "My dear, your garden is beautiful, but it is missing three things. It is missing the rare talking bird that knows and tells the truth, the singing tree that sings stories, and the golden water. If you get these, your garden will be truly enchanted and you will get everything you deserve!"

"Where will I find them?" asked Farina. The old woman replied, "You must travel towards Hindustan [India] for twenty days. Then you will meet an old man who will tell you all you need to know." After a while, the old lady thanked Farina and went on her way.

That evening, Farina told her brothers what the old lady said. The oldest brother, Farid, agreed to go. As he prepared to leave, he gave his gleaming dagger to his sister saying, "As long as the blade is clean, you will know I am safe." Then he set off on his long journey east. For twenty days and twenty nights, all was well. On the twenty-first day, the blade turned rusty. Farina was distraught with worry.

"I will go," said Firoz. Before he left, he gave a string of pearls to his sister saying, "While they glow, I am safe." For twenty days and twenty nights, all was well. Then on the twenty-first day, the pearls turned brown and dry. Farina, who was a spirited and brave girl, quickly disguised herself as a warrior for protection and rode off to save her beloved brothers. For twenty days and twenty nights, she rode swiftly. On the twenty-first day, she met an old holy man sitting under a tree. Even though his hair and beard were as white as snow, his eyes were bright.

"Have you seen my brothers?" she asked him. "They came here looking for the talking bird, the singing tree, and the golden water." The hermit replied sadly, "Many a young man has passed this way, never to return. I tried to help, but they forgot my advice and got into trouble." Farina begged him to help her find her brothers.

So he gave her a round, red rock and said, "Roll this up the mountain. If you reach the top, all will be well. However, do not, even for a moment, listen or pay attention to the multitude of voices you will hear on the way or you will turn into stone."

Farina rolled the rock up the mountain. As she climbed, she started hearing voices calling to her. She bravely ignored the loud, desperate voices and climbed higher and higher, till the voices faded and she reached the top. She found herself in an exquisite garden. The talking bird was waiting for her, while the singing tree was singing a sweet song and the golden water in the fountain appeared as pure liquid gold.

"Oh, Bird," said Farina, "this is all very beautiful, but where are my brothers?"

"I will help you," said the talking bird. "First, pick a branch of the singing tree to plant in your garden. Then fill that crystal jug with the golden water. I will lead you home. On the way, be sure to sprinkle drops of golden water on every rock you pass."

Brave Farina did as she was told and followed the bird down the mountain, sprinkling golden water on every rock she passed, and every rock turned into a young man. Farid and Firoz were among the dozens of young men who had come on this quest. They were happy to be rescued by their sister and went home. The talking bird built a little nest in their garden. The branch grew into a singing tree singing never ceasing melodies, and the golden water made their fountain sparkle like sunshine. Once more, there was peace, beauty, contentment, and happiness in their enchanted garden.

One day, the king of the land disguised as a hunter strayed into their garden. He had heard all about the wonders of this enchanted garden. The talking bird quickly flew to Farina and told her that this was their day of destiny, and the visitor was none other than the king himself. "King," said the talking bird, "ask them to show you what their father gave them before he died." Farid hurried off to bring the three gold coins their father had given them on his deathbed. The king looked carefully at the coins and saw his royal crest on the other side. Time lingered in that enchanted garden as the king felt a cloud lift from his memory. He remembered that he had made these three coins for his three children when they were born. "Where did you get these?" he asked Farid.

Before Farid could answer, the talking bird replied, "Your majesty, these are your long-lost children. They are Farid, Firoz, and Farina." The king felt faint with happiness. These were his children! He embraced his children. As they listened, the singing tree began to sing the whole story from the beginning. It sang about the kind gardener and his wife, about the brave deeds of Farina and her brothers. The king was enthralled by the story. He would spend the rest of his days to make up for all the lost time and love. Now, there was happiness and love in store for them, leaving no room for sorrow and bitterness in their hearts.

This fable illustrates the importance of bonds as families adapt to changes in the family and challenges in life. In the story, we read how three children are cared for and nurtured by adoptive parents who teach them the beauty of a garden. After the death of the adoptive parents, a challenging quest, and a bit of magic, the three grown children are reunited with their biological parents. Magic and mirth abound in their enchanted garden once again. The essence of the story is analogous to the purpose of this book: that during changes in family and challenges in life children can find comfort and solace in relationships with people they identify as family, biological or otherwise.

The term "family" has become more inclusive over the years (Belkin, 2011), no longer referring simply to a biological mother, father, and child. Today, the term often invokes images of children accompanied by one, two, or many adults of different genders, ages, and ethnicities. Parenthood is inherently stressful; however, children also represent an expansion of the self, purpose, fun, security, and motivation to be successful for many parents (Hoffman & Hoffman, 1973). In these ways, children are centrally located within the family structure, and it would stand to reason that any family counseling would include them. Alternatively, we know that including parents in work with children is tremendously helpful in achieving positive mental health outcomes (Carr, 2014), so it would make sense that parents are involved in child-focused therapies as well.

Historically, however, theorists and clinicians have been divided about including both parents and children in therapy, with many believing that parents and children should be treated separately or that one party should be omitted completely. For example, Virginia Axline believed it was unnecessary for parents to be present in play therapy, and Melanie Klein viewed parents as intrusive in the process (Carey, 1999). Carl Jung saw no reason to include children in therapy, as he considered children's problems to be reflections of unresolved parental issues (Wickes, 1988). Others made strong cases for the inclusion of both parents and children in counseling. In the field of family counseling, Carl Whitaker and David Keith (1981) noticed that change occurred more slowly when children were excluded from the process, and other prominent theorists and clinicians made similar, strong cases for including children in family counseling (e.g., Ackerman, 1970; Chasin & White, 1989; Minuchin, 1974). In play therapy, theorists identified the importance of parents' involvement in child treatment, resulting in the development of treatments such as Filial Therapy (Guerney, 1964) and Theraplay (Jernberg, 1979). Both approaches enhanced family interactions but neither provided opportunities to directly address family dynamics and marital issues.[2]

Today, many clinicians in the play therapy and family counseling fields continue to separate parents and children during therapeutic work. One study found that many family counselors excluded children completely from family sessions, while others included children but did not engage with them during sessions (Johnson & Thomas, 1999). Why the disparity? Many family counselors feel at a loss when it comes to actively including children in treatment (Haslam & Harris, 2011), particularly because children's engagement tends to involve less verbal expression (Landreth, 2012) and many family therapy training programs fail to adequately teach child-focused interventions (Oehlers & Shortland-Jones, 2013). They may struggle to incorporate play into their theoretical orientation, worry about the cost of acquiring toys and expressive arts materials, or fear appearing foolish or incompetent to the adult clients in the room (Gil, 2014).

For many play therapists, family issues are a common area of focus in their practices (Ryan, Gomory, & Lacasse, 2002), and some authors have suggested that play therapists may be more open to the idea of integrating family counseling and play therapy than family counselors are (Haslam & Harris, 2011). Yet, many play therapists feel inadequate in their ability to treat older, adult members of the family (Gil, 2014), and their openness to integrating play therapy with family counseling seems to decrease as children enter adolescence (Haslam & Harris, 2011). Furthermore, some play therapists may struggle to inject systemic thinking into their conceptualization of cases, and may miss opportunities to enhance treatment or utilize play as a means of family assessment as a result (Gil, 2014).

Finally, play therapists and counselors who expand their practice to include treating families invariably touch upon the issue of their own families of origin. Whenever counselors engage professionally with family systems, their own disaffected or disconnected familial themes may become activated.

For instance, relational dynamics, responsive communication, family traditions, and intergenerational elements passed down may activate the countertransference within the clinician's own family-of-origin subtext, as well as archetypal roles such as a caring mother and distant father (Green, 2014). These dynamic psychological issues are an inevitable part of every family's life. However, if counselors have not analyzed their own familial themes, and if they have not addressed their influence on the shaping of their behaviors in their adult lives, they are at risk for being psychologically triggered when they enter the dynamics of their clients' family systems. This may result in undermining their ethical ability to maintain the professional role of neutrality and may contaminate the transference. Training in family systems theory with an emphasis on exploring one's own family of origin is an essential mechanism to prepare mental health clinicians to work effectively with families (M. A. Paré, personal communication, April 8, 2015).

Family-based interventions have begun gaining popularity in the child treatment field (Kaslow, Broth, Smith, & Collins, 2012). This book was born out of this increasing enthusiasm for family involvement as well as a recognition that many play and family counselors still struggle to incorporate each other's philosophies into their work. Our hope is that this book will assist counselors in viewing referrals through a wider lens, considering how and where families can be integrated into children's therapy and how children can be actively involved in family work.

Through this book, we also aim to add meaningfully to the current literature on play in family counseling, keeping in mind the humanistic aim upon which much of play and family therapy is built. The power of the humanistic approach was elucidated by a family therapy pioneer, Virginia Satir (1972), who said, "feelings of worth can flourish only in an atmosphere where individual differences are appreciated, mistakes are tolerated, communication is open, and rules are flexible—the kind of atmosphere that is found in a nurturing family" (p. 13). Unfortunately, this powerful aspect of treatment is often overshadowed by current emphasis on standardized, evidence-based treatment protocols. Research on mental health disorders in children suggests that insight therapies such as family play counseling are effective because they foster positive psychological capacities for youth and their caretakers (Shedler, 2010). Furthermore, Shedler identified multiple factors specific to the insight-based approach that can be easily integrated within evidence-based treatment approaches: (a) focus on affect and expression of emotion, (b) identification of themes and recurring patterns, (c) focus on the therapy relationship, and (d) the exploration of fantasy life.

Thus, this book strives to provide the most current research-supported trends in family counseling interventions so that you, the mental health clinician, may incorporate them into your current practice competently. We intended for this book to clearly and practically link current scientific validation with play therapy interventions within a humanistic framework. The book is unique as many of the chapters include new research developed by the authors that substantiates the integration of play-based interventions within family counseling.

Part I of this volume includes various theoretical approaches that are integrative and humanistic in nature, including family based cognitive behavioral therapy (CBT), Theraplay, Filial Therapy, Jungian family play counseling, and Adlerian family play therapy. Part II examines assessment and family play counseling with various clinical groups, including children affected by autism, divorce, and trauma. Part III includes integrative applications in family play counseling, including the seminal work from Robert Jason Grant in autism, as well as a section on diverse and blended families, and finally Sueann Kenney-Noziska's well-written and insightful chapter on families experiencing sexual trauma. Part IV, the conclusion, provides the reader with information on competent clinical supervision with play therapists utilizing family counseling and vice-versa, as well as a chapter on the critical aspect of self-care in mental health work.

While not an exhaustive edition, we hope that you, the reader, will glean practical pieces of information to assist in furthering knowledge and awareness of the importance of play with families, especially those with young children, when providing psychotherapeutic services. We encourage the reader to seek out additional materials on this topic such as the family puppet interview (Irwin & Malloy, 1994), as well as the seminal books on family play therapy that inspired this volume, including Gil (2014) and Schaefer and Carey (1994). Also, we encourage the reader to seek out the newest work on conducting Filial Therapy with parents in group settings (Guerney & Ryan, 2013). Our book, which incorporates elements from these impressive collections, along with a commitment to professional development and supervised practice, will assist clinicians in furthering their competency in treating families with young children.

NOTES

1. "Thanks" to Kalpana Saxena, a professional storyteller residing in New Orleans, Louisiana, who wrote "The Garden of Enchantments" specifically for this book.
2. We are indebted to Mary Anne Paré for sharing her comprehensive knowledge of the history of integrating family counseling and play therapy.

REFERENCES

Ackerman, N. (1970). Child participation in family therapy. *Family Process, 9*, 403–410.

Belkin, L. (2011). A "normal" family. Retrieved March 15, 2015, from http://parenting.blogs.nytimes.com/2011/02/23/a-normal-family/.

Carey, L. (1999). *Sandplay therapy with children and their families.* Northvale, NJ: Jason Aronson.
Carr, A. (2014). The evidence base for family therapy and systemic interventions for child focused problems. *Journal of Family Therapy, 36*(2), 107–157. doi:10.1111/1467-6427.12032.
Chasin, R., & White, T. (1989). The child in family therapy: Guidelines for active engagement across the age span. In L. Combrinck-Graham (Ed.), *Children in family contexts: Perspectives on treatment* (pp. 3–25). New York, NY: Guilford Press.
Gil, E. (2014). *Play in family therapy* (2nd ed.). New York, NY: Guilford Press.
Green, E. J. (2014). *The handbook of Jungian play therapy.* Baltimore, MD: Johns Hopkins University Press.
Guerney, B. G. (1964). Filial therapy: Description and rationale. *Journal of Consulting Psychology, 28*(4), 303–310.
Guerney, L., & Ryan, V. (2013). *Group filial therapy.* London, England: Jessica Kingsley.
Haslam, D. R., & Harris, S. M. (2011). Integrating play and family therapy methods: A survey of play therapists' attitudes in the field. *International Journal of Play Therapy, 20*, 51–65.
Hoffman, L. W., & Hoffman, M. L. (1973). The value of children to parents. In J. T. Fawcett (Ed.), *Psychological perspectives on population* (pp. 19–76). New York, NY: Basic Books.
Irwin, E. C., & Malloy, E. S. (1994). Family puppet interview. In C. E. Schaefer & L. Carey (Eds.), *Family play therapy* (pp. 32–42). Lanham, MD: Jason Aronson.
Jernberg, A. M. (1979). *Theraplay®: A new treatment using structured play for problem children and their families.* San Francisco, CA: Jossey-Bass.
Johnson, L., & Thomas, V. (1999). Influences on the inclusion of children in family therapy. *Journal of Marital and Family Therapy, 25*(1), 117–123. doi:10.1111/j.1752-0606.1999.tb01114.x.
Kaslow, N. J., Broth, M. R., Smith, C. O., & Collins, M. H. (2012). Family-based interventions for child and adolescent disorders. *Journal of Marital and Family Therapy, 38*(1), 82–100.
Landreth, G. (2012). *Play therapy: The art of the relationship.* New York, NY: Brunner & Routledge.
Minuchin, S. (1974). *Families and family therapy.* Cambridge, MA: Harvard University Press.
Oehlers, K., & Shortland-Jones, R. (2013). Is family therapy including children? *Australian & New Zealand Journal of Family Therapy, 34*(3), 215–231. doi: 10.1002/anzf.1017.
Ryan, S. D., Gomory, T., & Lacasse, J. (2002). Who are we? Examining the results of the Association for Play Therapy membership survey. *International Journal of Play Therapy, 11*(2), 11–41.
Satir, V. (1972). *Peoplemaking.* Palo Alto, CA: Science and Behavior Books.
Schaefer, C. E., & Carey, L. (Eds.). (1994). *Family play therapy.* Lanham, MD: Jason Aronson.
Shedler, J. (2010, February–March). The efficacy of psychodynamic psychotherapy. *The American Psychologist, 65*(2), 98–109.
Whitaker, C. A., & Keith, D. V. (1981). Symbolic-experiential family therapy. In A. S. Gurman & D. P. Kniskern (Eds.), *Handbook of family therapy* (pp. 187–225). New York, NY: Brunner/Mazel.
Wickes, F. G. (1988). *The inner world of childhood: A study of analytical psychology.* Salem, MA: Sigo Press.

I

Integrative Approaches to Play in Family Counseling

Chapter One

Family-Based Cognitive Behavioral Therapy

Janine Shelby

Cognitive behavioral therapies (CBTs) are supported by a large, rigorous empirical base, and they have been soundly demonstrated to be effective for a wide range of adult and childhood disorders. Yet, studies also reveal notable attrition and only moderate-level response rates to the treatment (i.e., typically ranging from 50 percent to 80 percent; see Craske et al., 2014; Rey, Marin, & Silverman, 2011; Silverman et al., 2008). This leaves substantial room to improve upon existing CBT treatments. CBTs' traditional focus upon the individual may de-emphasize familial and other important environmental influences on children. Also, the CBT model has been questioned in terms of its developmental sensitivity. This chapter is written to reflect the view that CBT is most likely to be successful when familial issues and concerns are addressed, and play-based family therapy interventions can be used to achieve CBT goals in a developmentally sensitive and engaging manner. Several specific examples are presented in the following pages, along with a brief review of CBT's history, theory, and research base. Hopefully, this chapter will contribute to the budding movement to improve existing CBT practice by the inclusion of developmentally sensitive, family-focused psychotherapy interventions.

WHAT IS CBT? HISTORY, THEORY, AND CHARACTERISTICS

> Thoughts have power; thoughts are energy. And you can make your world or break it by your thinking. —Susan Taylor (Britt, 1990)

Near the turn of the twentieth century, Ivan Pavlov and B. F. Skinner founded the behaviorist movement, which introduced an alternative to the prevailing psychoanalytic therapy model that focused on intrapsychic motivations, drives, and influences. With the rise of behaviorism came understanding of classical and operant conditioning, and greater appreciation of observable behavior as opposed to subconscious or unconscious processes. In the 1960s, Aaron T. Beck, who developed cognitive therapy, and Albert Ellis, who established rational emotive behavior therapy (formerly "rational motive therapy"), played prominent roles in what is now the CBT *second wave*. This movement emphasized the importance of cognition (i.e., thoughts) in understanding human behavior and affect. During the latter two decades of the twentieth century, behaviorists and cognitive therapists merged to form what is today known as cognitive behavioral therapy (CBT).

Currently, there are dozens of theoretical approaches to psychotherapy. CBT differs from other psychotherapies by focusing on the interconnectedness and interdependence of a person's thoughts, emotions, and behaviors. CBT therapists, according to the Association for Behavioral and Cognitive Therapies (ABCT, 2015), seek "to help the client discover that he/she is powerful and capable of choosing positive thoughts and behaviors." By altering unhelpful cognitions and behaviors, clients can achieve more adaptive or desired ways of thinking, feeling, and behaving so that they may increase positive affect, decrease negative affect, try new rewarding activities, solve problems effectively, and/or use constructive ways of thinking about themselves, others, and the future.

CBT is not a single type of therapy, but a group of scientifically demonstrated treatments that share a common theoretical approach. The term "CBT" is used broadly to refer to cognitive therapy (CT), behavioral therapy (BT), and therapies that integrate cognitive and behavioral elements. Although they share some common features, CT differs from BT in their respective areas of emphasis. CT is based on the view that thoughts are the primary determinants of feelings and behaviors. For example, one student perusing the number of pages in a book chapter might think, "This is so long I will never finish it!" which might, in turn, lead to feelings of frustration and difficulty finishing the assignment. Another student reading the same assignment might think, "It's great that this chapter is long, because I will get to learn a great deal from it!" This cognition would likely lead to positive feelings and completion of the assignment. As shown in these examples, CT emphasizes how different interpretations of the same event lead to different emotions and actions. In contrast, BTs highlight the role of behaviors over thoughts in altering affect and cognition. In behavioral approaches, clients examine and modify the ways in which specific behaviors or thoughts are rewarded (and therefore likely to recur) within one's environment. For example, if a caregiver who complains that her child is often demanding gives him ice cream when he commands her to do so, the child's discourteous request style is rewarded and likely to be repeated. In child-focused BTs, caregivers learn to observe and change patterns of children's behavior by reinforcing only desired behaviors. They also learn to respond to children's undesirable behaviors in ways that make the unwanted behaviors less likely to recur (e.g., by implementing unwanted consequences or by refraining from providing rewarding consequences). As children's targeted behaviors are consistently addressed, new patterns of behavior emerge and can be maintained by the youngsters independently over time (e.g., the child learns to express desires politely).

There are hundreds of distinct CBT, CT, and BT manuals, but treatments falling under the CBT umbrella share several common characteristics. First, they are usually short term (i.e., often 6–20 sessions). Second, CBTs are designed to address specific diagnoses or symptoms; each CBT manual is matched to a particular disorder or set of disorders. CBTs are also structured and goal oriented, with progress toward objectives quantified, assessed, and tracked throughout the course of treatment. Lastly, CBTs involve some combination of techniques from a common pool of strategies (e.g., psychoeducation, exposure, self-monitoring, behavioral activation, coping skill enhancement, cognitive restructuring, contingency planning, and problem solving/communication skill development), depending on the client's problem or condition.

As a class of psychotherapy treatments, CBT is well established as an effective treatment approach. In fact, many CBTs are considered to meet the "gold standard" defined by several agencies, organizations, or task forces that rank treatments according to their level of scientific support (see Southam-Gerow & Prinstein, 2013). CBTs have been shown to be effective in the treatment of a wide range of childhood (Weisz, Weiss, Han, Granger, & Morton, 1995) and adult (Otte, 2011) mental health concerns. CBTs have been found to be particularly helpful for childhood internalizing disorders (Harrington, Whitaker, Shoebridge, & Campbell, 1998; Southam-Gerow & Kendall, 2000), such as depression and suicidality (Clarke, 1999; March et al., 2007), anxiety (Kendall & Hedtke, 2006), and trauma-related disorders (Cohen & Mannarino, 2000; Silverman et al., 2008; Stein et al., 2003). Although there is also strong empirical support for the use of BTs to address externalizing disorders, this chapter will focus on family-based CBT intervention strategies for internalizing disorders, where CBTs—as opposed to BTs—are more commonly used.

Are CBTs Applicable to Children?

Despite the support for the use of CBTs with youth from middle childhood through adolescence, only a small proportion of CBT studies have been conducted on youth younger than 8 years old (Grave & Blissett, 2004). Because CBT relies upon both sophisticated cognitive operations (e.g., metacognition, perspective-taking, and hypothetical reasoning) and well-developed verbal skills, developmental issues pose challenges to some aspects of the CBT model. Questions about CBTs' suitability for young children have led to a greater emphasis on developmentally sensitive treatment adaptations, and there is now widespread recognition that CBTs delivered to children and adolescents should be developmentally sensitive (Grave & Blissett, 2004; Knell & Dasari, 2015; McCarty & Weisz, 2007). Yet, few specific adaptations and guidelines have been provided (see Shelby & Berk, 2009; Ronen, 1998).

In contrast to the developmental challenges CBTs pose for young children, play therapy approaches are couched in developmental sensitivity. Beginning with Knell (1993) and continuing through the present, several practitioners have promoted blending CBT with play-based methods and/or incorporating cognitive and behavioral techniques within a play therapy paradigm (Drewes, 2009; Goodyear-Brown, 2002; Kenney-Noziska, 2008; Shelby and Berk, 2009). Despite the potential for mutual benefit, the play therapy and mainstream CBT literatures are not yet well integrated, though some recent publications (Cavett & Drewes, 2012; Drewes & Cavett, 2012; Lowenstein, 2014) have made strides toward greater use of cognitive behavioral play therapy (CBPT).

Family-Based CBTs

> Doing child psychotherapy is impossible without working with adults.
> —Friedberg and McClure (2002, p. 288)

Early CBT studies did not include active caregiver components in their protocols and most contemporary CBTs continue to emphasize individual work over caregiver collateral or family therapy. This focus on the individual child may mean that familial and environmental factors are not adequately considered in some CBT approaches (Wells & Albano, 2005). Research showing that family functioning is related to child functioning presents an additional challenge to the traditional, individual-focused CBT model. For example, greater family stress, parental critical expressed emotion, and negative parental behaviors are related to youth depression and caregiver-child reciprocal negative interactions (see Asarnow, Tompson, & Berk, 2005). Also, parental level of psychological support is associated with positive therapy outcomes for young children (Cohen & Mannarino, 2000). Fortunately, CBTs for children and adolescents have increasingly begun to include at least some family and/or caregiver components. Common CBT family/collateral treatment modules are listed in Figure 1.1.

Modules usually provided to caregivers alone during collateral sessions are not shaded, whereas components usually implemented in family sessions are shaded. Partial shading indicates that there are examples in the literature of the modules being delivered in either caregiver collateral or family-based sessions.

FAMILY PLAY THERAPY INTERVENTIONS

Below, CBPT interventions are proposed to correspond to some of the family-based CBT modules described in the literature. The interventions proposed here are not intended as a stand-alone treatment protocol; rather,

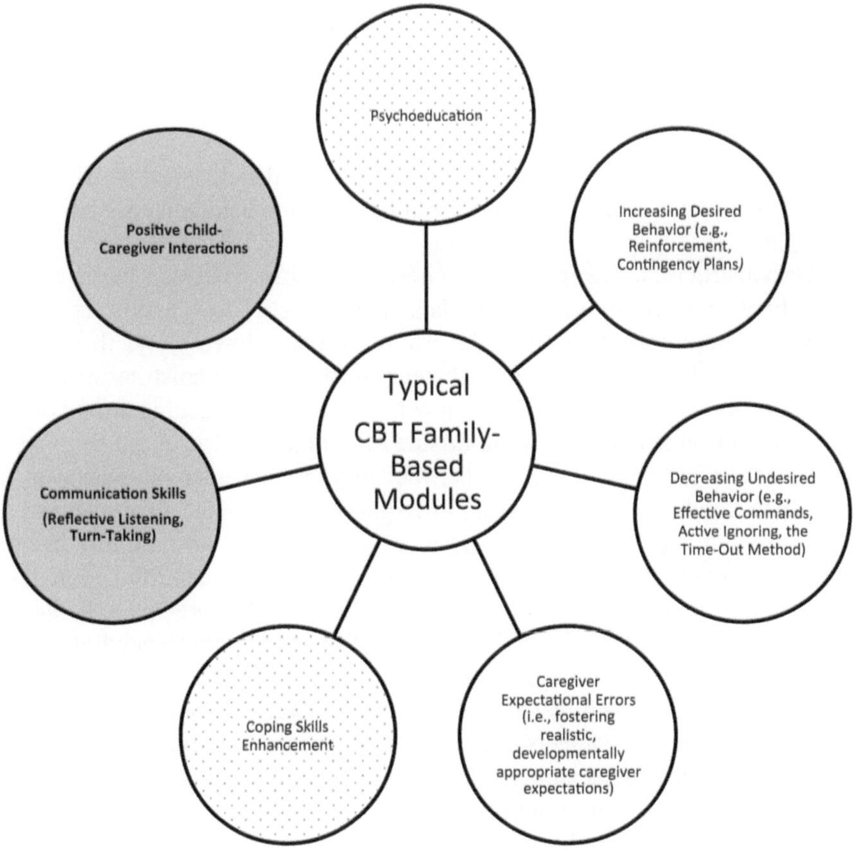

Figure 1.1. Common Elements of CBTs Involving Caregivers

these strategies are presented to illustrate ways in which typical CBT family components can be implemented in a play-based and experiential manner.

Expectational Errors

A common issue in parent-child psychotherapy is that parents have unrealistic and/or developmentally inappropriate expectations of their children. Many CBT interventions targeting parental expectations (i.e., unrealistic thoughts) have emphasized the use of psychoeducation, in which childhood development information is provided by the therapist or via written materials. Therapists then typically collaborate with parents to develop more realistic and/or suitable expectations of the children. Not all caregivers are responsive to the idea that their expectations are unrealistic, however, and some caregivers respond defensively to the therapist's efforts to provide corrective developmental information. Family-based, playful interventions, such as the one described below, can be beneficial by engaging caregivers in an enjoyable, play-based activity that demonstrates the concept without arousing negative parental reactions when the topic is presented.

The High Bar

This activity is based on the high jump, a track-and-field sport in which an athlete attempts to leap over a horizontal bar without dislodging the bar from its supports.

To construct the therapeutic prop needed for this activity, a bar is either assembled (e.g., from simple materials such as paper towel rolls taped together) or purchased (e.g., a limbo bar or wooden dowel), and then positioned in the therapy room using whatever means the therapist has available to support the bar (e.g., two hooks may be placed on the ceiling from which two cords provide a noose for either side of the bar, the bar might be placed atop stacked boxes or large blocks, the rungs of a ladder or ledges on a bookshelf might represent bars of different heights, or the therapist and a family therapy participant can support each end of the bar). In any event, family members are provided with balloons, beanbags, or a stuffed animal or doll that can be used to depict family members when they pretend to be high-jumping athletes during the activity, and the bar is initially placed at a low level, so the pitched objects can easily surpass it. After the bar is positioned and materials are disseminated, the family members are, one at a time, encouraged to toss their objects over the bar or pretend to compete in the high jump using their stuffed animals/dolls. After several successful "jumps," the bar is incrementally raised until no one can successfully get the objects over the bar (i.e., the bar may have to be positioned next to the ceiling such that it is unsurpassable). Then, the therapist explains that some parental expectations are extremely low, like the initial bar in the play therapy activity, and other parental expectations may be extremely high, like the current bar. Because there is no universal standard, the therapist elaborates, it can be difficult for caregivers to determine the best placement of their expectational bars. Usually, parents' placement decisions are based on factors like their children's skills and abilities, their own parents' expectations of them (the caregivers) when they were children, or their mood (the caregivers) at the time they are setting the standard of behavior. Though there is no single correct bar placement, there are general ranges in which children will likely succeed or fail. Sometimes, children succeed even when the bar is placed too far above their developmental capacity, but in these cases there may be long-term negative effects (e.g., fatigue, frustration, or anxiety) rather than a sense of accomplishment and pride. The goal is to place an expectational bar at a level that teaches children in a way that allows them to be successful and enthusiastic learners (at least most of the time). Following this brief description, the therapist then suggests the following five factors that can help parents set a particular expectational bar in a range that is right for their family: (a) developmental information, (b) the child's skills and abilities, (c) the child's current success rate meeting the expectation, (d) the child's positive or negative experience while attempting the task, and (e) information about what most parents—not merely adults in one's own family—expect of similar children (this may require behavioral experiments in which the therapist and caregiver obtain additional information, from research, by observing other caregivers when they are out in public, or by conducting surveys of other caregivers). This list is intended as a guide rather than as an exhaustive list of factors parents may consider when forming expectations of their children.

After this discussion, the family is asked to repeat the activity, again placing the bar at a low level, to individualize the concept for their family. With each object tossed, the caregiver identifies the child's chores, tasks, or behaviors that usually meet the caregiver expectational level. If the youngster agrees that the expectation is realistic to accomplish most of the time (as opposed to desirable, given that youth may not always prefer to complete chores or behave according to parental standards), he or she tosses an object over the bar. On the other hand, if the child disagrees with the caregiver's assessment (i.e., believing the standard is not realistic most of the time), the item is placed on a list that will later be examined by the pretend high jump field referee. Next, the caregiver and child are asked to name several areas of expectation that the child does not usually surpass. These areas are also added to the referee's list. Then, the family and therapist evaluate the items on the referee's list using the five criteria named earlier. Each item is discussed with respect to each of the five criteria. For example, expecting a cognitively delayed three-year-old to wait quietly for an hour while her mother has a phone conversation would be examined in terms of its develop-

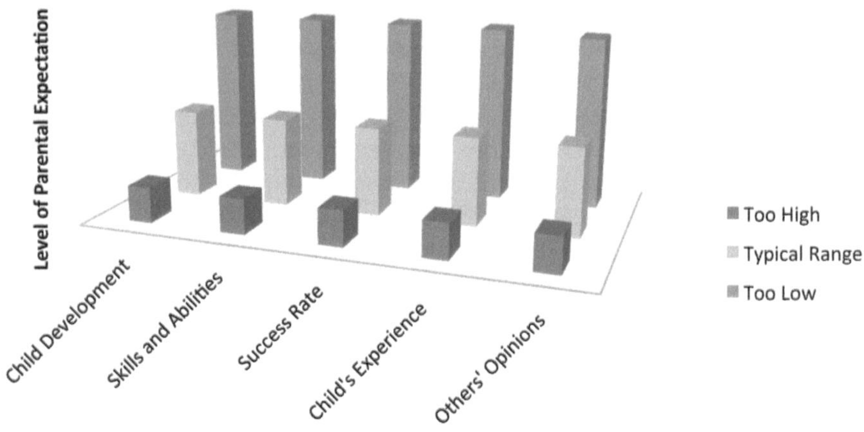

Figure 1.2. Expectational Bar Criteria

mental bar (i.e., this is too high an expectation for the developmental capacity of a three-year-old child), skills and abilities bar (i.e., this child has additional difficulty functioning in an independent and self-sustaining manner relative to other same-age children), success rate (i.e., this child is not likely to have been able to meet the parent's expectation in the past), child experience (i.e., the child probably feels frustrated and anxious when trying to meet the parental expectation), and typical caregiver expectations (which would be estimated by the caregiver or investigated for discussion in future sessions). In this example, the bar was set too high on each of the five criteria, though sometimes there is variability across the criteria. Family members may enjoy maneuvering the bar in the therapy room to reflect caregivers' conclusions about each of the criteria. Caregivers are advised that too high a bar in even one area warrants consideration of adjusting the bar. During the discussion, the therapist can emphasize how the child's success with a lower bar can eventually motivate him or her to attempt a higher-bar performance, but failure inhibits motivation and impedes future success. After each criterion has been considered, the caregiver determines based on the totality of the data whether the overall bar for the item should be lowered, raised, or left as it is. As the final step in the intervention, the caregiver selects one or two specific areas where he or she agrees to lower the expectational bar, and indicates the appropriate height at which the bar in the therapy room should be placed to represent the new, expected standard of behavior at home (i.e., reflecting whether the degree to which the current standard will be adjusted by repositioning the bar in the therapy room). The child then successfully tosses the object over the new, more appropriately placed bar; caregivers define the new expectation so that the child understands it; and the homework assignment is to apply the adjusted expectation and contingency plan at home (e.g., using praise, rewards, and/or negative consequences). In subsequent sessions, family members discuss their progress at home, and additional expectational errors are targeted.

Positive Parent-Child Interactions and Communication

Though they may not be aware of their communication styles, many caregivers of youth receiving clinical mental health services use overly negative methods of interacting with their children. Some young people also use patterns of overly critical behavior when they interact with each other or their parents. The following strategy is proposed to increase interpersonal cognizance and positive familial interactions.

Relationship Soup

To depict positive interactions, the therapist requires three ingredients for the *relationship soup* activity.

First, an ingredient is provided that is nice to eat (e.g., grapes) to represent positive familial interactions (e.g., positive verbalizations about the other

Recipe Book

Relationship Soup:

Ingredients:	Cooking Materials:
Grapes	Large Pot or Bowl
Large Paper Clips	Stirring Spoon
Hot Sauce	Serving Bowls
Whipped Cream	Spoons

To large bowl, add one grape per positive caregiver-child interaction. Add one paperclip for each apathetic interaction, such as boredom or disinterest. Add one dash of hot sauce for each negative statement. After 5 minutes, add whipped cream, mix ingredients, and serve them. Decide if you want to eat the soup. If it is unappetizing, change the ingredients! Try again, until the relationship soup is good to eat.

Figure 1.3. Relationship Soup

person or displays of affection). To demonstrate apathy, the therapist uses a second, large and clean but inedible ingredient (i.e., jumbo, washed paper clips). Third, to show critical or other negative familial interactions, the therapist presents an ingredient with a strong odor and taste (e.g., hot sauce) that would be incompatible with the pleasant food. Using these items, the therapist demonstrates how interactions between family members dictate their relationship soup recipe (i.e., behaviors will be coded by adding an ingredient to the soup that represents the family members' interactions). Using a large pot or bowl, the therapist describes what each ingredient connotes, demonstrating that correction or criticism during family special time earns a drop of hot sauce to the family soup. Positive statements (e.g., compliments and praise) or positive nonverbal displays (e.g., smiling at each other or expressions of affection) earn one grape per positive behavior, and indicators of boredom (or, for caregivers and teenagers, excessive self-interest) mean that something inedible (e.g., a large paper clip) is dropped in the pot. Next, the therapist role-plays positive, apathetic, and negative behaviors with a family of dolls or imaginary family members, while family members practice "rating" the therapist by using the food items that correspond to each behavior. When they use the recipe items correctly to code the therapist's behaviors, family members are then asked to create their own family *soup* by discussing an event in the child or adolescent's day or engaging in play together for 5 minutes, while the therapist codes the family members' behavior by adding food items to the soup pot to reflect each observed behavior. At the end of the 5-minute practice period, a family member is asked to add whipped cream to the ingredients the family earned during their 5-minute interaction. The mixture is then stirred and served to each member. As family members examine the concoction, the therapist asks them whether they would enjoy eating the *soup.* Although they are not asked to actually eat the mixture (i.e., if it contains an unpleasant combination of ingredients), family members quickly discover that a small amount of hot sauce (i.e., criticism or negativity) ruins the dish. Also, the paper clips (i.e., apathy or self-absorption) pose unappetizing barriers to enjoying the dish.

After a discussion of whether their interactions at home are similar to the *soup* created during their therapy interaction, the therapist explains that they can alter their relational patterns just as the recipe can be modified to produce a more pleasant relationship soup. Then, multiple 5-minute familial interactions are coded during subsequent practice periods and/or sessions. Therapists should record the number of positive, apathetic, and negative statements made during each practice period, and monitor the family's progress over time. The intervention is successful when family members consistently respond in positive ways to each other in order to create an edible soup during their family special time, where they may eventually enjoy eating the soup they create with their familial interactions. Family members are encouraged to schedule positive family time, or make *relationship soup*, at home on a regular basis as their skills improve.

Communication

Many parents believe that if they disagree with their children or teenagers, it is not important to listen to their opinions. However, difficulty validating or taking the young person's perspective impedes effective caregiver-child communication. Moreover, some caregivers discount their children's perspectives based on the belief that they (the adults) have the sole, correct view of situations and circumstances. The technique proposed below is a brief intervention designed to promote intrafamilial empathy, validation, and perspective-taking skills between caregivers and their children.

Judging a Book by Its Cover

In this intervention, the therapist prepares each side of a book or piece of construction paper with a different photograph or picture on each side. Without exposing the pictures on the opposite side to either party, the therapist places the book at eye level between caregiver and child (or between parents on one side and children on the other), so that, unbeknownst to them, each person or group sees a different picture than the other. The therapist then asks each family member to describe what he or she sees. Because they see different pictures, their descriptions differ. The therapist might then ask each family member to persuade the other of the accuracy of his or her own perspective (without yet revealing the picture on the alternative side to the other family members). Finally, the therapist shows the family members both sides of the book and describes how they are both correct, but that different family members are seeing their own perspective of the same object. Using this demonstration, the therapist and family members then discuss the futility of trying to convince the other that one perspective is correct and another is incorrect, as well as the fact that curiosity about another's perspective feels better to everyone than insisting only one perspective is correct. It should be emphasized that holding regard for their children's perspective does not necessarily mean caregivers are bound to set rules based solely on the young person's perspective; rather, rules are easier to enforce when children's feelings are understood and considered. A situation from the family's own experience involving discrepant caregiver-child views is then selected, and family members are encouraged to share what each sees as other family members listen with curiosity and without judgment or correction.

Problem Solving

Many caregivers feel so overwhelmed by their complex life situations and/or the child's behaviors that collateral or family sessions are filled with complaints or problems. When concerns are or feel urgent to caregivers, they may find it difficult to focus on only one issue at a time, which hinders problem resolution. This intervention is designed to help caregivers prioritize and focus on a small number of issues at a time.

Deck of Concerns

In this intervention, therapists ask caregivers to write all their concerns on index cards, listing one issue per card. After the caregiver has completed the index card *deck of concerns*, the caregiver is asked to place each card in one of three piles (e.g., the "must be addressed now" pile is placed in front of the caregiver, and the "it can wait" and "I'm not sure" piles are to the left and right). After the caregiver has sorted the cards, the therapist and caregiver examine the items in the "not sure" pile, placing each concern where it best fits after discussing it. Then, the "now" pile cards are rank ordered by the caregiver and only the top-priority cards are agreed to be the focal points of the session. A step-by-step action plan is listed on the back of the top-priority card after the therapist and caregiver discuss the necessary steps toward resolving the issue. The caregiver takes the card home as a reminder of what specific steps need to be accomplished during the week. The *deck of concerns* also provides both structure and treatment plan goals for future sessions.

Children can engage in this activity to identify their concerns, and a separate pile can be introduced for issues that are "for grown-ups to solve" if the child's concerns involve areas of adult responsibility. This technique can be used in family sessions to promote perspective taking by asking caregivers to complete a set of cards for concerns they believe their youth experience. After the young people identify and rank their concerns with their own set of cards, their list and rankings are contrasted with the caregivers' (or other family members') to assess how similar adult perspectives of the children's concerns are, as well as to enhance communication and caregiver awareness of children's thoughts and feelings.

Mindfulness and Coping

Although coping is frequently addressed in individual CBTs for children, caregivers may model affect dysregulation behaviors and inadequate coping strategies. Family-based mindfulness activities are enjoyable ways families can build distress tolerance, regulate affect, and enhance coping skills.

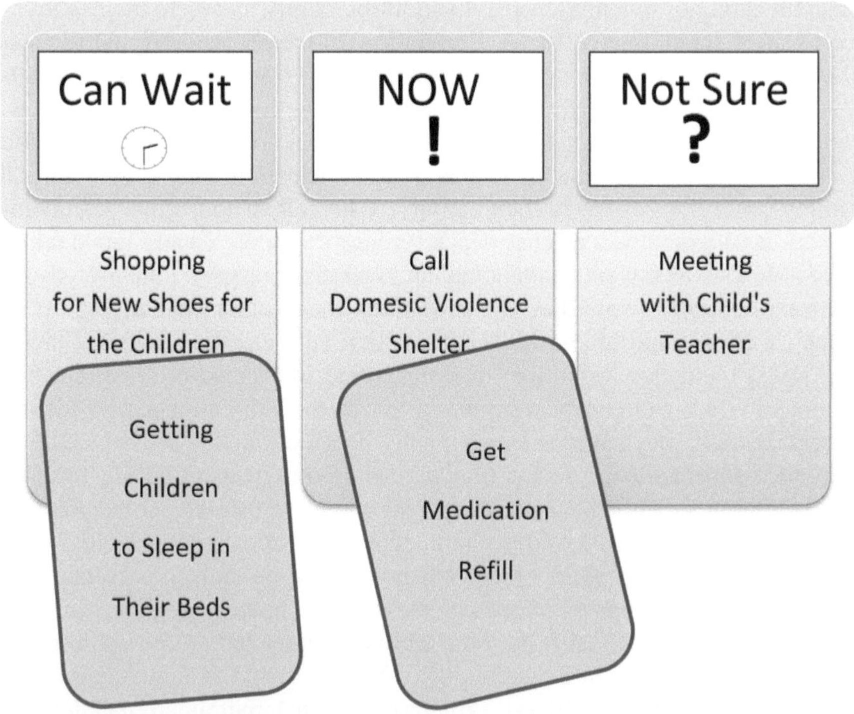

Figure 1.4. The Deck of Concerns

Mindfulness/Coping/Distress: Tolerance Stations

In this activity, at least a dozen unique coping and/or mindfulness stations are set up in the therapy room. At each station, the family member is asked to remain attentive and silent as he or she puts his entire focus on the activity for a period of 30 seconds to one minute, depending upon the age of the youngest child in the family. Some activities involve pleasant and soothing sensations (e.g., smelling vanilla extract, moving sand in a sand tray, squeezing a stress ball, or placing one's hand in a bowl of shaving foam).

Other activities involve mind-body integration (e.g., standing on one leg, or sitting with one's eyes closed). Activities can also involve repetitive motion, such as moving beads one-by-one on an abacus or transferring individual small stones from one pile to another. Other activities are more cognitive in nature, and involve the instruction to remember a favorite moment or silently repeat a positive self-thought. Some activities may also involve slightly noxious or challenging experiences (e.g., holding a small weight in one's hand while the arm is outstretched at a 90-degree angle from the body, placing one's hand in a bowl of ice, or staring at unwrapped chocolate bars without eating or touching them). In addition, family members may be invited to sit or stand quietly, focused on their own breath, while trying to clear their minds of thoughts by returning focus to their respiration. After each 30-second to 1-minute period, family members rotate through each station (i.e., with one family member per station). During the activities, therapists should calmly remind family members that if their attention strays, they should simply return their focus to their activity. When all stations have been completed, family members discuss which stations they enjoyed and found relaxing, which stations were challenging, and how they sustained themselves for the required period of time at the stations they found challenging. With practice, these mindfulness skills can assist family members with maintaining affect regulation when they feel distressed in a range of situations and settings. When caregivers become skilled in the mindfulness activities, a caregiver-child play station can eventually be added. In this station, children play for a short period (i.e., 2–5 minutes) while caregivers mindfully observe their children's affect, behaviors, and play narrative themes. At the completion of the time period, the adults nonjudgmentally describe to the child what they observed in their child's play. When this is successful, caregivers might then be asked to engage in special playtime at home using the skills of remaining present, focused, curious, and nonjudgmental as the child plays. Additional caregiver-child dyadic play skills are taught to facilitate interactive play, but this mindfulness skill provides an important foundation for positive caregiver-child interactions, including play. Family members may be asked to set up their own mindfulness stations at home and practice mindfulness stations consistently at home.

CASE STUDY

Gabrielle had a stern look that made her seem much older than her 11 years. She presented for therapy with her mother, Ms. G., and baby sister, Samantha. Gabrielle's father had not been part of her life since he abandoned the family when she was an infant, and she did not enjoy her relationship with her mother's boyfriend of one year, Mr. M. Gabrielle found less joy in her life than she used to, but she retained her interest in fashion and style. In fact, she spent hours drawing clothing and designing outfits to wear to school. Ms. G., who worked long hours as a seamstress, had spent most of Gabrielle's early years trying to support herself and her daughter. She did not understand Gabrielle's depressed and irritable mood, now that they had the added emotional and financial support of Mr. M., which allowed Ms. G. to work shorter hours.

It was important to Ms. G. that Gabrielle succeed in school, so her daughter would not have to face the hardships Ms. G. had endured as a high school dropout and young mother. Although Gabrielle wanted to choose her own school attire and to enroll in an after-school sewing club, Ms. G. insisted that Gabrielle wear the optional uniform and refrain from getting "sidetracked" with nonacademic interests. As a result, Gabrielle became increasingly sullen and withdrawn, and she had what Ms. G believed to be a "disrespectful and terrible" attitude (e.g., insolent, negative, and ungrateful for the new home and other benefits Mr. M.'s income provided). Another point of contention was Gabrielle's refusal to call Mr. M. "Dad," which Ms. G. believed was respectful. Ms. G. sadly reported that it was no longer enjoyable to spend time with her daughter. Gabrielle failed to complete her additional chores now that Samantha demanded Ms. G.'s attention when Ms. G. returned home from work. Similarly, Gabrielle's grades declined, and she did not complete her homework assignments thoroughly. To exacerbate an already tenuous situation, Gabrielle was expected to accompany her stepfather on weekends on his quest to earn extra income by recycling aluminum cans. Although Gabrielle liked Mr. M. most of the time, she felt jealous of the attention her mother gave him and she felt embarrassed about the prospect of her school friends seeing her digging in public trash bins. Ms. G expressed that she loved her daughter, but she felt overwhelmed with a new job, a new baby and partner, and now, Gabrielle's psychological issues impacting the family. After the school counselor reported to Ms. G that she believed Gabrielle might meet criteria for a mild depressive disorder, Ms. G. referred her to a therapist.

As part of her CBT homework assignment, Gabrielle began engaging in pleasant activities to elevate her mood, including spending special time with her mother on Sunday afternoons while the baby napped. Her mother received psychoeducation about depression and the importance of allowing her daughter to engage in enjoyable activities, including scheduling pleasant mother-daughter special time and social outings (i.e., behavioral activation). Gabrielle also learned that her thoughts could influence how she felt, so she focused on altering thoughts that were untrue and/or unhelpful (e.g., whereas she had formerly told herself that her mother hated her and her stepfather had ruined her life, she now told herself that her mother loved her even when they disagreed). She also concluded that there were still some enjoyable things about her life, and that some things had improved since Mr. M. joined the family. In addition to using this standard CBT approach, the therapist used play-based therapeutic activities. When the therapist realized that Ms. G. had unrealistically high expectations for Gabrielle (i.e., to assume the bulk of the housework, complete homework, and contribute to the family income, while sacrificing age-appropriate socialization and free time), the family engaged in the High Bar activity. Ms. G. understood that she expected too much of her daughter when she realized that Gabrielle had never had a successful week in which she was able to perform all of her household duties and homework to her mother's satisfaction. Ms. G. also became aware that these expectations contributed to Gabrielle's sense of hopelessness and lack of motivation. When the therapist noticed the mother's tendency to comment on her daughter's shortcomings more frequently than Gabrielle's strengths, they participated in the Relationship Soup activity during therapy. Because they both liked to cook, they giggled when their interactions during the 5-minute practice period forced them to mix the incompatible ingredients they had earned. Ms. G. realized, to her surprise, how often she made negative comments about her daughter, and Gabrielle noticed how her own sulking, nonparticipation, lack of eye contact, and shoulder shrugging added inedible ingredients to their *relationship soup*. This activity together with the corresponding homework assignment to practice positive interactions at home helped them improve their communication patterns. When the stepfather was invited to participate in a *relationship soup* session, he easily and enthusiastically contributed positivity to the interaction. In spite of the change in their behavior toward each other, Ms. G. continued to show difficulty understanding Gabrielle's perspective about her desire to choose her own clothing, call her stepfather figure by his first name, socialize often with peers, and refrain from collecting cans. The Judging a Book by Its Cover activity was helpful in demonstrating that Ms. G.'s view was only one of two equally accurate views, and the activity served as a building block for more productive, empathic conversations and compromises. Ms. G. ultimately agreed on a compromise that felt comfortable to Gabrielle (e.g., free dress on Fridays, joining in the social club in exchange for collecting cans one weekend per month, and choosing an affectionate nickname for Mr. M.). At this point, the family members had many tools for successful interactions and Gabrielle's depression symptoms decreased. Only when they experienced sporadic emotional outbursts did family members have difficulty acknowledging the other's perspective and remaining positive in their communication style. So, to enhance their affect regulatory and distress tolerance capacity, as well as to strengthen their coping skills, the family began each session by engaging in mindfulness stations, and continued this practice outside of the therapy sessions. They reported that this led to a general sense of calm at home, as well as increased emotional attachment between Mr. M. and Gabrielle. The play-based, experiential approach to family CBT increased engagement in the treatment, decreased defensiveness, and made the sessions both enjoyable and eagerly anticipated by the clients.

CONCLUSION

Despite the increased recognition that developmentally sensitive and family-focused interventions are likely to be beneficial for young CBT recipients, CBTs combining either play-based or family-based interventions are under-represented in the literature compared to those that are primarily individual focused. CBTs that combine *both* play- and family-based interventions are even more rare and only beginning to emerge. Granted, the degree to which adding family therapy components to efficacious treatments adds to treatment effects needs clarification (Asarnow, Tompson, & Berk, 2005), and more CBPT research is necessary to determine the added value of play over traditional CBT. Yet, indirect factors, such as childhood developmental research and the relative influence of caregiver, familial, and contextual factors on young children, support the inclusion of both play- and family-based interventions into CBTs. This chapter was written to contribute to the emergent literature that supports such a blend, and to encourage more widespread integration of family therapy, play therapy, and CBT.

REFERENCES

Asarnow, J. R., Tompson, M. C., & Berk, M. S. (2005). Adolescent depression: Family-focused treatment strategies. In W. M. Pinsof & J. L. Lebow (Eds.), *Family psychology: The art of the science* (pp. 425–450). Oxford, England: Oxford University Press.

Association for Behavioral and Cognitive Therapies. (2015, March). *About psychological treatment: What is Cognitive Behavior Therapy (CBT)?* Retrieved from http://www.abct.org/Information/?m=mInformation&fa=_WhatIsCBTpublic.

Britt, D. (1990, June 3). *The relentlessly upbeat woman behind spirit of essence : magazines: Editor Susan Taylor's personal blend of hope and encouragement attracts 4 million, mostly black readers.* Retrieved from http://articles.latimes.com/1990-06-03/news/vw-879_1_susan-taylor.

Cavett, A. M., & Drewes, A. A. (2012). Play applications and trauma-specific components. In J. A. Cohen, A. P. Mannarino, & E. Deblinger (Eds.), *Trauma-focused CBT for children and adolescents: Treatment applications* (pp. 124–148). New York, NY: Guilford Press.

Clarke, G. N., Rohde P., Lewinsohn P. M., Hops, H., & Seeley J. R. (1999). Cognitive-behavioral treatment of adolescent depression: Efficacy of acute group treatment and booster sessions. *Journal of the American Academy of Child and Adolescent Psychiatry, 38*(3), 272–279.

Cohen, J. A., & Mannarino, A. P. (2000). Predictors of treatment outcome in sexually abused children. *Child Abuse & Neglect, 24*(7), 983–994.

Craske, M. G., et al. (2014). Randomized controlled trial of cognitive behavioral therapy and acceptance and commitment therapy for social phobia: Outcomes and moderators. *Journal of Consulting and Clinical Psychology, 82*(6), 1034–1048.

Drewes, A. A. (2009). *Blending play therapy with cognitive behavioral therapy: Evidence-based and other effective treatments and techniques*. New York, NY: Wiley.

Drewes, A. A., & Cavett, A. M. (2012). Play applications and skills components. In J. A. Cohen, A. P. Mannarino, & E. Deblinger (Eds.), *Trauma-focused CBT for children and adolescents: Treatment applications* (pp. 105–123). New York, NY: Guilford Press.

Friedberg, R. D., & McClure, J. M. (2002). *Clinical practice of cognitive therapy with children and adolescents*. New York, NY: Guilford Press.

Goodyear-Brown, P. (2002). *Digging for buried treasure.* Nashville, TN: Self-published.

Grave, J., & Blissett, J. (2004). Is cognitive behavior therapy developmentally appropriate for young children? A critical review of the evidence. *Clinical Psychology Review, 24,* 399–420.

Harrington, R., Whittaker, J., Shoebridge, P., & Campbell, F. (1998). Systematic review of efficacy of cognitive behavior therapies in childhood and adolescent depressive disorder. *British Medical Journal, 316,* 1559–1563.

Kendall, P. C., & Hedtke, K. A. (2006). *The coping cat workbook* (2nd ed). Ardmore, PA: Workbook Publishing.

Kenney-Noziska, S. (2008). *Techniques, techniques, techniques: Play-based activities for children, adolescents and families*. West Conshohocken, PA: Infinity Publishing.

Knell, S. M. (1993). *Cognitive-behavioral play therapy.* Northvale, NJ: Jason Aronson.

Knell, S. M. & Dasari, M. (2015). Cognitive behavioral play therapy for anxiety and depression. In L. A. Reddy, T. M. Files-Hall, & C. E. Schaefer (Eds.), *Empirically-based play interventions for children*, 2nd ed. Washington, DC: American Psychological Association.

Lowenstein, L. (2014). *Cory helps kids cope with sexual abuse: Playful activities for traumatized children.* Toronto, Ontario, Canada: Champion Press.

March, J., Silva, S., Petrycki, S., Curry, J., Wells, K., Fairbank, J., Burns, B., et al. (2007). The treatment for adolescents with depression study (TADS): Long-term effectiveness and safety outcomes. *Archives of General Psychiatry, 64,* 1132–1143.

McCarty, C. A., & Weisz, J. R. (2007). Effects of psychotherapy for depression in children and adolescents: What we can (and can't) learn from meta-analysis and component profiling. *Journal of the American Academy of Child and Adolescent Psychiatry, 46*, 879–886.

Otte, C. (2011). Cognitive behavioral therapy in anxiety disorders: Current state of the evidence. *Dialogues in Clinical Neuroscience, 13*(4), 413–421.

Rey, Y., Marin, C. E., & Silverman, W. K. (2011). Failures in cognitive-behavior therapy for children. *Journal of Clinical Psychology, 67*(11), 1140–1150.

Ronen, T. (1998). Linking developmental and emotional elements into child and family cognitive-behavioural therapy. In P. Graham (Ed.), *Cognitive-Behaviour Therapy for children and families* (pp. 1–17). Cambridge, England: Cambridge University Press.

Shelby, J. & Berk, M. J. (2009). Play therapy, pedagogy, and CBT: An argument for interdisciplinary synthesis. In A. A. Drewes (Ed.), *Blending play therapy with cognitive behavioral therapy: Evidence-based and other effective treatments and techniques* (pp. 17–40). New York, NY: Wiley.

Silverman, W. K., Ortiz, C. D., Viswesvaran, C., Burns, B. J., Kolko, D. J., Putnam, F. W., & Amaya-Jackson, L. (2008). Evidence-based psychosocial treatments for children and adolescents exposed to traumatic events. *Journal of Clinical Child & Adolescent Psychology, 37,* 156–183.

Southam-Gerow, M. A., & Kendall, P. C. (2000). Cognitive-behavior therapy with youth: Advances, challenges, and future directions. *Clinical Psychology and Psychotherapy, 7,* 343–366.

Southam-Gerow, M. A., & Prinstein, M. (2013). Evidence base updates: The evolution of the evaluation of psychological treatments for children and adolescents. *Journal of Clinical Child & Adolescent psychology, 43*(1), 1–6.

Stein, B. D., Jaycox, L. J., Kataoka, S. J., Wong, M., Tu, W., Elliott, M. N., & Fink, A. (2003). A mental health intervention for school children exposed to violence: A randomized controlled trial. *JAMA, 290*(5), 603–611.

Weisz, J. R., Weiss, B., Han, S. S., Granger, D. A., & Morton, T. (1995). Effects of psychotherapy with children and adolescents revisited: A meta-analysis of treatment outcome studies. *Psychological Bulletin, 117,* 450–468.

Wells, K. C., & Albano, A. M. (2005). Parent involvement in CBT treatment of adolescent depression: Experiences in the Treatment for Adolescents with Depression Study (TADS). *Cognitive and Behavioral Practice, 12*(2), 209–220.

Chapter Two

Including Families in Theraplay with Children

Evangeline Munns and Catherine Munns

I love, because I am loved. —Eric Fromm

Near the beginning of its history, Theraplay started to include parents as well as the child in its treatment protocol. The focus has not only been on helping parents become sensitive and responsive to the basic needs of the child including acceptance, warmth, and nurturance, but also encouraging delightful, fun interactions that could bring joy to both parent and child (Booth and Jernberg, 2010; Munns, 2000). Shared happiness and joy can help to heal (Panksepp, 1993). This approach has led to comments from children such as "I never want this to end" (from an emotionally troubled adolescent in a Theraplay session) or "This is the most precious time in the week for me and my son" (from a father in a father/son Theraplay group). Comments such as these reflect the strong, positive feelings that can grow between a parent and child in Theraplay. Shared exhilaration and laughter can bring a sense of attunement and affective resonance with each other. Such experiences contribute to a child's feeling of being connected, to have a "zest for life" and optimism later on (Panksepp, 1993; Stern, 1995; Sunderland, 2006). Shared positive affect has been related to a number of desirable outcomes in typically developing children, such as increased compliance, social skills, frustration tolerance, etc. (Kochanska and Aksan, 1995; Laible and Thompson, 2000).

Theraplay was founded by Dr. Ann Jernberg, a psychologist working with the Head Start programs in Chicago, Illinois, in 1967 with a goal of trying to build stronger attachments between the Head Start mothers and their children. Today, Theraplay is practiced around the world in 44 countries

(Booth and Jernberg, 2010). It has been used in private, clinical, hospital, and school settings using family and group formats. An increasingly popular format has evolved using group Theraplay in schools called "Sunshine Circles" where teachers and their assistants have led groups (Schiefer, 2009). Teachers frequently report that the children seem to become more aware of each other, know their peers' names sooner, are more caring and kind toward each other, and are less aggressive.

Theraplay is a short-term, structured, economical model of play therapy. It is considered a short-term intervention (typically 12–24 sessions but can be longer depending on individual needs). Each session is structured and led by an adult. It is conducted with minimal cost (no toys are used). Although language is used during Theraplay, it is not considered a verbal therapy (no probing questions nor interpretations are made with the child during sessions, although reflections of how the child might be feeling are sometimes given). The goals of Theraplay are primarily to enhance the healthy attachment between parents and their child, to increase the self-regulation of the latter, and to increase the self-esteem and trust of all family members. Hopefully, this is done in an atmosphere of fun and delight. Theraplay is applicable to all ages (from infants to adults) (Munns, 2005, 2008) and to a wide range of social, emotional, and behavioral difficulties (Munns, 2009). Theraplay is particularly effective with foster children, adopted children, and stepchildren where attachments have been disrupted or never formed in the first place or for those on the autism spectrum where forming positive relationships can often be problematic (Booth and Jernberg, 2010; Munns, 2000, 2009, 2011).

CURRENT RESEARCH AND THEORY

Theraplay is based on attachment theory with the belief that the first relationship a child has with its chief caregiver is the most important one in its life, as it forms the template for all other relationships. If this first relationship is not a healthy, secure one, then all subsequent relationships will be affected. Theraplay attempts to rectify this first attachment by replicating early interactions that typically occur between a young child and its parent (primary caregiver), thus fulfilling basic needs that may have been unmet earlier in the child's life. Thus, Theraplay starts with the child's emotional age rather than his or her chronological age. Touch is the sensory system that is most advanced in the newborn (Sunderland, 2006). Much positive touch is employed in the Theraplay process, because in normal parent/child interactions with very young children, there is a lot of physical contact (Gerhardt, 2004). Along with this, therapists guide the parents toward more attunement to their child's verbal and nonverbal cues during the interplay of their reciprocal exchanges. The parent is an essential component in all aspects of the Theraplay process—from assessment and conceptualization, to therapeutic work in session, to conducting homework sessions with his or her child.

Theraplay Research

There is a growing body of evidence supporting the effectiveness of Theraplay (Coleman, 2010; Munns, 2014; Wardrop and Meyer, 2009;). This includes studies using randomized control groups or matched controls (Munns, 2014) which have shown that Theraplay aids in significantly reducing aggression (Franke, 2007; Lender and Lindaman, 2007; Wettig, Franke, and Fjordback, 2006), lowers internalizing symptoms (Sui, 2009), and improves self-esteem (Sui, 2009). Other studies have indicated that Theraplay can increase empathy of young single mothers, as well as increase attachment scores between parents and their children (Wardrop and Meyer, 2009). In language-disordered children who received Theraplay, social and emotional functioning and language expression have increased significantly compared to controls (Ritterfeld, 1989). Externalizing behavior decreased significantly in a group of clinical children and their parents who received Theraplay (Munns, Jensen, and Berger, 1997). These findings are also often confirmed by clinical observations from therapists, teachers, and parents. Theraplay has been rated as demonstrating "promising research evidence" by the California Evidence-Based Clearinghouse for Child Welfare (Booth, Lindaman, and Winstead, 2014).

Related Neuroscience Research

Credibility for Theraplay's treatment approach has grown partly because of support for its underlying tenets from the field of neuroscience (Hart, 2008; Perry and Szalavitz, 2006; Schore, 2005; Siegel, 2011). Theraplay aligns well with neurosequential programming (Perry and Szalavitz, 2006), which is evidence based. Treatment begins first at the level of the client's stage of brain development regardless of his or her chronological age. For example, if a child was neglected or traumatized when very young, then treatment would start by stimulating the lower brain (brain stem, cerebellum, and connecting neural networks), which governs our survival needs, movements, and physiological regulation. Perry's neurosequential programming begins with daily, repetitive, patterned activities designed to help the lower brain to mature using somatosensory, rhythmic activities (Gaskill and Perry, 2014). Likewise, Theraplay also begins with activities one might normally do with a young child, such as sensory-motor, rhythm, and touch activities that would stimulate the lower brain.

Since the brain develops in a hierarchical manner, each part of the brain is dependent upon the adequate maturation and organization of the preceding part. Therefore, treatment would start with the lower part, and once that part was functioning well, programming would proceed to using activities to stimulate the next higher level. This means that a wide variety of treatments are included in neurosequential programming, but timing is the key in determining which treatments are used first. In both neurosequential programming and Theraplay, there is a progression to using more chronological age-appropriate activities later in treatment.

When treating a person who has been chronically traumatized, it is important to note that the individual may have an overactive amygdala (a key component of the middle or emotional brain), which keeps the individual in a high alarm or stress state. With such an individual, the neurosequential model focuses on activities designed for emotional expression and regulation of feelings. In Theraplay, activities vary from stimulating ones to calming, soothing ones in an effort to help the individual toward self-regulation. Lassenius-Panula and Makela's (2007) research study of young children and their parents found a significant lowering of the stress hormone cortisol after receiving Theraplay. A number of therapists emphasize the need to create a sense of safety and self-regulation first before any kind of treatment can take effect (Baggerly and Green, 2014; Gaskill and Perry, 2014; van der Kolk, 2006).

The neuroscience field also supports Theraplay's emphasis on stimulating the right hemisphere of the brain, which processes sensory motor perceptions, social emotional experiences, creativity, etc. The right hemisphere is important for the development of empathy and self-regulation (Schore, 2005). Increasing empathic sensitivity and affect regulation are often main goals in Theraplay.

Touch Research

Previously it was mentioned that Theraplay includes a lot of physical contact in an effort to foster attachment between parent and child. Touch is the most advanced sensory system in the newborn, and the infant requires positive, affectionate touch in order to thrive. Numerous animal and human studies have shown the importance of touch (Field, 2001; Field and Reite, 1985; Ford, 1993; Gerhart, 2004; Makela, 2005; Sunderland, 2006). Because positive, close, bodily contact can activate the release of calming hormones such as opioids and oxytocin, the child's arousal system can be soothed and regulated through touch while promoting attachment between parent and child at the same time (Field, 2001; Nicholson and Parker, 2009; Sunderland, 2006). Reduced stress response is important, since research indicates that high levels of cortisol can negatively impact brain development (van der Kolk, 2005, 2006).

MAIN THERAPLAY DIMENSIONS

There are four underlying principles that guide Theraplay therapists: structure, engagement, nurture, and challenge. These principles were originally based on observations by Dr. Jernberg of typical parent/child interactions:

Structure

Normally young children are structured by their parents, thus helping to make their environment safe, predictable, and organized so the child feels safe and secure. Daily routines for eating, sleeping, playing, etc. and clear directions for behavior help the child to feel regulated. In Theraplay sessions, games with easily understood directions such as "Red light, Green light" or "Mother may I?" are used where the child, in order to play the game, has to follow the rules. This dimension is stressed for deregulated, impulsive, and acting-out children or for those who are used to being in control (parentified children).

Engagement

Parents ordinarily participate with their young child in hundreds of playful, enjoyable encounters, leaving the child with a sense of connection and positive shared affect with the parents. The child also learns he or she can be a source of delight to the parents. In Theraplay, many of the activities bring a sense of shared fun and laughter to the participants. Some of the engaging activities in Theraplay include mirroring (imitating each other's body movements), passing funny faces, cotton ball throw and catch, etc. This dimension is emphasized for children who are withdrawn, fearful, depressed or those on the autism spectrum.

Nurture

This dimension is the most crucial one for all children. All children need to be nurtured in order to feel valued, important, soothed, and loved. Consistent nurturing is needed as well for basic survival needs to be met such as eating, drinking, warmth, etc. In Theraplay nurturing activities include feeding the child a snack, powdering or putting lotion on "hurts" or "boo-boos" on the hands of the child, giving the child a sip of juice from a juice box while cradling and rocking the child, giving manicures or pedicures, or games involving backrubs, etc.

Nurture is especially important for children that have been traumatized or abused, but because they have experienced negative touching in the past, the activities often need to be modified, including a very gentle, sensitive approach on the part of the therapist. As mentioned before, nothing is forced and the child is not coaxed. If the child says "no" or nonverbally indicates he or she is uncomfortable, then the activity is stopped or modified until the activity becomes acceptable to the child. For example, if the child does not want lotion put on his or her "hurts," then the activity might be changed to hand prints where powder is smoothed on the palms of the child and then they are pressed on a dark-colored piece of construction paper, revealing a hand imprint left on the paper (provided the child wants to do this). After experiencing this safe kind of touch from an adult, the child can usually relax and accept the nurturing that he or she so very much needs.

Nurture is also important for aggressive, acting-out children who usually are in trouble with adults and often do not receive much nurturing. These children can develop tough exteriors, but can feel quite vulnerable emotionally inside.

Challenge

This dimension helps children believe they can master things and take age-appropriate risks. In our Western society, with its emphasis on achievement, children are often challenged too often or beyond their developmental abilities. Care is taken in Theraplay to gear challenging activities to the child's developmental level of ability. Challenging activities can lead to a sense of mastery, self-confidence, and self-esteem.

Challenging activities in Theraplay include the following: throwing beanbags into the arms of the adult, paper punch, rising together from a sitting to a standing position by holding one's partner's hands, balancing pillows on the head or feet, jumping from pillows, etc. Challenging activities are emphasized for children who have been overprotected, fearful of making mistakes, afraid of taking risks and also for children who need a safe way to express some of their aggressive feelings. For example, a Theraplay activity called "sword fight" with rolled-up newspapers allows for a safe release of aggressive feelings. Certain dimensions are emphasized for certain types of difficulties (i.e., structure and nurture for an aggressive, impulsive child, or engagement, nurture, and challenge for a withdrawn child).

INTEGRATIVE FAMILY PLAY THERAPY TREATMENT, PLANNING, AND PROTOCOL

The initial interview with the parents includes a thorough developmental, social, and family history including at times the family histories of each parent. The marital relationship can also be briefly discussed. This is followed a week later by a family assessment session using the Marschak Interaction Method (MIM), which is a semistandardized method of observing family interactions and relationships. This session is videotaped and later reviewed in a feedback session with the parents where their strengths as well as their difficulties are discussed. Goals are set in collaboration with the parents. The fundamentals of Theraplay are briefly discussed. A commitment to try to attend each session on a regular basis (usually one session per week per half hour of Theraplay followed by a half hour of parent counseling) is encouraged. Note that in traditional Theraplay programming, the half hour of parent counseling would not take place after each Theraplay session. Instead, parents would come alone for a parent counseling after three or four Theraplay sessions. It is crucial to work more closely with the parents in order for good treatment generalization to take place. It is also recommended to have a practice session with the parent(s) before Theraplay begins with a child. In this practice session the parents get a chance to experience some of the activities their child would be receiving and in the process gain a better understanding of the purpose of the activities. This is also a time where parents can begin to connect their feelings and experiences to their own childhood histories.

The Theraplay sessions with the child and therapist then begin while the parents observe from a one-way mirror or corner of the room, ideally with an interpreting therapist, who is there to answer their questions and to help the parents become more attuned to their child's cues. This observation lasts for four or five sessions where the therapist models positive interactions with their child. This is followed by parents joining the activities and interacting directly with their child under the guidance of the therapist. Gradually the activities are led by the parents while the therapist starts taking a secondary role, so the primary attachment becomes stronger with the parents. Parents are also encouraged to try Theraplay activities at home each week. This homework is very important so that generalization of treatment effects can become stronger. The homework activities are discussed at the end of each Theraplay session, during the parent counseling session (Mahy and MacQuarrie, 2000).

When the referral problems at home and school have ameliorated or subsided significantly, the Theraplay treatment comes to an end with a final party session where the growth of the child is noted and celebrated. Four follow-up Theraplay sessions are planned to occur within a year from the end of treatment.

Treatment Plan

The treatment plan is briefly outlined below:

Session 1: Parental interview for developmental child and family history.
Session 2: Marschak Interaction Method (MIM) assessment, which is videotaped.
Session 3: Feedback of MIM and goals are discussed.

Session 4: Demo and practice of Theraplay activities with parents.
Sessions 5–8: Parents observe their child and therapist playing together.
Sessions 8–15 (or more): Theraplay sessions (including parents as well as their child) followed by optional parent counseling. (Note that in session 9 or 10 homework is assigned: Theraplay activities are chosen by parents to practice at home. Progress is discussed in parent counseling sessions.)
Final/party session: Determined by progress made at home and school. A party is held in the last session which involves favorite Theraplay activities of the child and parents, with the latter leading the activities. Party hats are exchanged and favorite food such as a cake brought by the parents and drinks are consumed. The strengths and growth of all family members are discussed.
Follow-up sessions: Four follow-up Theraplay sessions are tentatively scheduled to take place within a year.

Sample Theraplay Agenda

A typical agenda for a Theraplay session might consist of the following:

Entrance: Family members form a single line behind the therapist, who leads the group into the room modeling different actions that everyone behind the leader copies (e.g., slow, fast, big, small, tiptoe steps, waving arms, etc.). The leader finally stops at a cluster of cushions or beanbag chairs in a corner or center of the room, where everyone sits down.

Hello Song (or special handshake): The therapist starts a simple song where everyone's name is mentioned (e.g., "Hello Johnny, hello Mom, hello Dad, I'm glad you've come to play").

Checkup or Inventory: The therapist notes two or three positive features of the child (e.g., "Johnny, I see you've brought your shiny, brown hair and your sparkly blue eyes") and sometimes notes something about each parent (e.g., "Mom, you've brought your rosy cheeks, and Dad, you've brought your warm smile"). Often the parents are asked to notice one positive thing about their child (and sometimes about each other).

Taking Care of Hurts: The therapist looks for "hurts" (scratches and bruises on each hand of the child), which she or he lotions or powders with baby powder. If parents themselves have come from abusive or neglectful backgrounds, the therapist may (in later sessions) take care of the "hurts" on the parents' hands as well. Also, in later sessions, the therapist asks the parents to put lotion on the "hurts" of their child. If the family group includes siblings, the children in later sessions can put on lotion on the "hurts" of each other, thus learning to take care of each other.

Theraplay Activities Related to Main Dimensions: Three or four Theraplay activities such as hand stacking, pass a funny face, blowing cotton balls to each other, catching soap bubbles, passing a gentle touch, etc.

Feeding: Favorite snack of the child (potato chips, pieces of fruit, etc.) is fed to the child.

Good-bye Song: Everyone holds hands while singing "Good-bye Johnny, good-bye Mom, good-bye Dad and [therapist's name], we're glad you came today." This might be followed by a group hug.

As mentioned before, a parent counseling session is provided following the therapy session where the activities could be debriefed and progress at home and school could be reviewed. If the child is old enough (i.e., an adolescent), he or she can be included in the discussion occasionally. With younger children, a co-therapist could take the child to play outside or do crafts, etc., in a separate room. If this is not possible, then the child would be directed to stay in a corner of the room with quiet toys or books while the adults talk.

Two Practical Interventions

The Theraplay agenda described above can be expanded beyond the identified child in two practical interventions. First, the Theraplay model can incorporate all of the siblings besides the referred child, particularly if there is severe sibling rivalry or scapegoating apparent in the family dynamics (Loweth, 2000; Wood, 2000). Second, a multifamily model can be used, especially if there are long waiting lists, where more than one family is experiencing similar difficulties with children approximately the same age (Manery, 2000; Sherman, 2000). This format has been very effective in family groups consisting of parents and their adoptive children (Finnell, 2000) and with homeless mothers and their children (Rubin, 2000). The multifamily model provides added benefits such as greater opportunities for children to socialize with their peers and for the parents to support each other.

CASE STUDY

Alan was a 4-year-old boy who was so aggressive and noncompliant that his single mother had decided to "give him up." The mother described Alan as "a little monster" and that he had turned out to be just like her ex-husband, whom she despised. She described Alan as always being resistive to almost everything, impulsive, and aggressive. The mother reported that Alan would continually provoke her so she would become enraged quickly. She had come to a point where she did not want him in her home. Alan had a 10-year-old sister who achieved well academically, was easily compliant, and was described as "an angel" by her mother. Previously mother and children had participated in traditional family therapy, which was unsuccessful. The family therapist referred this family for Theraplay in a last, desperate bid to keep the family intact.

After an initial family and developmental history took place, MIM was administered and video recorded. The MIM video was reviewed and goals were set by the mother and therapists. It was decided that the main dimensions to be focused on were structure and nurture for Alan with the hope that he would become more cooperative with adults and less aggressive and impulsive. For the mother, it was important that she become more positive and accepting, more attuned to Alan's needs, and to learn to enjoy her son. The main goal was to create a healthy, strong attachment between mother and her child.

During the first few Theraplay sessions, where the mother observed (from a one-way mirror) Alan and his therapist playing together, she remarked to the co-therapist (interpreting therapist) beside her that "I don't see how this play is going to help my son!" She was hostile and rejecting. The interpreting therapist encouraged her to just keep on observing for a few sessions and to see if any changes might occur. Fortunately, Alan behaved mainly in a positive manner with his therapist, who focused on noting his strengths and gave clear structure to the activities. Alan, at first quiet and cautious, soon started to relax and enjoy himself under the warm, accepting manner of the therapist. Additionally, he was very controlling at first, but with the consistent, firm limits placed by the therapist, he became more cooperative. The mother changed as well and was starting to see some of the positive qualities of her son.

After four sessions the mother entered the room and began playing directly with her son under the guidance of both therapists. At first, Alan started to act out when his mother began to participate (old patterns can often emerge when a parent first joins in). However, with firm, clear directions from the therapist and the emphasis on "no hurts" (a strong Theraplay rule), he settled down and became more cooperative. Engaging activities like "tossing a balloon in the air," "cotton ball blow," "cotton ball guess," and "pass a funny face" emitted laughter from both of them.

Since this mother had come from a childhood where she had been rejected and neglected by her own mother, when the activity "taking care of hurts" came about, the interpreting therapist put lotion on the mother's "hurts" on her hands. She then asked the mother to nurture her son by putting lotion on his "hurts." In the parent counseling session later, the therapist mentioned how beautifully she had done this nurturing activity and the mother answered, "I could never have done that if you had not done it to me first." This illustrates how some parents need to experience nurturing themselves first, before they can do this with their child. In the Theraplay model, the therapist plans for this nurturing of the parent first.

Alan and his mother progressed well with an emphasis on nurture and structured activities where directions were clear and simple. Alan's impulsive behavior was attended to by the therapists and he was quickly redirected each time. Overall, he developed greater self-regulation regarding impulsivity. He learned to follow the directions of simple games like "Red light, Green light," "What time is it, Mr. Wolf?" (stop and go games), and "Mother may I." He responded positively to the nurturing activities such as previously described (taking care of "hurts"), feeding, and games involving hugs and back rubs. His favorite activity was being rocked in a blanket in his mother's arms. His improved behavior generalized to the home, where he became much more compliant with his mother's requests and she became more accepting and affectionate. As he felt better about himself and felt more closely attached to his mother, he became less aggressive with his sister.

In the parent counseling sessions the mother gained some insight into the possibility that she was projecting some of her negative feelings of her husband onto her son. Toward the end of treatment, a suggestion was made to the mother that she might seek psychotherapy for herself, in order to help resolve some of her resentment toward her former husband. Four checkup sessions were held during the year, where the family demonstrated continued improvement.

The above case illustrates how Theraplay can help a parent and child become closer in their attachment to each other and how negative behavior can be improved significantly. This case illustrates as well how important it can be to integrate the parent into treatment where some of the needs of the parent can be met, as well as the child's needs. Treatment effects are then more likely to generalize to the home and to be longer lasting.

CONCLUSION

Theraplay is a model of treatment that attempts to provide the crucial experiences that a child needs (and sometimes that a parent needs first) to feel securely attached, accepted, valued, and loved by his or her chief caregivers. This means that it is essential to integrate parents into treatment with their child. Theraplay attempts to replicate what normally occurs in the interactions between parents and a young child. It is guided by the empirical research from neuroscience and the importance of touch, and employs a parallel approach to neurosequential programming. Theraplay is a short-term and structured approach that includes healthy physical contact, and strives for self-regulation of the child. Attunement and warm responsiveness from the parent to the child is modeled and encouraged. It is applicable to a wide age range and social, emotional, and behavioral difficulties, particularly those involving attachment issues. An atmosphere of focusing on positive strengths of both child and parent, warm nurturance, and lively engagement creates conditions that bring fun and joy to the family, which is conducive to true healing.

REFERENCES

Baggerly, J. & Green, E. (2014). Mending broken attachment in displaced children. In C. Malchiodi and D. Crenshaw (Eds.), *Creative Arts and Play Therapy for Attachment Problems,* New York, NY: Guilford Press, 275–293.

Booth, P. & Jernberg, A. (2010). *Theraplay: Helping parents and children build better relationships through attachment-based play* (3rd ed.). San Francisco, CA: Jossey-Bass.

Booth, P., Lindaman, S., & Winstead, M. (2014). Theraplay in reunification following relational trauma. In C. Malchiodi and D. Crenshaw (Eds.), *Creative Arts and Play Therapy for Attachment Problems,* New York, NY: Guilford Press, 139–158.

Coleman, R. (2010). Research findings that support the effectiveness of Theraplay. In P. Booth and A. Jernberg (Eds.), *Theraplay: Helping Parents and Children Build Better Relationships Through Attachment-Based Play,* San Francisco, CA: Jossey-Bass, 85–97.

Field, T. (2001). *Touch.* Cambridge, MA: MIT Press.

Field, T. & Reite, M. (1985). *The psychobiology of attachment and separation.* New York, NY: Academic Press.

Finnell, N. (2000). Theraplay innovations with adoptive families. In E. Munns (Ed.), *Theraplay: Innovations in Attachment-Enhancing Play Therapy*, Lanham, MD: Jason Aronson, 235–256.

Ford, C. W. (1993). *Compassionate touch: The role of human touch in healing and recovery*, New York, NY: Simon & Schuster.

Franke, U. (2007). *An analysis of the therapeutic treatment process using Theraplay with oppositional, defiant children and shy withdrawn children.* Paper presented at the Third International Theraplay Conference, Chicago, IL.

Fromm, E. (1963). *The art of loving.* New York, NY: Bantam Books.

Gaskill, R. & Perry, B. (2014). The neurobiological power of play. In C. Malchiodi and D. Crenshaw (Eds.), *Creative Arts and Play Therapy for Attachment Problems*, New York, NY: Guilford Press, 178–194.

Gerhardt, S. (2004). *Why love matters: How affection shapes a baby's brain.* New York, NY: Brunner-Rutledge.

Hart, S. (2008). *Brain, attachment, personality: An introduction to neuroaffective development.* London: Karnac Books.

Kochanska, G. & Aksan, N. (1995). Mother-child mutually positive affect, the quality of child compliance to requests and prohibitions, and maternal control as correlates of early internalization. *Child Development*, 66(1), 236–254.

Laible, D. & Thompson, R. (2000). Mother-child discourse, attachment security, shared positive affect, and early conscience development. *Child Development*, 71(5), 1424–1440.

Lassenius-Panula, L. & Makela, J. (2007). *Effectiveness of Theraplay with symptomatic children ages 2–6: Changes in symptoms, parent-child relationships, and stress hormone levels.* Paper presented at the Third International Theraplay Conference, Chicago, IL.

Lender, L. & Lindaman, S. (2007). *Research supporting the effectiveness of Theraplay and the Marschak Interaction Method.* Paper presented at the Third International Theraplay Conference, Chicago, IL.

Loweth, D. (2000). Bringing the sibling into Theraplay: A family system view. In E. Munns (Ed.), *Theraplay: Innovations in Attachment-Enhancing Play Therapy*, Lanham, MD: Jason Aronson, 95–102.

Mahy, A. & MacQuarrie, J. (2000). Theraplay and parent counselling. In E. Munns (Ed.), *Theraplay: Innovations in Attachment-Enhancing Play Therapy*, Lanham, MD: Jason Aronson, 79–93.

Makela, J. (2005). Kostetuksen merketya lopsen kehelyksena. (The importance of touch in the development of children). *Finnish Medical Journal Review*, 14, 1542–1549.

Manery, G. (2000). Dual family Theraplay with withdrawn children in a cross-cultural context. In E. Munns (Ed.), *Theraplay: Innovations in Attachment-Enhancing Play Therapy,* Lanham, MD: Jason Aronson, 151–194.

Munns, E. (2000). *Theraplay: Innovations in attachment-enhancing play therapy.* Northvale, NJ: Jason Aronson.

Munns, E. (2005). Theraplay with adolescents. In L. Gallo and C. E. Schaefer (Eds.), *Play Therapy with Adolescents*, Lanham, MD: Jason Aronson, 30–47.

Munns, E. (2008). Theraplay with zero- to three-year-olds. In C. E. Schaefer, S. Kelly-Zion, J. McCormick, and A. Ohnogi (Eds.), *Play Therapy for Very Young Children*, Northvale, NJ: Jason Aronson, 157–170.

Munns, E. (2009). *Applications of family and group Theraplay.* New York, NY: Jason Aronson.

Munns, E. (2011). Theraplay: Attachment-enhancing play therapy. In C. Schaefer (Ed.), *Foundations of Play Therapy* (2nd ed.), Hoboken, NJ: John Wiley & Sons, 275–296.

Munns, E. (2014). Group Theraplay. In E. Prendiville and J. Howard (Eds.), *Play Therapy Today*, New York, NY: Routledge, 163–178.

Munns, E., Jensen, D., & Berger, L. (1996). *Theraplay and the reduction of aggression.* Unpublished Research, Blue Hills Child and Family Center, Aurora, Ontario.

Nicholson, B. & Parker, L. (2009). *Attached at the heart: Eight proven parenting principles for raising connected and compassionate children.* New York, NY: iUniverse.

Panksepp, J. (1993). Rough and tumble play: A fundamental brain process. In K. B. MacDonald (Ed.), *Parents and Children Playing*, Albany, NY: SUNY Press, 147–184.

Perry, B. & Szalavitz, M. (2006). *The boy who was raised as a dog.* New York, NY: Basic Books.

Ritterfeld, U. (1989). Theraplay auf dem prufstand: bewertung des therapieerfolgs am beispiel sprachauffalliger vorschulkinder (Putting Theraplay to the test: Evaluation of therapeutic outcome with language disordered preschool children). *Theraplay Journal*, 2, 22–25.

Rubin, P. (2000). Multifamily Theraplay groups with homeless mothers and their children. In E. Munns (Ed.), *Theraplay: Innovations in Attachment-Enhancing Play Therapy*, Lanham, MD: Jason Aronson, 211–234.

Schiefer, K. (2009). *Sunshine Circles manual.* Wilmette, IL.: The Theraplay Institute.

Schore, A. (2005). Attachment, affect regulation, and the developing right brain: Linking developmental neuroscience to pediatrics. *Pediatrics in Review*, 26, 204–217.

Sherman, J. (2000). Multiple family Theraplay. In E. Munns (Ed.), *Theraplay: Innovations in Attachment-Enhancing Play Therapy.* Lanham, MD: Jason Aronson, 195–210.

Siegel, D. (2011). *The whole-brain child.* New York, NY: Delacorte Press.

Stern, D. N. (1995). *The motherhood constellation: A unified view of parent-infant pathology.* New York, NY: Basic Books.

Sui, A. (2009). Theraplay in the Chinese world: An intervention program for Hong Kong children with internalizing problems. *International Journal of Play Therapy*, 18(1), 1–12.

Sunderland, M. (2006). *The science of parenting.* New York, NY: DK Publishing.

van der Kolk, B. A. (2005). Developmental trauma disorder: Towards a rational diagnosis for children with complex trauma histories. *Psychiatric Annals*, 401–408.

van der Kolk, B. A. (2006). Clinical implications of neuroscience research in PTSD. *Annals of the New York Academy of Science,* 1071, 277–293.

Wardrop, J. & Meyer, L. (2009). Research on Theraplay effectiveness. In E. Munns (Ed.), *Applications of Family and Group Theraplay*, Lanham, MD: Jason Aronson, 17–24.

Wettig, H., Franke, U., & Fjordbak, B. (2006). Evaluating the effectiveness of Theraplay. In C. Schaefer and H. Kuduson (Eds.), *Contemporary Play Therapy*, New York, NY: Guilford Press, 103–105.

Wood, S. (2000). Treatment of a sexually abused child in the context of sibling rivalry. In E. Munns (Ed.), *Theraplay: Innovations in Attachment-Enhancing Play Therapy*, Lanham, MD: Jason Aronson, 140–148.

Chapter Three

Incorporating Parents in Young Children's Psychotherapy

Filial Therapy

Glade L. Topham and Risë VanFleet

> Relationships that are "connecting" and allow for collaboration appear to offer children a wealth of interpersonal closeness that supports the development of many domains, including social, emotional, and cognitive functioning. —Daniel Siegel (2001, p. 78)

Filial Therapy (FT) is a specialized treatment approach developed by Bernard and Louise Guerney (Guerney, 1964) in which parents are taught the skills of Child-Centered Play Therapy (CCPT). In FT training, parents learn CCPT skills that they then apply during special, one-on-one play sessions with each of their children, ages 3–12. Filial therapists initially supervise the play sessions providing specific, targeted feedback to foster parents' skill development, parents' attuned and responsive caregiving, and parents' ability to reflect on their own and their children's internal experiences in interaction. As parents develop these competencies they are able to create a context within the special playtimes, and eventually more broadly within the parent-child relationship, that facilitates child healing, growth, and healthy development.

One of the strengths of the FT approach is its simplicity and straightforwardness. The simplicity of the approach allows overwhelmed parents with few resources to quickly make progress and gain confidence. Furthermore, the clear-cut skills and structure of FT make it an ideal treatment model for new therapists or therapists who have had little experience working with parents and children conjointly. FT avoids pathologizing children or parents and eschews a linear or medical model of assessment and treatment. Instead, FT focuses on family members' strengths and capacities to overcome and work through challenges, and the parent-child relationship is viewed as the primary mechanism for change (Topham & VanFleet, 2011). Similar to many models of family therapy, FT takes a "socialization-as-intervention" approach (Cavell & Elledge, 2007). FT focuses on addressing the family's presenting problems, while also assisting families in developing and maintaining processes and patterns of relating to each other that promote healthy development and positive outcomes for all family members. In this way, it is at once an intervention and a prevention approach.

Since Bernard and Louise Guerney developed FT over 50 years ago, a number of different group models have been adapted from the original FT group (Landreth & Bratton, 2006; VanFleet, Sniscak, & Faa-Thompson, 2013; Wright & Walker, 2003). Although each model is slightly different than the others, there are more similarities than differences, and the research and theoretical foundation for FT presented in this chapter applies across models. However, the specific treatment details provided are in reference to VanFleet's depiction of the individual filial family therapy model, developed over 20 years ago (see VanFleet, 2014 for a detailed description of the model). Note that the term "parent" is used throughout the chapter to refer to primary caregivers (i.e., biological parents, foster parents, grandparents, adopted parents, and so on).

CURRENT RESEARCH AND THEORY

Theoretical Foundation

Client-Centered Play Therapy (CCPT) theory guides the primary parent-child interaction of FT. Parents learn the CCPT principles and skills and, with support, apply them to create a context in which their children can work through and gain mastery over worries, insecurities, loss, and other challenges. The therapist-parent interaction, which also follows CCPT principles through the therapist's supportive, accepting, and empathic approach to the interaction, reinforces this process. Additional theoretical influences from family systems, attachment, psychodynamic, and cognitive behavioral theories can be found in FT (Guerney & Ryan, 2013; VanFleet, 2014). FT utilizes a family systems lens to focus on *all* parent-child relationships within the family system, regardless of whether or not they are directly implicated by the family in the presenting problem. Attachment theory's influence can be seen in the emphasis placed on helping parents develop sensitivity and responsiveness to their children while respecting and supporting child autonomy. The influence of psychodynamic theory is found in the attention paid to the symbolic meaning of children's play and brief discussions with parents regarding dynamic issues that might prevent attunement and responsiveness. Cognitive behavioral theory skills such as reinforcement, shaping, and vicarious learning facilitate the process of training parents in FT skills (Guerney & Ryan, 2013; VanFleet, 2014).

Empirical Support

Research has consistently demonstrated that, when compared to wait list control groups, participation in FT is associated with significantly greater increases in parent communication of acceptance, involvement with children (e.g., Kidron & Landreth, 2010), respect for children's feelings and expression of them, validation of children's emotions (e.g., Kidron & Landreth, 2010), and recognition of the need for and support of children's autonomy and independence (e.g., Kidron & Landreth, 2010). Similarly, parents who participate in FT report decreases in parental stress (e.g., Bratton et al., 2013), heightened awareness of their children's internal experiences, more realistic ideas of what is developmentally appropriate for their children (e.g., Lahti, 1992; Wickstrom, 2009), increased awareness of their own behaviors in interactions with their children, and a greater understanding of the impact of their behaviors on their children (Lahti, 1992).

A number of positive child outcomes have also been found for children participating in FT. These include reduced behavior problems (Bratton et al., 2013; Kidron & Landreth, 2010; Smith & Landreth, 2003), increased ability to cope with negative emotions and to express them to parents (Lahti, 1992), increases in child self-esteem (Smith & Landreth, 2003), and decreases in internalizing symptoms (e.g., Smith & Landreth, 2003). The positive effects of FT for both parents and children have been found with a wide range of presenting problems and with families from diverse cultural and ethnic backgrounds (see VanFleet, Ryan, and Smith 2005, and Guerney and Ryan, 2013, for a review).

FAMILY PLAY THERAPY PLANNING AND PROTOCOL

Filial Therapy Skills

In FT, four skills are taught to parents: empathic listening, limit setting, structuring, and child-centered imaginary play.

Empathic Listening

Empathic listening is fundamentally about parent attunement to and reflection of the child's behaviors and inner experiences (i.e., emotions, desires, intentions, etc.) during play. As a child lines up figures a parent might reflect the basic behaviors of the child such as "you are lining up those guys," but would also try, through observation, to discern and reflect the intentions, desires, and feelings of the child. For example, after a child struggles and then succeeds to get toy figures to stand up correctly a parent may reflect, "At first it was hard to get those to stand up and so frustrating, but you stuck with it and kept figuring it out until you got it to work. You are so excited that you figured it out!" Parents offer their undivided attention to their child and avoid any intentional or unintentional direction of the play, such as asking questions, using praise, or answering questions.

Limit Setting

Limits are kept to a minimum to create a context in which children are free to play in the ways they want or need without fear of judgment, correction, or redirection. It is important that during special playtimes, children feel a sense of control over themselves and their play. Limits typically include not damaging toys or the playroom and not hurting the parent or self. Other limits may be implemented if parents are unable to tolerate specific child behaviors (e.g., swearing), but these are kept to a minimum. The therapist works with the parent to develop tolerance for a wide range of behaviors during the filial playtime. There are three levels to the limit-setting process: setting the limit, providing a warning, and enforcing the consequence. Each level includes specific language that simplifies the process for parents and establishes predictability for children. If a child was about to draw on the walls with a crayon the parent would *set the limit*: "[Child's name], one of the things you may not do in the special playroom is draw on the walls. But you may do almost anything else." The statement is ended in this way to return the child's attention to the permissive nature of the playroom. If the child later moved to draw on the walls the parent would *provide a warning*: "[Child's name], one of the things you may not do is draw on the walls. If you choose to draw on the walls you will have to leave the special playroom, but you can do almost anything else." Finally, if the child persisted in trying to draw on the wall a third time, the parent would *enforce the consequence:* "[Child's name], you chose to draw on the walls. Our special playtime is over." And the parent would gently guide the child out of the room.

Structuring

In general, the structuring skill is used to introduce the special playtime, to prepare the child for the end, and to ultimately transition out at the end. Parents are taught to introduce the playtime by saying, "[Child's name], it is time for our special playtime. You can do almost anything you want to do in the special playroom. If there is something that you may not do, I'll let you know." The parent gives two warnings prior to the end of the playtime: at five minutes and one minute: "[Child's name], we have five minutes left of our special playtime." At the end of the playtime the parent says, "[Child's name], our special playtime is over." The parent also stands up and moves toward the door to signal to the child the end of the playtime. If the child resists, the parent reflects the child's emotions but reasserts that the playtime is over and gently guides the child out of the room: "You are having fun and don't want to leave, but our special playtime is over."

Child-Centered Imaginary Play

In child-centered imaginary play the children are the actors and directors, with parents playing out the roles the child wants them to play. When parents are invited by the child to join in the play, parents generally discontinue verbally reflecting and immerse themselves in their role in play. If the child's directions are unclear, parents work to discern the child's wishes without asking the child for direction, which might disrupt the child's play. Through this process, parents develop increasing attunement to their child as they struggle to sense what the child most needs from them in play. For example, a parent whose child invited her into dinosaur play may sense his need to be strong and to win. In the dinosaur battle, as she is being defeated, she may exclaim, "You are beating us. Ah, you are just too strong for us. We are trying to fight you back but you are too big, too fast, too powerful for us!"

Five Phases of Treatment

There are five phases of FT treatment: (1) assessment, (2) training, (3) supervised play sessions, (4) home play sessions, and (5) generalization and discharge (see VanFleet, 2014, for a detailed description of the FT skills and process). The order of phases remains consistent across cases regardless of presenting issue; however, the length of each phase may vary depending on parents' needs, how quickly parents progress, and the severity and nature of the presenting problem.

Assessment

The first two sessions are typically set aside for assessment. Parents attend the first session without children. This is important, as the goals of the first session are to build a relationship with parents, to learn about the parents' concerns regarding the child and the family, and to conduct a developmental and relationship history on the child and the family. Children are invited to attend the second session with their parents. At the beginning of the second session, the therapist meets with the entire family to begin building a relationship with the children and help them become comfortable with the playroom. The therapist also conducts a play observation. Family members are instructed to play as they normally would at home for 20 minutes while the therapist observes from an unobtrusive position in the room. At the end of the 20 minutes, the therapist meets alone with the parents to discuss his or her observations and to learn from parents how representative the play observation was of what happens at home. If the therapist is satisfied with what has been learned during the assessment, the therapist may choose to make a recommendation of FT at the end of the second session.

Training

The training phase, lasting three to four sessions, is devoted to helping parents learn the play session skills prior to the filial play sessions. The first of the training sessions includes brief, 10- to 20-minute *demonstrations* of the play session skills with each of the children in the family, ages 3–12. Parents observe the play demonstrations and take notes for later discussion. During that discussion, the therapist helps the parents understand the connection between the therapist's behaviors in the demonstration sessions and the four play session skills. In addition, the therapist may briefly discuss the purpose for and rationale of the different play session skills, including the ways in which the skills and FT process will likely help the parents reach their treatment goals.

The therapist provides more *direct instruction* on the four play skills during the second session of the training phase, providing examples of how each of the skills is used. The therapist also provides opportunities for parents to briefly try the skill. Toward the end of this session the therapist conducts a brief role play with each parent. The parents are asked to focus on utilizing only the empathic listening skill while the therapist plays with two or three toys at a slow pace. The therapist plays in a deliberate manner with exaggerated emotional displays and provides brief positive coaching to facilitate parent success and help parents begin to develop confidence.

The final element of the training phase is the *mock play session* in which the therapist plays the role of the child while also providing in-the-moment feedback to parents as they practice. Typically, two sessions are devoted to these role plays with each parent participating in at least two 10- to 15-minute mock play sessions followed by feedback discussion. The therapist may decide to do a third mock play session with parents in cases where parents are slow in developing the skills or in cases where the parents and/or therapist anticipate that the child's behaviors may be particularly challenging to the parents (e.g., particularly aggressive or sexualized play). In the mock play sessions, the therapist provides opportunities for parents to practice all four play session skills through showing obvious emotion, inviting the parent into play at least once, and making an obvious move toward breaking a limit. As parents improve in skills, the therapist may increase the degree of difficulty for parents and may begin to act out challenges that are anticipated from the child.

Supervised Play Sessions

After completing the training sessions, parents begin the filial play sessions with their children. The first parent-child play session is typically 20 minutes, with future sessions lasting around 30 minutes. If parents have multiple children between the ages of 3 and 12 participating, however, play sessions may be shortened to 15–20 minutes each, and/or the therapy session may be extended beyond typical 50-minute sessions to 90-minute sessions. If two parents are participating, parents take turns in play sessions with their children, and if circumstances allow, the nonparticipating parent unobtrusively observes the other parent's play sessions along with the therapist. During the play sessions, the therapist takes detailed notes in order to provide specific feedback to each parent. The observing parent is invited to participate in the feedback session listening and asking questions but not in offering his or her own feedback.

The therapist typically starts with one or two pieces of positive feedback and then solicits the parent's reaction to the play session. This is an important part of the discussion, as it allows the therapist to help the parent work through any negative reactions/interpretations that might prevent the parent from being completely present for the child during play sessions. It may also provide a port of entry for the therapist into parent beliefs and needs that interfere more generally with the parents' ability to be sensitive and responsive in the parent-child relationship. Asking for parent input early on also clearly demonstrates the collaborative working model typical of FT and permits full parent participation in discussing their strengths as well as challenges. Next, the therapist provides detailed positive feedback on the four play session skills, with one or two recommendations for improvement. The last element of the feedback discussion is typically a discussion of the themes and developmental issues demonstrated in the child's play. Initial feedback discussions are concentrated primarily on parent skills with much less time spent on the nature of the child's play. However, as parents progress in treatment this typically flips, with much of the feedback discussion in later sessions focused on child play. These discussions foster parent awareness of and attunement to the internal world of their children.

Home Play Sessions

By the fifth or sixth play session, parents typically have a pretty good handle on the play session skills and are prepared to transition play sessions to their home. In anticipation of this transition, the therapist has been assisting parents in putting together an inexpensive set of toys and in problem solving when and where parents will hold home play sessions to avoid interruptions. After the transition to home sessions, parents are encouraged to conduct one half-hour play session each week with each of their children. Depending on the parents' success with the play session skills at home, the therapist may space discussion sessions out to every other week while the parents continue to hold weekly sessions with their children. During the sessions, therapists review home play sessions with parents, answer questions, address issues that come up, and help parents talk through their own reactions and experiences in the play sessions.

Generalization and Discharge

Therapy sessions are also used to help parents generalize the play session skills to everyday parent-child interaction. Using the empathic listening skill, parents learn to listen to, accept, and validate their child's emotional experience. They provide scaffolding support to their child, providing as much (but not more) help as their child needs in problem solving the situation. Parents are encouraged to use the same three-step limit-setting sequence outside of play sessions. In addition, the therapist helps parents identify limits and consequences appropriate for their child. Parents use the structuring skill outside of play sessions by learning to anticipate their child's needs and challenges, preparing the child for transitions, and structuring the child's environment to facilitate success. Parents generalize the child-centered imaginary play skills to parent-child (one-on-one) activities, such as making cookies or playing a game together. In these activities, parents follow the child's lead as much as possible while giving the child their undivided attention. The final few sessions during the discharge phase are typically spaced out, with one final supervised play session to complete treatment.

ONE OR TWO PRACTICAL INTERVENTION(S)

FT is a strengths-based approach, and the therapist relies heavily upon supportive scaffolding to help parents incrementally build competence and confidence. This approach helps therapists avoid becoming discouraged in their work with parents who initially struggle to make progress. Instead of focusing on how far a parent has to go to reach mastery, the filial therapist focuses attention on what is going well for the parent and on the next step for the parent in his or her development. This supportive, scaffolding approach can be seen in how filial therapists help parents build the play session skills, develop attunement to their children, and increase in reflective awareness of self and the relationship with their children.

An example of scaffolding in the process of parent skill development can be found in the mock therapy sessions in which the therapist plays the role of child and provides specific feedback to the parent. The therapist regulates the degree of difficulty of the mock session based on parent ability. For example, as the parent is initially getting a feel for the skills the therapist's play is simple and deliberate with obvious cues for the use of the skills such as obvious emotion, clear evidence that a rule is about to be broken, and a clear invitation to join the therapist (as the child) in play. The feedback is overwhelmingly positive, with a few suggestions for improvement. Much of the feedback is focused on recently developed skills and abilities and those that are emerging or just beyond the parent's current abilities. For example, a therapist may tell a parent with fewer skills, "Nice job here paying attention to what I am doing and avoiding taking lead of the play. You could even add a description here of something you see me doing. If you were describing what I am doing, what might you say?" Assuming the parent responds with a description of something the therapist is doing the therapist would then praise the success, "Perfect description! That really helps me as a child feel like you are 100 percent focused on and invested in what I am doing." In this way the therapist helps the parent develop his or her skills in a positive and encouraging way.

The therapist scaffolds the parent's awareness of the child and the child's play during feedback discussions by gently inviting the parent to reflect on what the child might be experiencing, feeling, or needing. In the case where a parent had low awareness of the child, the therapist may do more of the work focusing the parent's attention on meaningful play session behaviors. For example, a therapist might make the following observation: "Johnny seemed to spend a lot of his time lining up and organizing and categorizing all of the toys during the session. What do you think that was about for him?" Or, for a parent who struggled to attune to child inner experience, a therapist might ask, "When he finally got that last block to stay on the top of the tower, and he hopped up on the couch with a big smile, what do you think he was thinking and feeling?" The therapist may share personal observations and offer his or her own thoughts on what might be going on for a child, but only as needed. A primary focus of the discussion is inviting the parent to reflect and hypothesize about child behavior and internal experience.

Finally, the therapist uses scaffolding during the feedback discussions with parents about their own experience in play sessions with the child. The goal here is to help parents become increasingly aware of their own thoughts and feelings and how those reactions impact their responses to the child in play. For parents who are more aware, the therapist may simply offer a general prompt to guide parent reflection: "What did you notice about your reactions to Tim in play?" Or "What were the times when you noticed the strongest reaction in yourself to Tim's play?" For parents who demonstrate less awareness the therapist may do more to direct the parents' attention: "I noticed that when Tim was ordering you around you had a little bit of a reaction; you got kind of quiet and your face turned a little red. What do you think was going on for you in that moment?" If the parents are in a position to continue to engage in reflection, the therapist may scaffold their reflections toward an understanding of what they brought to the interaction that may have influenced the way they saw or experienced their child in the moment. These discussions can help parents take responsibility for the things that prevent them from being fully present for the child. It also helps them develop the capacity to reflect on their own as they continue to encounter feelings and thoughts that block responsiveness.

CASE STUDY

As is customary with case studies, all identifying information has been disguised or removed, and in some aspects, a composite of several families is used. The case study that follows shows an accurate depiction of the FT process.

Background: The Mercers

Rob and Ila Mercer had two children, ages 6 and 4. They came to therapy because the 4-year-old, Randy, had not adjusted well to his diagnosis of juvenile-onset diabetes, made one year earlier. Although he was medically stable, Randy had developed behavioral and emotional problems that were upsetting for the entire family. The parents reported that their 6-year-old, Mellie, was "mature for her age" and caused no problems. They were proud that she seemed so responsible, but they also worried aloud that the problem with Randy took away from the attention that she received. Rob and Ila reported that the diagnosis and subsequent family events had created tension in their relationship. They had been drifting apart prior to this, and now they found themselves in more frequent arguments. They could not agree on an approach with Randy, and they often worked at counterpurposes. Ila said she felt so bad for Randy having to have multiple injections and finger sticks for his blood glucose tests every day, as well as the restricted eating that signaled that he was "different." She reported that she often gave in to him when he fussed, trying to placate him with new toys, watching television past his bedtime, and other concessions. Rob believed that Randy would cope much better if he was not "babied" quite so much. He often found himself being the primary disciplinarian. When he tried to follow through on certain limits, he felt undermined by Ila.

Although Randy accepted his injections without trouble, he frequently protested when they pricked his finger for the blood glucose tests. He cried, ran away from them, and threw tantrums. They said they sometimes simply let the tests slide, but at other times, they had to hold him down. Ila said that she also could not tell the difference between "bad behavior" and "when his sugars were out of kilter." For a period, she had been testing his blood sugar even more frequently whenever he misbehaved, trying to determine whether it was "behavior" or "diabetes" causing the problem. In the past month, Randy had begun throwing tantrums more frequently and in more situations, such as when he couldn't get something at the store that he wanted, when he was told to brush his teeth, and at bedtime. Rob noted that when Ila paid attention to Mellie for longer than a few minutes, Randy would get between them, fussing if Ila didn't turn her attention back to him. Both noted that Mellie was a good girl who "gave in to" Randy. If she had a toy or item that he wanted, Mellie gave it to him when he fussed.

The therapist empathically listened to Rob and Ila during their first meeting, asking questions periodically. The therapist's empathy helped them feel accepted rather than judged, and they opened up further about their worries. As the session closed, it was apparent that they were worried about the "little monster" that Randy was becoming. They wanted their sweet boy back without the behavioral acting out that was consuming most of their family time. They wanted to have more fun as a family and to prevent diabetes from running their lives. They also wanted to make sure they were managing Randy's diabetes well while still helping him to feel normal.

The therapist obtained a release to speak with Randy's doctor, who later commented that Randy's medical condition was stable and his tests of long-term glucose control were within the acceptable range. The problem appeared to be triggered by the diabetes and its management, but was now primarily behavioral and interpersonal in nature.

Family Play Observation and Recommendations

During the second meeting, Rob and Ila brought Randy and Mellie to the playroom. The therapist observed them for approximately 20 minutes, and then Randy and Mellie were invited to play in a secure waiting area where other interesting toys were arranged. It was just around the corner from the playroom where the therapist continued the meeting with the parents, so any need for supervision of the children could be readily addressed.

The therapist asked Rob and Ila how similar their family playtime had been to the way things were at home. They mentioned that Randy's way of interrupting other family members when they were interacting with each other, rather than him, was very common. He had done this several times with each of them and especially when Mellie was interacting with Ila. They also mentioned that his whining when he had to share one toy with Mellie was also typical, often the first sign of an impending tantrum. The three also discussed positive aspects of the family playtime and the therapist's observations. There was warmth in their interactions, and it showed that they genuinely loved each other. The therapist mentioned how both parents were trying very hard to be attentive to both children. They also discussed one incident during the play session when Randy grabbed a toy from Mellie. Rob had begun to reprimand him verbally, and Ila cut in and said, "It's okay this time. He had a rough time at dinner tonight." The therapist discussed this without judgment, simply asking the parents if this was an example of the different styles they each had when handling Randy's behavior. They agreed that it was.

Because the family dynamics had been altered rather significantly by the diagnosis and subsequent management of Randy's diabetes, the therapist recommended FT as the primary treatment. It was believed that FT would provide Randy with an increased sense of control over his world and a more appropriate outlet for his confused feelings. Additional anticipated benefits include providing Mellie with more attention as well as an opportunity to express her own feelings, a way to allow the children's respective development to unfold in a more positive direction, a means for both parents to gain greater understanding of their children, and the building of more secure attachments and better relationships with both of them. In addition, it was expected that FT would help parents align their parenting practices and decisions, which would likely help reduce some of the tensions in their marriage.

FT Play Session Training

During the next session, the therapist held 20-minute individual play sessions with both Randy and Mellie while Rob and Ila watched from a corner of the room. They had a clipboard with paper on which they could write their observations and questions about the play sessions. Randy's play was generally aggressive in nature. Mellie started out somewhat timid in her play, moved to some nurturing play, and then finished with two dolls arguing and fighting.

After Randy and Mellie left the room, Rob and Ila told the therapist they were not surprised by Randy's play, although they were concerned about it. They were startled by the aggressive nature of Mellie's play, however, and expressed worry that this approach might cause her to become aggressive, too. The therapist empathically listened to their concerns: "You couldn't believe she would play that way, and you're having second thoughts. . . . You really wouldn't want this approach to make her become aggressive." The therapist then went on to explain a bit more about the method, how the CCPT sessions help children express themselves in symbolic ways, and that the overall process was designed to help them work through feelings and become better adjusted emotionally, socially, and behaviorally. She went into some detail to help allay their fears, and they both agreed to move forward with FT at the end of the session.

The next three sessions were devoted to training Rob and Ila, using the approach outlined earlier in this chapter. During the mock play sessions, Ila had some difficulty stating limits and using a firmer tone of voice, but with coaching and a little more practice she did better. Rob struggled a bit with the child-centered imaginary play. He was able to play the roles very well, but he tended to lead them rather than follow the child's (therapist role-playing the child) lead. More attention and practice was devoted to that skill for him. At the end of their second full mock session, Rob and Ila felt ready to begin sessions with their children.

Early Parent-Child Play Sessions

Rob played with Randy for the first FT play session. Randy repeated his themes of aggressive play with the bop bag. Rob utilized empathic listening while observing Randy's play, using some of the phrases the therapist had used in the demonstration session, which also applied here. He refrained from leading the play, catching himself twice when he began to suggest a move. Randy also found some dinosaurs and had them fight each other. He laughed throughout this play, and at the end, a T-Rex came and pushed something at the smallest dinosaur. He did not explain this, and Rob had trouble finding something to say.

Ila then played with Mellie. Mellie went to the sand tray. She selected female figures to dance in the sand (the beach), and she then said they were going shopping for sandals. After 10 minutes, she asked her mother to take two of the figures and follow her through the imaginary store (also in the sand tray) to buy things they needed for their party on the beach. Ila was able to reflect Mellie's feelings during the play ("They really like dancing on the beach. . . . They are eager to go buy some things. . . ."), and she also followed along with the play when she was given the characters to use.

Both parents had completed excellent first play sessions. During the discussion afterward with just the therapist and the parents, they both commented how hard it was to hold back on the usual things they would say and do, but they understood that it was important. The therapist was able to provide them with specific positive feedback on the many things they did well, and discussed the more difficult moments with them. She covered things Rob might say during the T-Rex play should it occur in the future and suggested some deeper-level feeling reflections that Ila could use with Mellie. They discussed what the play might mean. This focused on Randy's aggressive play and its possible relation to his feelings about his (sometimes) intrusive medical treatment and lack of control. The discussion also included focus on relationship building in Mellie's play.

During the next session, Mellie played cautiously with Rob, again relying on doll figures and the sand tray. She also held a tea party with the soft large dolls, but there was no dissension among the dolls this time. She included her father in the tea party, and poured water and served a meal for him. Randy's aggressive play with the bop bag was still there, and Ila started out providing some excellent empathic responses to it. She seemed to understand him much better, seeing that other feelings and dynamics were at play below the aggressive play. His play shifted when he began punching the bop bag so that it would hit Ila. At first she moved away, but he persisted in hitting the bag so that it would hit her. Ila tentatively set a limit: "It's not nice to try to hit me. Let's play something else." Again at the end, the therapist provided feedback to each of them, highlighting the many positive aspects of their skills and the sessions. They both were feeling quite good about the process except Ila knew that her limit had been "wimpy." The therapist helped her rephrase that limit and they practiced briefly so Ila could get a firm, but not punitive, tone of voice. The preponderance of positive feedback made it easier for both parents to hear the suggestions for improvement. They also discussed play themes. Relationship building seemed to continue in Mellie's play, and Randy's aggressive play had crossed its first boundary. The therapist listened to the parents' concerns and fears, and then discussed how this limit-testing behavior was actually a "good" thing—that it showed that the process was working already. Since limit-testing and control issues were part of the pattern at home, it was to be expected that they would surface in the play sessions as well. The discussion deepened as the therapist explained how the lack of control that Randy probably felt about having diabetes had come out in some of his bad behavior—that the bad behavior was perhaps his attempt to feel more in control. She went on to suggest that the play sessions would gradually provide him with a greater sense of control over something that would be more acceptable—control over the play. Very often, as this theme is coupled with solid boundaries when needed, the externalizing behaviors at home disappear.

Later Supervised Parent-Child Play Sessions

The therapist observed three more sessions in which the parents each played with one of the children. Mellie began to share more of her feelings, selecting themes where two characters frequently became upset with each other. In one particularly telling scene, a family was eating at the table in the dollhouse. The boy of the family had a tantrum and destroyed everything in the house. To convey this, Mellie created a scene of chaos but did not actually destroy anything. Rob and Ila needed some help understanding this uncharacteristic behavior in Mellie. Eventually, they began to recognize Mellie's awareness and feelings about the family's struggles with Randy. The therapist reassured them that they were on the right path, and that it was wonderful that they were beginning to see her point of view that she had hidden so well.

Randy continued aggressive play, never again pushing past the boundaries. Both parents were able to reflect his aggressive feelings, frustrations, tensions, and anger as shown in his play. During the fifth session, he picked up a doctor puppet, then threw it on the floor and jumped on top of it several times. Rob and Ila were amazed to see him express his feelings so directly toward the medical figure. By this time, they understood that this was part of his therapeutic process and were not worried.

In the meantime, there had been some early signs of improvement at home. The only intervention to this point was the FT, but Randy began verbalizing some of his feelings more readily rather than acting them out. Mellie seemed less shy and was more willing to talk with her parents. Rob and Ila reported that they were trying to ensure that Mellie had some time of her own with them, especially at bedtime.

Home Play Sessions and Generalization

Rob's and Ila's skills improved with each session, and after their fifth play sessions alternating with one of the children, the therapist discussed the transition to the home sessions. They set up the play sessions in their den and removed the toys at the end until the next time. Things began to improve dramatically after the third home sessions, the eighth sessions overall. Randy had played with the medical kit they had included, serving as the doctor to the dolls that were there. He was a bossy and unpleasant doctor, telling his patients what they should do and how they would die if they did not follow his instructions. The way this play evolved demonstrated Randy's strong anxiety about his disease, not merely the dislike of the needles and tests. Once this emerged from beneath his acting out, Ila and Rob were able to listen empathically to his fears ("The patients are scared about what the doctor is telling them. It's a scary thing.") and anger ("His patients are mad—really mad—because they don't like their diseases. . . . That boy really hates that doctor because he's so mean."). Randy's tantrums and oppositional behaviors lessened considerably in daily life.

Mellie went through a period of anger themes, symbolically showing her distress more clearly. At the same time, she seemed more relaxed and participated more actively in the family. After one powerful session in which Mellie became a doctor and performed surgery on her mother to "make everything better," Rob and Ila expressed relief that they had discovered the feelings that Mellie had been hiding.

Because Rob and Ila were very skilled at this point and the sessions were going well, the therapist began helping them generalize the use of the skills in everyday life. As they began using the FT skills regularly, the remaining problems seemed to dissipate. The tantrums stopped because Randy had an outlet for his feelings, and he felt more in control. His parents were more understanding of his feelings about his disease, his diet, and his treatment, and he no longer had to "show" them. Mellie was getting more attention and feeling more a part of the family. She no longer deferred to Randy on everything. This led to more sibling spats, but Rob and Ila understood that this was healthier than for her always to be yielding to her younger brother. Rob and Ila reported that they were more consistent over time and with each other. They rarely argued about parenting issues anymore. Ila was able to set limits with Randy without worrying about tantrums, and Rob felt closer to both children. They were pleased with the results in a relatively short span of time, and they were committed to continuing the play sessions as long as the children were interested in them. They had become adept at applying the skills in everyday life, and they began planning their discharge from therapy. The formal therapy ended after the parents had held a total of 12 sessions with each child, and they continued having play sessions after therapy ended. They knew they could return to see the therapist should any new problem arise.

CONCLUSION

FT is an empirically supported form of family therapy that incorporates parent-child play sessions as a means of building secure attachment between parent and child, providing greater attunement and acceptance of feelings, and developing greater parent confidence and competence. It is a straightforward psychoeducational model that offers great flexibility for a wide range of child and family problems. Research, as well as clinical evidence, points to its effectiveness in fostering positive change in all family members—parents and children alike. FT has been adapted into a variety of formats, and it can easily be used in conjunction with other forms of treatment, including individual play therapy, group work, and other forms of family therapy. More information about its methods and applications can be found in Guerney and Ryan (2013), VanFleet (2014), and VanFleet and Guerney (2003), as well as at www.play-therapy.com and www.nire.org.

REFERENCES

Bratton, S. C., Ceballos, P. L., Sheely-Moore, A. I., Meany-Walen, K., Pronchenko, Y., & Jones, L. D. (2013). Head start early mental health intervention: Effects of child-centered play therapy on disruptive behaviors. *International Journal of Play Therapy*, *22*(1), 28–42. doi:10.1037/a0030318

Cavell, T. A., & Elledge, L. C. (2007). Working with parents of aggressive, school age children. In J. Briesmeister & C. Schaefer (Eds.), *Handbook of parenting training: Helping parents prevent and solve problem behaviors* (3rd ed., pp. 379–423). Hoboken, NJ: Wiley & Sons.

Guerney, B. (1964). Filial therapy: Description and rationale. *Journal of Consulting Psychology, 28*, 303–310.

Guerney, L., & Ryan, V. (2013). *Group Filial Therapy: The complete guide to teaching parents to play therapeutically with their children*. Philadelphia, PA: Jessica Kingsley.

Kidron, M., & Landreth, G. (2010). Intensive child parent relationship therapy with Israeli parents in Israel. *International Journal of Play Therapy, 19*, 64–78. doi.org/10.1037/a0017516

Lahti, S. (1992). An ethnographic study of the filial therapy process. *Dissertation Abstracts International: Section B: The Sciences and Engineering, 53*(8-A), 2691.

Landreth, G., & Bratton, S. C. (2006). *Child parent relationship therapy (CPRT): A 10-session filial therapy model.* New York, NY: Routledge.

Siegel, D. J. (2001). Toward an interpersonal neurobiology of the developing mind: Attachment relationships, "mindsight," and neural integration. *Infant Mental Health Journal, 22*, 67–94. doi:3.0.CO;2-G" TARGET="_blank" http://dx.doi.org/10.1002/1097-0355(200101/04)22:1 67::AID-IMHJ3 3.0.CO;2-G

Smith, N., & Landreth, G. L. (2003). Intensive filial therapy with child witnesses of domestic violence: A comparison with individual and sibling group play therapy. *International Journal of Play Therapy, 12*, 67–88. doi.org/10.1037/h0088872

Topham, G. L., & VanFleet, R. (2011). Filial therapy: A structured and straightforward approach to including young children in family therapy. *Australian & New Zealand Journal of Family Therapy 32*, 144–158. doi.org/10.1375/anft.32.2.144

VanFleet, R. (2014). *Filial Therapy: Strengthening parent-child relationships through play* (3rd ed.). Sarasota, FL: Professional Resource Press.

VanFleet, R., & Guerney, L. (Eds.). (2003). *Casebook of Filial Therapy*. Boiling Springs, PA: Play Therapy Press.

VanFleet, R., Ryan, S. D., & Smith, S. K. (2005). Filial Therapy: A critical review. In L. A. Reddy, T. M. Files-Hall, & C. E. Schaefer (Eds.), *Empirically based play interventions for children* (pp. 241–264). Washington, DC: American Psychological Association.

VanFleet, R., Sniscak, C. C., & Faa-Thompson, T. (2013). *Filial Therapy groups for foster and adoptive parents: Building attachment in a 14 to 18 week family program*. Boiling Springs, PA: Play Therapy Press.

Wickstrom, M. (2009). The process of systemic change in filial therapy: A phenomenological study of parent experience. *Contemporary Family Therapy: An International Journal, 31*(3), 193–208. doi:10.1007/s10591-009-9089-3

Wright, C., & Walker, J. (2003). Using Filial Therapy with Head Start families. In R. VanFleet & L. F. Guerney (Eds.), *Casebook of Filial Therapy* (pp. 309–329). Boiling Springs, PA: Play Therapy Press.

Chapter Four

Psyche and System

Integrating Jungian Play Therapy into Family Counseling

Mary Anne Paré

Everything depends on everything else. —Haida First Nation saying

It was Jesse,[1] age four and a half, who first introduced me to the concept of the integration of play therapy and family counseling in 1989. This little guy, with flaming red hair and temperament to match, arrived at our family-based therapeutic day program from the third daycare he had been asked to leave within a year. There were legitimate reasons for these removals: refusal to join circle time, disruption at naptime, and biting other children. By the time he came through our door, Jesse's parents, Miriam and Robert, who also had an 18-month-old and two day jobs, were emotionally stretched thin. In the intake meeting, they avoided eye contact with each other. This child and his parents clearly were in need of psychosocial support.

Miriam and Robert described Jesse as the "24-hour cyclone" in their family. Aside from the disruption caused by the inevitable phone calls from daycares, life at home had become filled with negatives: Don't bite your sister, don't put food in your shoes, and don't pour Mommy's shampoo down the toilet. Sleep deprivation and parental disagreements had damaged the quality of the marital relationship. Robert had conflicts with his boss. Miriam's younger brother, Charlie, had recently died. Both parents recognized that Katie, the 18-month-old, was not getting the attention she needed.

Along with the day program for children, the couple attended weekly evening meetings with a counselor. It was only after their fears of "expulsion" from the therapeutic center subsided that they could acknowledge the impact of the stress upon their relationship. However, it was only when Jesse brought home a drawing with a smiling sun that Miriam and Robert finally disclosed deep-rooted anxiety about their son. In infancy, Miriam's siblings had nicknamed Jesse "Charlie Junior" because his red hair and emerging personality were so like those of his uncle Charlie, who was also his godfather. In adolescence, Miriam's brother had spiraled down from "golden boy" to "black sheep." His death the previous year, resulting from an overdose of OxyContin and other street drugs, left the family uncertain whether the death was accidental. Miriam and Robert traced the "cyclone" in their family to around the time of Charlie's death. Might their son's extreme behaviors be related to parental responses due to worries about similarities between Jesse and his deceased uncle?

Meanwhile, Jesse and I had an hour-long, weekly session in the play therapy room. After sessions of disasters with crashing cars, collapsing block towers, and drowning animals, Jesse introduced a Saint Bernard dog who came to the rescue of the many victims in his play. Over a number of weeks, the drowning diminished and the pleasurable water play increased. Then the Saint Bernard carried a baby doll into the water basin, and Jesse asked me to help him give it a bath. His play was transforming, as was he.

One day, as Jesse and I were on the way to the play therapy room, he stopped at the door of the parent room, where Miriam and Robert and I had met that morning before they joined the children in the yard for outdoor play. "Someday I'd like to go in there for a shat," he said. It took me a few moments to translate this into "chat," which is what Jesse had intended to say. It wasn't until later, when I was completing my session notes, that I registered what he was proposing: he wanted to join his parents and me in our sit-down talk time. As I thought about it, the logic of this request began to sink in. In the couple sessions, the parents experienced blame and anxiety about their son. In play therapy, this little guy was moving into healing play. If we were all in the same room, might that increase the potential for change? When I raised this at our next team supervision session, the group was wary: How long would Jesse last in the toyless setting of the parent room? Alternatively, could his parents let go of their worries and anger to join in Jesse's imaginative play in the play therapy room? My supervisor ended with a pertinent question: "If you were to work with the two generations together, who would supervise you?"

I began to look at the play and family counseling literature to build a new foundation on which to practice. Could I incorporate compatible theoretical building blocks from which to develop a practice that addressed the family as an interconnected system? Back at the therapeutic center with Jesse and his parents, there was a new development. The parents separated after an explosive fight and refused to come in together to address this crisis. In individual meetings, deeper issues around sexuality surfaced and I began to understand the complexity of the couple's conflict. While the opportunity for parent-child sessions with this particular family had slipped away, I realized there were others families with which the integration of the two modalities might be useful. Once again, I turned to the literature, this time renovating my work with children and families. In this chapter, the theoretical integration of Jungian Family Play Counseling will be described (Paré, 2013; Paré & Allan, 2006). The application of this model, including the role of the therapist, toys and playroom, play, and engagement with the family system will be discussed and illustrated in a case study.

LITERATURE REVIEW

Extensive reading and researching of the literature encouraged me to integrate the Jungian play therapy model in which I had been trained with family therapy theory and practice. Though Jung lectured and gave seminars on children, this aspect of his teachings was only published posthumously in 2008 in a book called *Children's Dreams*. In 1929, Francis Wickes, a Jungian analyst, wrote extensively on children but emphasized Jung's belief that therapists should work with children's parents, as Jung considered children to be acting out the unresolved conflicts and unconscious aspects of their parents (Wickes, 1988). Fordham, a British Jungian analyst, believed that the archetype of the Self is activated in childhood and that children can and should be seen and treated alone (Fordham, 1996). Subsequently, Jungian practitioners have focused on treating the child (Allan, 1988; Green, 2014; Sidoli & Davies, 1988) and generally refer parents to other professionals. Lois Carey (1999) developed a Jungian approach to working with parents and children using sandplay. The Jungian Family/Play Counseling model (Paré, 2013; Paré & Allan, 2006) in this chapter emphasizes the importance of working as a team with parents and including both generations in therapy whenever the goals of the work reinforce an integrated approach.

Jungian play therapy involves, as a central tenet, the transformative potential within image, symbol, and archetype. Jung conceptualized the unconscious as a storehouse within which solutions and healing were located and which would be accessible in the safety of a transference relationship (Allan, 1988). Archetypes or symbols are the language of the unconscious, and children are fluent in this language in their play. The practice of Jungian play therapy affords children "sufficient psychological space in an emotionally protected environment or *vas* (container), so that personal development (i.e. individuation) materializes. Individuation characterizes progress[ion] from psychological fragmentation towards wholeness" (Green, 2014, p. 34).

Wachtel (1992) identified flexibility and a readiness to shift perspective as hallmarks of an integrative approach. To expand play therapy practice to include the family system, one is faced with the task of "remodeling" practice by rethinking theory. Drawing on commonalities and compatible differences within the theoretical concepts of both play and family counseling, play therapy practitioners can expand their repertoire for working with parents and children together. This approach gives recognition to the interconnection of family and facilitates an understanding of children's behaviors from systemic as well as behavioral and intrapsychic perspectives.

An integrated practice of Jungian play/family counseling entails first meeting with parents, then, when indicated, the whole family. Next, a plan is developed with parents about who should be engaged in counseling and when. If children need individual play therapy, parents are included either at beginnings or endings of sessions, or via phone calls between sessions. Siblings, parents only, and whole-family sessions may be scheduled as the work progresses, depending on evaluation of how the therapeutic involvement is bringing about change in family dynamics. Assessment entails an initial extensive family history with genogram, and continues throughout therapeutic involvement, as shifts in family dynamics direct the course of counseling. Termination is indicated when individual needs are understood and being met, family interactions have shifted from a focus on pathology to one of well-being, and parents identify that their goals for treatment have been achieved.

The Role of the Therapist

In play therapy, the relationship between children and therapists is central (Landreth, 2012), with the transference-countertransference relationship acting as the catalyst to healing (Allan, 1988). A safe container is created, through the design of the room, the choice of materials, and the therapist's presence. Within this container, the children's feelings can emerge to be felt and be understood. The therapist's goal is to be fully present and engaged with the child. In family counseling, the neutral therapist's presence as a neutral party within the family dynamics creates the potential for healing within the family (Becvar & Becvar, 2013). Again, a safe space is created, this time for all members to experience being together in a different way. Reflecting, questioning, and directing family members in facilitative interactions with each other creates the opportunity for new ways of feeling and thinking about oneself and each other. The family myth has the potential to be deconstructed and transformed. The therapist acts as a bridge to connecting family members, to enable change to happen within the family (Freeman, 1992).

In integrated Jungian family/play counseling, the therapist's role is expanded to include aspects of the functions of both play and family therapist. Therapy doesn't begin, necessarily, until a trusting relationship is established with children. Equally critical is the therapist's ability to join with all family members. The therapist determines when/if parents and/or children need individual sessions and when/if including the whole family will enhance the therapeutic process. Therefore, the therapist has the dual role of the transference relationship with the child and of facilitator of change and reparation occurring within the family. Just as the play therapist is often in the roles of both witness and guide in the play therapy process, this position can act as a powerful catalyst for change within the family.

The Role of Symbol

In play therapy, the materials provide a language for the child's self-expression (Allan, 1988). Toys and miniatures are the "words" that represent internalized concepts or feelings, and the child chooses and manipulates play materials to explore, make sense of, and transform difficult emotions, beliefs, and memories. Symbols bridge the gap between concrete experience and abstract thought most efficiently (Piaget, cited in Green, 2014). Carl Whitaker, a founding father of family therapy, utilized the term "symbol" to represent the primacy of the unconscious in the dynamics of the family (Whitaker & Keith, 1981). In family counseling, members utilize symbols in the form of words and stories, rather than play materials. The spoken word is used to express introjects and constructs in the family's story. The family mythology is present in all interactions and, by creating opportunities for new ways of interrelating, the family story can be edited and rewritten. The externalization of the problem allows for new and unique outcomes to be explored (White & Epston, 1990). In integrated Jungian family/play counseling, both the language of symbols and cognition are accessed. The therapist creates the opportunity for an interweaving of talk and play in order to include children and parents and to allow for the exploration of both paths to change and healing.

Mechanisms of Change

At the core of the play therapy process is the transference relationship between therapist and child. The child projects both positive and negative aspects onto the therapist, and the symbolic language of play accesses and activates the healing potential of the psyche. In family counseling, dynamics, beliefs, history, patterns, and roles are explored. New interactions create new ways of experiencing one another and being together. In integrated Jungian family/play counseling the process of change is expanded, so that healing and growth can occur unconsciously, through symbol, and consciously, with dialogue and interactions.

In the case of Jesse and his family, for example, a safe transference relationship had already been established between Jesse and the therapist.

Change was occurring on the symbolic level with Jesse's catastrophic play externalizing the distress he was feeling and with the emergence of the healing archetype of the Saint Bernard dog. Furthermore, the parents had identified the projection and anxiety embedded in the family story of Jesse's connection to his dead uncle, who could be conceptualized as the archetype of the "black sheep." The conflict between the parents had likely resulted in triangulation within the family, with Jesse acquiring the position of the identified patient. Had the work continued, an integrative approach would have addressed the family dynamics and projection on the adult level, which would have enabled Jesse's parents to experience their son in new interactions and meaningful play.

INTEGRATIVE FAMILY/PLAY COUNSELING TREATMENT PLANNING AND PROTOCOL

The Jungian family/play counselor who has done the foundational work of integrating theory and expanding practice will approach referrals with the recognition that each family[2] is unique. A primary skill for the Jungian play/family counselor, from the very beginning of counseling, is the ability to interweave the languages of symbol and words in practice. This calls for fluency with both, as well as an intuitive sense of when to use which language, depending on the family's needs. If there has been a family fight, the first intervention may be for each family member to draw the fight and then tell the story of their picture. Alternatively, puppets, the ball as a "talking stick," or the basket of balls with feeling faces may be used to help describe what happened. Then the family might move to the sand tray(s) to create images of how they want it to be when the problem is "all better." The ages of the children, the parents' comfort level and skill with play and degree of agitation in the family system will guide the practitioner in which language is best suited at any given time in the session.

Drawing on systems theory allows the Jungian play counselor to track the influence that roles, beliefs, values, and family history have on the presenting problem. The therapist builds hypotheses about the meaning each member places on the presenting problem. For example, what is the shadow side of this family? Who is taking the role of provocateur, enabler, facilitator? Is there a golden child, a black sheep, a wicked stepmother? How might a belief that higher education is critical for success influence the parents' feelings toward their learning-disabled child? In turn, how might this impact the child's sense of self? How has the fire that destroyed the family home created fear that keeps the parents from allowing their children to be free to explore the world? The hypotheses that are generated by these issues guide the therapist's choices of who come in, the directions of conversations and play, as well as interpretations of symbolic material.

In this integrated model, there is a continuum of session attendees, including an individual child, sibling group, couple, or whole family, depending on what is at the forefront of the work at any time. Consultation with parents assists in decisions about who attends during each stage of treatment. For example, children may come individually when parental anxiety is high due to problem behaviors, whereas the couple may attend first to address problematic marital dynamics. Nevertheless, all family members are included, in some way, from the beginning of counseling to emphasize that the treatment process is aimed to help the whole family. Children can be asked what their parents told them about coming to see the therapist (Chasin, 1994) and often experience great relief to know their parents are talking with someone about family matters.

Early Phase of Treatment

In the early phase of counseling, the Jungian family/play counselor assesses the potential for families to address problems together using play and talk. Situations where bringing parents and children into the playroom together would be advantageous include those where:

- children are uneasy about being in the playroom with the therapist (i.e., very young children, fear of strangers, experience of abuse, language difficulty, beginning stage, previous negative experience of counseling by parents or children);
- parents show the ability to manage their own anxiety to be present for children;
- acting out has become the primary way the child is being heard in the family;
- children's security of attachment has been disrupted by events in family life (i.e., illness, death, separation, major moves).

On the other hand, parent-child integration is contraindicated in situations where:

- parents are struggling with emotional issues to the degree that this makes them inaccessible to children in the counseling setting;
- children need privacy and separate space to deal with issues of trauma and /or feelings that they want to protect parents from;
- parents' own process of healing might result in disclosing experiences or information that would burden the child;

- children or parents are unable to move out of a reactive position, even in play;
- the family's themes activate family-of-origin issues in the therapist that inhibit her or his neutrality (i.e., supervision required beforehand).

Initial sessions also provide information as to how best to provide a therapeutic experience for each client family. Meeting with the parents first allows for their concerns to be heard without having to modify them in front of their children (Chasin, 1994; Wachtel, 1992), and different parental perspectives provide important insight into family interactions. Parents know their family best, while therapists have the experience and training to be helpful in a wide range of issues. Working as a team can create the changes in line with the family's hopes and goals. Children's behavior is considered as an attempt at communication; the adults can collaborate to develop hypotheses as to what the child is attempting to express. The initial session is also the time to address issues of confidentiality; at each developmental stage there are different guidelines for children's confidentiality needs (Miller, 1994). Parents are informed about any relevant therapeutic directions if/when the professional is working with children on their own.

Middle Phase of Treatment

Throughout treatment, sessions involve ongoing assessment and joining with members. When all family members attend, directed play creates structure, as the family become familiar with the therapist, the room, and the process. From a Jungian play therapist perspective, interventions are also on a continuum, from active processes such as directing, structuring, playing a role, linking, and interpreting behaviors, to passive processing such as reflecting and observing (Allan, 1988; Green, 2014). The therapist uses knowledge of the family to determine the direction of each therapeutic hour, and the unique style of the family and ages of the children best determine the degree of structure in talk and play sessions. When parents respond well to the therapist's modeling of engaging in child-directed play, this modality is ideal, as the unconscious material opened up often identifies the "problem" and activates the healing potential within the psyche and the system. When the session involves talking about difficult issues, the therapist speaks to the child's level of understanding. Meanwhile, children are given the opportunity to practice putting their feelings into words in a safe environment. Everyone can have input in problem solving and discussion, whether it be in words or in play.

Structured games are an engaging way to bring family dynamics and symbols into early sessions. Activities can be as simple as throwing a ball back and forth, with the person holding the ball being the one who gets to speak (it is remarkable how a resistant child will scramble to get his or her turn at the ball). A collection of balls with faces with a range of emotions can be useful tools when families are telling stories of difficult events; each person can choose the ball that fits how he or she felt. The myriad of innovative techniques detailed in a wide range of books on interventions for individuals and families suggest that the only limits on activities are therapists' and children's imaginations (e.g., Gil, 2014; Jernberg & Booth, 2001; Kaduson & Schaefer, 1997, 2001, 2003; Lowenstein, 2010).

When the child is attending individual sessions, it is essential to continue the teamwork model of working with parents. Practitioners may spend an hour with a child client weekly while parents are with their children the other 167 hours. Whenever possible, having parents in the playroom at the beginning of a session to describe how things are going, both the positives ("We had fun at the zoo") and the difficult ("Sally wet her bed four times"), without comment or judgment, confirms that the therapist knows about the children's lives between sessions. Parents are asked to hang their "disciplinarian hat at the door" so that they can be free to join their children in play. The rules of the room are different from every day and it is the therapist's job to enforce them (no one gets hurt, nothing broken on purpose, otherwise free choice during child-directed time). When there are concerns about children's behavior, the therapist models how to interact around the issues, allowing parents to be in a different role in the therapeutic space. If parents have difficulty with this arrangement, this is discussed at the adult level. The rationale is that this is a time to experiment with new ways of interacting to enhance family dynamics. Having the parent join in the latter part of a session so children can share any thoughts or feelings about their play brings the parent into the symbolic process. It also provides the basis for phone calls or follow-up meetings to discuss the child's progress.

Final Phase of Treatment

Jungian family/play counseling enters the termination phase when the presenting problem is no longer the main focus of family interactions. Deeper understanding and positive transference relationships will have enhanced family life and parents and children will have integrated alternative, supportive, and playful ways of addressing family issues. The therapist and family discuss the possibility of regression during times of high stress in the family, and parents are encouraged to call with concerns after treatment ends. If parents do call, the therapist generally meets with parents for a follow-up appointment to examine patterns, relate current issues with the earlier work, and review what interventions that were useful for the family. Children seldom need to come in again. When children are having significant struggles, offering checkups allows them to be in control of choosing if/when they need to come in again. The ultimate goal of the Jungian family/play therapist is to retire herself or himself from the family, knowing deeper understanding, strengthened relationships, problem-solving skills, and playfulness have made them better prepared for their lives together.

INTERVENTION

The *House* intervention evolved from the work of Carla Sharp, who developed the Build-a-House assessment tool (1995). In this assessment, families constructed a house from play materials at the beginning of counseling. The layout of the building, the choice of symbols, and the interactions of family members provided Sharp with insights into strengths and problem areas within the family's dynamics. Paré's version of the House expands the therapist's role as observer to include an interactive facilitation role. The technique offers a means of assessment as well as a game that can be used as an initial introduction to the playroom for parents and children together. It asks the question, "What is your family like?" inviting the family to respond on a metaphorical level.

The timing of introducing the house-building game in treatment depends on the uniqueness of each family and the issues that it brings to counseling. This technique may be counterindicated in the initial phase if there has been a recent separation or divorce, or if children are new to a foster or adoptive home. Some families choose to return to the game at different phases of the work, as a symbolic way of marking their progress and integrating what they have learned in counseling. Deciding when to conduct the intervention within the therapeutic hour is also important. When the family first enters the playroom, most children want to explore the room and the play materials, and parents may be feeling awkward and unsure of themselves. The therapist can suggest that the adults join the children in the play area, and he or she converses with the parents based on observations of the children: "The children are showing us what they like best. Mom, what were your favorite things to play when you were their age?" This conversation can continue to expand: "Dad, did you play like this with your siblings when you were little?" Children generally love to hear stories of parents' childhoods and are adept at the multitask of listening and playing. This is a way to integrate child-directed play and adult-focused interactions, which allows for a comfort level at all ages. It is also a way of introducing multigenerational themes and has the potential to begin exploring family history. If the talk agitates children or if there is conflict over toys, the attention returns to the present moment and provides the opportunity to address family dynamics: "Mom, is this fight over the teddy bear similar to what might happen at home?"; "Dad, could you see if you can help the kids sort this out?" Once the family has spent some time getting to know the room, the materials, and the therapist, the suggestion of the house-building game can be introduced.

Materials for this intervention include a large set of blocks, sand tray miniatures, and dollhouse furnishings. If neither a sand tray nor dollhouse is available, small toys that include human and animal figures, trees, fences, and vehicles will suffice. Blocks can also act as furniture. Prior to the introduction of the game in session, the therapist explains it to the parents. Once the activity is introduced, the therapist oversees it; his or her first task is to *clarify guidelines*: "This game is for the whole family. Together you get to build a house from these blocks. You can then add anything you want to the house. The only rule is that everyone agrees on how you want it to be."

Once the family begins, the second task of the therapist is to *reflect the process*, sometimes when a child is unwilling to participate. Since parents have already been briefed on the game, they know it is their job to respond to the child, using parental skills to explore feelings and encourage involvement. If parents have difficulty playing this role (due to their own emotional issues or simply their own discomfort with play), the therapist supports them in the parental task: "Dad, do you suppose Laura is feeling shy . . . or mad about being here today?" or "Mom, do you think Jimmy isn't sure what to build? Maybe you could help him?" The therapist also models flexibility: "How about we do the building game first, and then we'll get the Play-Doh out?" or "How about using some of the Legos to construct the house?" If the child's resistance cannot be redirected, it is likely best to revert to child-directed play, thus modeling the versatility that is needed with young children. It is important for therapists to remember that the symbol of a house is a potent one, and it may stir up many feelings in children and/or parents at this early stage of counseling.

When the family does engage in building a house together, the role of the therapist involves *keeping the process on track*: "Dad, I notice that Jimmy has put a tiger in the garage you built. Is that okay with you?"; "Mom, you said everyone would have their own rooms and now all the beds have been moved into one bedroom. Is that the way you want it?"; "Laura, how about you check with everyone about how many cats the family wants to have?" Within this role, the therapist also makes sure that everyone is in agreement with the final creation.

The game of house building gives the therapist a wide-ranging introduction to how the family works, as well as information as to how each member might respond to play-based interventions. It will likely raise issues that can be returned to in future sessions. Interactions highlight leaders, followers, mediators, helpers, provocateurs, resisters, and enablers, as well those who are playful, critical, distracted, avoidant, supportive, and positive. The choices the family makes in the construction of the house also provide insights into boundaries (e.g., walls between rooms), secrecy (e.g., a roof on the house), and individuation (e.g., one child builds separately). Other additions such as people, animals, furniture, and belongings tell about the family as well. Variations might include two houses for separated families or for including grandparents, foster homes, or respite families who are actively involved in child care. The final role of the therapist in this intervention is to debrief with the parents. Ideally, this occurs in a follow-up appointment without the children present. Parents' experiences in the session, and their observations can be very useful. The concept of working as a team to decide the direction and focus of the work draws on parents' potential to contribute to the healing process.

CASE STUDY

Kate, 7 years old, was referred to counseling because she showed signs of dissociation in the classroom setting. Her school counselor described her as struggling, both academically and socially. Kate's father, Ben, reported a history of broken attachments and traumatic events. Kate had lived with her biological parents, Ben and Betty, and her half-brothers, Karl and Ken, until the age of 3. After significant parental conflict, Betty separated from Ben and severed all contact between him and the children. The children were exposed to drugs, alcohol, and related crimes. Ben pursued his parental rights through the courts. When a judge granted Ben regular access, Betty left the country with the three children. An international agency found the mother and children, and they were returned to Canada. After a long and complex court case, the judge ruled that Betty would maintain custody of her two sons, but she was denied both custody of and access to Kate. Kate was currently living with Ben, who was a relative stranger to her, and a new stepmother, Carol,

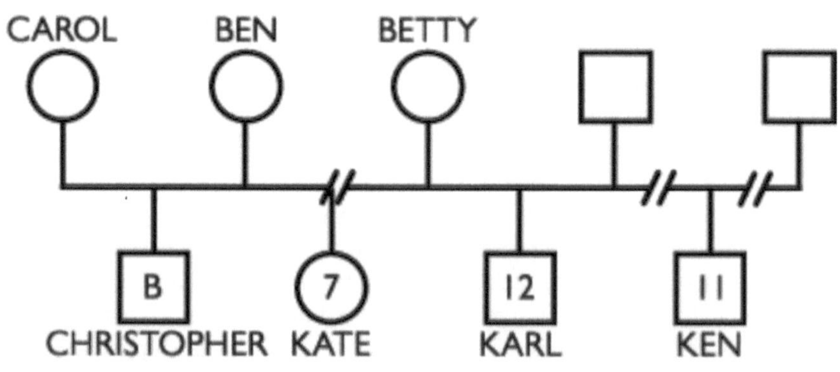

Figure 4.1. Kate's Family Genogram

who was expecting in five months. As well, Kate had lost all contact with her biological mother and half-brothers, the only family she had really known.

Where to begin the work? This child would clearly benefit from play therapy, and yet this was a family in crisis. Ben and Carol had no family support within visiting distance, and their first year of marriage had been dominated by Kate's abduction, the search for her, and a series of ongoing court cases. These events had devastated their finances and created a climate of chronic stress in their relationship. Meanwhile, despite her history of neglect and chaos, Kate was greatly missing her mother and brothers, and she challenged Ben and Carol in their parental roles. The therapist conceptualized that there were four significant therapeutic groupings in the work with this family: (1) father-daughter, (2) daughter alone, (3) stepmother and daughter, and (4) family all together. Because the court order denied contact between Kate and her biological mother, it was not possible to include Betty in the counseling, but her influence in this family was a constant presence, and she played a significant part in the therapist's conceptualization of the family process.

The Parent-Child Relationship

Parent-child therapy began with Kate and Ben together after the initial assessment meetings indicated that Kate was ambivalently attached to her father and that Ben was capable of playful interaction with his daughter. Ben brought Kate to early morning sessions and entered the play for 30 minutes. The school counselor joined Kate at the end of the hour and delivered her to her classroom. The play involved Play-Doh, clay, and painting, and it was clear that Kate wanted her father to create with her and witness her artistic creations. Conversations between Kate and Ben ranged from bedtime routines and agreed-upon consequences to Ben's responses to Kate's questions about her mother, brothers, and early history. In the final father-daughter session, Kate decided to hold court in the playroom. Her biological mother had recently mounted a legal challenge to the custody arrangement, which was again raising stress levels in the family. With Kate directing, Ben, the therapist, and Kate alternated the roles of judge, lawyers, and parents. In this play, Kate "spoke" to the judge and her mother, verbalizing her sadness, her anger, and, after long deliberation, her wish to stay with her father.

The Marital Relationship

In debriefing phone calls with parents after sessions, marital issues were raised and the therapist assessed that this couple was at risk for separation. Weekly appointments with Ben and Carol were initiated to address the traumatic history, as well as parenting and couple issues. The work focused on each hearing one another recount the pain of recent years and rebuilding trust in the relationship. It became clear that there was also a negative transference-countertransference between Kate and her stepmother. It was difficult for Carol to separate her resentment toward Betty from her feelings toward Kate. Ben, who continued to fear another abduction, was overinvolved with Kate and underinvolved with his pregnant wife.

Healing the Wounded Mother Archetype

The parent-child sessions had strengthened Kate and Ben's attachment. With the assurance that Kate was showing increasing ability to manage school and friends, Ben was encouraged to direct his energies toward himself, his marital relationship, and his wife's pregnancy. Individual play therapy focused on the theme of the negative archetypal maternal figure that Kate was projecting onto her stepmother. Kate often chose sandplay, using the figure of the Wicked Stepmother from Snow White. Kate buried, lost, found, embraced, reburied, yearned for, gave gifts to, raged at, and lost again this figure. As the story evolved, Kate seemed to be piecing together the archetypal Bad Mother/Good Mother split. There were times when the mother figure nurtured, and others times when she cut Play-Doh "babies" into pieces with a plastic knife.

The issue of the imminent arrival of the baby also arose in Kate's sandplay. Naturally, she had ambivalent feelings about this sibling, having missed out on a secure early attachment experience with her father. The playroom's baby doll underwent a range of abusive parenting interventions and was then left naked by an open window. Over the treatment duration of the play, the representation of the maternal figure softened. The Wicked Stepmother moved to a less prominent place in the sand picture. New characters found a princess that had been lost and built a sand castle for her, surrounded by fences and jewels. The baby doll was retrieved from its abandoned position and given a bath.

The Family System

A critical aspect of the work with this family was next. The couple's work had strengthened Ben and Carol's relationship and individual play therapy had reduced the negative transference between Carol and Kate. The arrival of the new baby, Christopher, gave Carol a sense of legitimacy as a mother. This opened the possibility that she had something to give and receive from joint play sessions with Kate. In these sessions, there was a lot of baby doll/real baby play, an all-girls' tea party (while Christopher napped), and talk about the family Kate would make when she grew up. When Carol's mother came to help out with the baby, Kate invited her new "Nana" to join her in the playroom, which she did.

House-Building Intervention

The final session with the family included Kate, Ben, Carol, and Christopher. Kate served an elaborate tea party and distributed the contents of a treasure chest to all family members. She then asked if the family could build a house. This game had been suggested earlier in the counseling, but Kate had declined to play. The house developed into a castle with thrones for each family member and a kitchen table piled high with food. Carol added a garden and patio. When Ben suggested building bedrooms, Kate became unfocused. She wandered off and returned with materials to construct another house. She placed the Wicked Stepmother figure and two children on beds and built a wall to surround the property. When asked about it, she said, "Another family lives there." Having constructed a representation of home for her biological mother and half-brothers, Kate seemed pleased with herself. She returned to the family's "castle" and created a bedroom that she declared was for her and her baby brother. Next, Kate went through the basket of animals, grabbing the largest snake, and circled the castle with the snake. This was a delicate moment for Ben, Carol, and the therapist, as they shared later during a phone call. To each of them, the symbol of the snake seemed threatening and menacing. However, the weeks of working together had prepared them to be in the moment. "Wow. Look at that big snake," Ben said. "It goes all around the house," reflected Carol. "Yes," said Kate, beaming. "It's a guard snake. No one can hurt anyone in this house now." Kate then asked that her baby brother be placed in her lap and posed with him beside the house for a photograph of the home the family had created.

Follow-up contact found Kate managing her schoolwork and friends more successfully. She continued to both "love" and "hate" her little brother in a way her parents described as "pretty normal." With the final court case behind them, Ben and Carol said their family was moving on in their life together as they had always hoped.

CONCLUSION

Within play therapy's core principles exist the precepts of Jungian theory. The transference relationship and access to the unconscious through symbol activates the healing potential in the child (Allan, 1988; Green, 2014; Jung, 1966). However, the child exists within the interdependent system of the family; what happens to the child happens to the family and what happens to the family happens to the child. Interacting in both symbolic and verbal languages offers the family a range of ways to understand one another and discover new ways of being together. The process of change is activated on both a conscious and unconscious level.

Furthermore, the integration of play with family counseling strengthens both therapeutic approaches (Gil, 2014) and creates a powerful synthesis in the treatment of children and families (Miller, 1994). Grounding the therapeutic process in both intrapsychic and systemic theory, while drawing on similarities within these theories, allows therapists to engage with families in ways that respond to each person's and each system's unique and multilayered needs.

NOTES

1. All names and identifying information have been changed to protect client confidentiality.
2. The term "family" represents any system involved in raising the children and "parent" includes any adult who is providing regular care for children.

REFERENCES

Allan, J. (1988). *Inscapes of the child's world: Jungian counseling in schools and clinics.* Dallas, TX: Spring Publications.

Becvar, D. S. & Becvar, R. J. (2013). *Family therapy: A systemic integration* (8th ed.). Upper Saddle River, NJ: Pearson.

Carey, L. (1999). *Sandplay therapy with children and their families.* Northvale, NJ: Jason Aronson.

Chasin, R. (1994). Interviewing families with children: Guidelines and suggestions. In C. Schaefer & L. Carey (Eds.), *Family play therapy*, (pp. 57–70). Northvale, NJ: Jason Aronson.

Fordham, M. (1996). *Children as individuals* (3rd ed.). London: Karnac Books.

Freeman, D. (1992). *Multigenerational family therapy.* New York, NY: Haworth Press.

Gil, E. (2014). *Play in family therapy* (2nd ed.). New York, NY: Guilford Press.

Green, E. (2014). *The handbook of Jungian play therapy with children and adolescents.* Baltimore, MD: John Hopkins University Press.

Jernberg, A. & Booth, P. (Eds.). (2001). *Theraplay* (2nd ed.). San Francisco, CA: Jossey-Bass.

Jung, C. G. (1966). *The Collected works of C. G. Jung, vol. 16: The practice of psychotherapy: Essays on the psychology of the transference and other subjects.* Princeton, NJ: Princeton University Press.

Kaduson, H. & Schaefer, C. (Eds.). (1997). *101 Favorite play therapy techniques.* Northvale, NJ: Jason Aronson.

Kaduson, H. & Schaefer, C. (Eds.). (2001). *101 More play therapy techniques.* Northvale, NJ: Jason Aronson.

Kaduson, H. & Schaefer, C. (Eds.). (2003). *101 Favorite play therapy techniques* (Vol. 3). Northvale, NJ: Jason Aronson.

Landreth, G. L. (2012). *Play Therapy: The art of the relationship* (2nd ed.). New York, NY: Brunner-Routledge.

Lowenstein, L. (Ed.). (2010). *Creative family therapy techniques.* Toronto, Ontario: Champion Press.

Miller, W. (1994). Family play therapy: History, theory and convergence. In C. Schaefer & L. Carey (Eds.), *Family play therapy*, (pp. 3–19). Northvale, NJ: Jason Aronson.

Paré, M. A. & Allan, J. A. (2006). *Symbol and relationship: An integration of Jungian play therapy and systemic theory.* HAPT Annual Conference, Honolulu, HA.

Paré, M. A. (2013). *Psyche and system: Integrating play therapy and family therapy in theory and practice.* COAP, Bend, OR.

Sharp, C. (1995). *Use of play in family assessment.* Workshop presentation, APT Annual Conference, San Francisco, CA.
Sidoli, M. & Davies, M. (Eds.). (1988). *Jungian child psychotherapy: Individuation in childhood.* London, England: Karnac Books.
Wachtel, E. (1992). An integrative approach to working with troubled children and their families. *Journal of Psychotherapy Integration, 2*(3), 207–224.
Whitaker, C. A. & Keith, D. V. (1981). Symbolic-experiential family therapy. In A. S. Gurman & D. P. Kniskern (Eds.), *Handbook of family therapy*, (pp. 187–225). New York, NY: Brunner/Mazel.
White, M. & Epston, D. (1990). *Narrative means to therapeutic ends.* New York, NY: W.W. Norton.
Wickes, F. G. (1988). *The inner world of childhood: A study of analytical psychology*. Salem, MA: Sigo Press.

Chapter Five

Adlerian Family Play Therapy

Terry Kottman and Kristin K. Meany-Walen

Feelings of worth can flourish only in an atmosphere where individual differences are appreciated, mistakes are tolerated, communication is open, and rules are flexible—the kind of atmosphere that is found in a nurturing family.
—Virginia Satir

Adlerian family play therapy is encapsulated in this quote from Virginia Satir, one of the pioneers of family therapy. Adlerian family play therapy combines two intervention strategies: family play therapy and Adlerian therapy. This combination provides a forum to help families learn to create the atmosphere Satir described, resulting in families that foster feelings of worth in all family members.

Family play therapy is a modality that "invites family members to engage with one another in ways that are mutually satisfying and relationally edifying" (Czyszczon, Riviere, Lowman, & Stewart, 2015, p. 186). It is a relative newcomer into the field of counseling. Sweeney and Rocha (2000) suggested that "family play therapy is a truly inclusive intervention for the presenting family with young children, providing both the therapist and other family members with a more complete picture of family dynamics and processes" (p. 36).

Adlerian therapy has been critical to the evolution of both family therapy and play therapy (Miller, 1994). Prochaska and Norcross (2010) contend that "Adler's ideas have quietly permeated modern psychological thinking, often without notice. It would not be easy to find another author from which so much has been borrowed from all sides without acknowledgment than Alfred Adler" (p. 91). Adlerians believe that Alfred Adler was a pioneer in just about every avenue of the counseling profession—the first cognitive-behavioral therapist, the first holistic therapist, the first positive psychologist, and the first family therapist (Watts, 2010). Adlerians have been providing family counseling since the 1920s (Gladding, 2007; Sherman, 1999) and play therapy since the 1980s (Kottman & Meany-Walen, in press).

The purpose of this chapter is to describe Adlerian family play therapy. First, current research and theory will be reviewed. Second, Adlerian family play therapy treatment planning and protocol will be explained. Third, two practical interventions will be described. Finally, an Adlerian family play therapy case study will be provided.

CURRENT RESEARCH AND THEORY

Current Research

Although there are no published research studies on Adlerian family play therapy, there is a developing body of research showing the effectiveness of Adlerian play therapy (e.g., Meany-Walen, Bratton, Kottman, 2014; Meany-Walen, Bullis, & Kottman, & Dillman Taylor, in press; Meany-Walen, Kottman, Bullis, & Dillman Taylor, in press). In their randomized controlled study of 58 elementary school children, Meany-Walen and colleagues (2014) found that children receiving Adlerian play therapy demonstrated a statistically significant reduction in behavior problems compared to the control group. Results showed large treatment effects. In addition, teachers reported a statistically significant reduction in their stress related to the children.

Adlerian family therapy has been described in many articles, chapters, and books (e.g., Bitter, 2014; Bitter, Roberts, & Sonstegard, 2002; Christensen, 2004; Gladding, 2007; Sherman & Dinkmeyer, 1987). Pfefferle and Mansager (2014) demonstrated how to use the Adlerian family diagnostic process as an intake and treatment planning tool. They included a case study and examples of interventions used with families. Sperry (2011) described Adlerian family counseling strategies for working with families in which one member had a personality disorder. He conceptualized and diagnosed the family unit aside from the individuals who made up the family. Sperry shared ideas on what might be helpful in improving family members' relationships and the family functioning. Bitter and Byrd (2011) used disclosure and storytelling in the family therapy process and offered ways to incorporate them in Adlerian family therapy. Lastly, Carlson and Robey (2011) included a description of key Adlerian tenets and a case study illustrating how to use Adlerian family therapy with a blended family. Although these examples do not have research to support their effectiveness, they do provide readers with examples of various adaptations and ways to facilitate Adlerian family therapy.

Adlerian Theory

"Adlerians believe that human beings are essentially social, purposeful, subjective, and interpretive in their approach to life" (Bitter, 2014, p. 133). These concepts can be applied to family play therapy. A main reason a counselor would use Adlerian family play therapy is that the family is the first, and most important social, context for its members. People have a need to belong and gain significance, and the family provides a forum for trying to do just this (Gladding, 2007). Family members learn and exercise communication skills, problem-solving tactics, and relationship-building strategies in the context of their families. They are a continuous influence on one another. "Any movement by the individual or the family creates movement in all other components of the system" (Dinkmeyer, 1997, p. 456). This makes family play therapy an incredibly powerful process. Adlerian family play therapists explore how each member gains a sense of belonging and significance in the family and use play therapy strategies to encourage members to shift negative patterns of belonging to more positive ways of connecting.

Because Adlerians consider all behavior purposeful, one key in understanding individual family members is to consider the purpose or goal of their behaviors.

> Typically individuals move away from feelings of inferiority toward feelings of growth, completeness, and wholeness. The individual strives to overcome perceived difficulties. Such behavior is described as goal-directed, future-oriented, teleological, or purposive. Purposive behavior is an important assumption, as it guides the Adlerian family counselor in developing strategies for behavioral and attitudinal change. (Christensen, 2004, pp. 8–9)

The Adlerian family play therapist uses play therapy techniques to investigate the goal of each member's behavior and to help family members shift their goal toward more socially appropriate positive goals. In most cases, these goals are out of the individual's awareness, so the therapist must gently reveal them to clients by making guesses about the purposes of their behavior.

Adlerian psychology is a phenomenological theory, meaning that Adlerians believe reality is perceived subjectively (Christensen, 2004). More emphasis is put on the individual's interpretation of what has happened than on what actually happened. The role of Adlerian family play therapists is to explore the subjective views of each family member and to help members understand the stance other members take on various situations and family struggles. Because many families have children, one method of gaining an understanding of the younger family members is to use play as a vehicle for communication (Sweeney & Rocha, 2000).

Other important theoretical concepts in Adlerian family play therapy are inferiority feelings, lifestyle, and social interest. Adler believed that all individuals strive to compensate for feelings of inferiority that develop from the discrepancy between their self-ideal and self-assessment (Ansbacher & Ansbacher, 1956; Maniacci, Sackett-Maniacci, & Mosak, 2014). People can deal with inevitable feelings of inferiority in three ways: overcompensating, giving up, or using them as a challenge. Quite often, in families, there are patterns of dealing with inferiority feelings. The Adlerian play therapists can help clients learn to recognize their patterns and develop coping strategies (Kottman & Ashby, 2015).

Lifestyle is the basic orientation to life based on each individual's unique pattern of perceptions regarding self, others, and the world, which dictates how he or she must think, feel, and behave (Dinkmeyer, 1997). As each family member's lifestyle is explored, the influence of the family atmosphere (the general affective tone of the family) and family constellation (psychological birth order) on each member and on the family dynamics is considered. In Adlerian family play therapy, an understanding of both the individual member's lifestyles and the family's lifestyle is developed. Adlerian family play therapists identify patterns that might suggest discouragement in individual members or places where the parents and children are "locked in repetitive, negative interactions based on mistaken goals that motivate all parties involved" (Bitter, 2014, p. 128). Play therapy strategies are used to help family members learn to understand themselves and one another and to learn new patterns of interaction.

Adler (1979) believed that all human beings are born with an innate capacity to develop community feeling or social interest. This aptitude must be fostered through upbringing and appropriately encouraged to develop cooperation and contribution (Yang, Milliren, & Blagen, 2010). The Adlerian family play therapist assesses the social interest in individual family members and the capacity of family members to foster and support social interest in one another. Based on this assessment, the Adlerian family play therapist designs activities to encourage enhanced social interest in members and to teach parents to foster a higher level of social interest in the children and in the entire family.

ADLERIAN FAMILY PLAY THERAPY PLANNING AND PROTOCOL

There are four phases in Adlerian family play therapy: building relationships, exploring lifestyles, helping members gain insight, and reorienting/reeducating (Kottman & Ashby, 2015). The Adlerian family play therapist guides family members through the phases in a journey to create a space where individual differences are appreciated, mistakes are tolerated, communication is open, and rules are flexible. This process is facilitated by using questioning strategies and observing the family members engaging in free play, directed activities, art techniques, and sand tray experiences.

Building the Relationship

The first phase, building the relationship, actually lasts throughout the process as the counselor continually cultivates connection with family members (Kottman & Ashby, 2015; Kottman & Meany-Walen, in press). This process can start in an initial meeting with the parents, in which the counselor begins to build rapport with parents and starts the process of collecting the family history. Alternatively, the counselor can begin the process by including the entire family in the first session. In the initial session with the entire family, the counselor uses play to begin the process of connecting with various family members and to assess family dynamics. It is often helpful to ask, "What does everyone know/think about coming here?" to get each member's perceptions of the problem or family issues. The counselor can also ask the family to make a joint sand tray or group drawing showing what is going on that brings the family into therapy or individual sand trays or drawings to show each member's perception of the presenting problem or goal for the outcome of therapy. During this initial family meeting, the counselor demystifies the counseling process by exploring confidentiality, goals for therapy, and rules the family wants to have for their interactions in sessions (e.g., take turns talking, no put-downs, etc.).

In the first few family play therapy sessions with the entire family, the counselor asks the family to engage in free family play as a vehicle to observe typical family interactions and family dynamics. The counselor is either quiet during this process or uses nondirective play therapy skills like tracking, restating content, reflecting feelings, and returning responsibility to the family members during these sessions. Sometimes the counselor asks questions about what is happening between members in the session or about specific situations in their interactions outside the sessions. Initially, limits are not set in order for the counselor to see how parents handle situations in which limits would be appropriate.

It is important for the counselor to be encouraging in the process of building relationships with family members (Kottman & Meany-Walen, in press). To be encouraging in family play therapy, a counselor will do the following:

1. Value family members as they are, not as their reputation indicates or as others hope they will be, but as they really are.

2. Have faith in family members' abilities. This faith helps to win their confidence. It will also help them develop self-respect and a belief in themselves.
3. Give equal recognition for effort and for successful completion of tasks.
4. Help each family member discover his or her place in the family and begin working and interacting positively from that position. This is done throughout the entire therapy process by modeling, coaching, and role playing.
5. Plan for success. Provide toys and materials that every member of the family can master and use creatively.
6. Identify strengths and assets rather than weaknesses and mistakes. Point out specific instances of progress and positive movement during the session as it happens.
7. Use clients' individual interests to trigger conversation. Show involvement by talking about things that are important to them.

Exploring Lifestyles

In this second phase of Adlerian family play therapy, the counselor explores the lifestyle of various family members and the family through observation, directive play, sand tray, art techniques like the Family Art Assessment (DeOrnellas, Kottman, & Millican, 1997; Landgarten, 1981; Sutherland, 2008), and adventure therapy strategies (Ashby, Kottman, & DeGraaf, 2008; Kottman, Ashby, & DeGraaf, 2001). These strategies allow for a systematic exploration of individual assets, family strengths, family atmosphere, family constellation, goals of misbehavior, personality priorities, Crucial Cs (i.e., connection, capability, counting, and courage), lifestyle convictions, and mistaken beliefs (Bitter, 2014; Christensen, 2004; Kottman & Meany-Walen, in press). This information helps the counselor conceptualize the lifestyle of each family member and the family. Since Adlerian family play therapy is a strength-based approach to working with families, the counselor also discovers the emotional, behavioral, and attitudinal strengths of individual family members and of the family as a whole.

Family atmosphere is the characteristic pattern established by the parents and presented to the children as a standard for social living (Dewey, 1973). It is the climate of the family

> created through an alchemy of parental characteristics: attitudes toward the children, discipline philosophies, lifestyles, family values, family atmosphere of their own family of origin, the marital relationship, parenting skills, assets, and any personal problems or life circumstances that might reduce their ability to provide warmth, respect, or structure for the children. (Kottman & Ashby, 2015, p. 37)

The family atmosphere is unique to each family and has a great impact on the formation of the children's lifestyles and on how family members react to and interact with one another (Bitter, 2014). In the process of exploring family atmosphere, the counselor investigates family values, family rules, communication patterns, boundaries, and hierarchy. It is also important to explore who in the family has the power.

Although the family constellation consists of the parents, children, and extended family members, the usual emphasis in Adlerian therapy is on the psychological birth order of the children in the family. Children often have certain personality traits that are characteristic of their ordinal position of birth order (Yang et al., 2010). The usual positions described in the Adlerian literature are the only, the oldest, the second, the middle, and the youngest child (Bitter, 2014). The "typical" oldest child might be bossy, the only child may expect to be the center of attention, the second child might be highly competitive, and so forth.

> These five positions represent vantage points from which children view the world. It is not the position, however, that counts, but rather the meaning and interpretation the child gives to that position. In this sense, every person's birth position is unique and uniquely defined. (Bitter, 2014, p. 135)

Many things can affect the psychological position, like chronic illness, disabilities, time interval between live births, stillbirths, etc. The counselor considers family constellation to identify how each member finds a place in the family system. For instance, the counselor ponders questions such as: How does each child interact with the parents? How does each child get along with the other children? Which of the children are allied with each of the parents? How does each child react to family rules? Which child embodies each family value?

The goals of children's misbehavior were first postulated by Rudolph Dreikurs, who suggested that all misbehavior can be attributed to children striving for attention, power, revenge, or proof that they are inadequate (Dreikurs & Soltz, 1964). In order to recognize which is a particular child's goal in a specific situation, the counselor contemplates the child's misbehavior, the reactions of adults who are interacting with the child, and the child's reaction to discipline or correction. Because many of the families that come for play therapy have a child whose goal of misbehavior is power, it is important to consider the family dynamics that might create or support a child having this as his or her goal. The child whose goal is power usually comes from a family in which the following circumstances exist: (a) the child does not have reasonable or appropriate power and responsibility; (b) the child has excessive amounts of power and responsibility; or (c) the family is chaotic, disorganized, and lacking in a sense of structure and safety. It is important to make a distinction among these three dynamics of the power-seeking child in order to select an intervention that meets the family's need.

The mistaken goal patterns between adults and their children must also be considered. Bitter et al. (2002) suggested that when parents and children are locked into a negative pattern, the adults may be striving toward the mistaken goals of (a) demonstrating adequacy (proving they are "good" parents), (b) asserting control over their children, (c) seeking revenge against their children for perceived hurts or threats, and/or (d) demonstrating inadequacy as parents. These mistaken goal patterns are identified by asking parents questions about the family dynamics when children are misbehaving, watching the family members as they play together, or setting up play situations in which the misbehavior might occur in a session. This assessment of mistaken goals will guide the counselor in developing suggestions for parents.

Assessment of personality priorities is another method that Adlerians use to conceptualize clients and guide treatment planning (Dillman Taylor, 2013; Kfir, 2011; Kottman & Meany-Walen, in press; Pew, 1976). Personality priorities are patterns of behavior and reactions that are based on the individual's convictions about how he or she acquires belonging, significance, and a sense of mastery. The personality priorities are superiority, control, comfort, and pleasing. During family play therapy, counselors look for the priority (or sometimes two) that serves as an organizing pattern of coping with situations and relationships. Counselors ponder the following questions (adapted from Dewey, 1978): (a) What is this family member striving to achieve within the family?; (b) What does this member need to feel that he or she belongs and is significant?; (c) What does this member need to feel a sense of mastery of various situations within the family?; (d) What is this member trying to avoid?; (e) What does this member complain about?; (f) What happens when this member is struggling to cope with family situations?; (g) How do other family members react to this person? In the Adlerian family play therapy process, it is often helpful to consider family members' personality priorities in deciding how to explain things to them, in couching recommendations for shifts in family dynamics and parenting strategies, in suggesting possible activities for the playroom, and so forth (Kottman & Ashby, 1999; Kottman & Meany-Walen, in press).

The Crucial Cs (i.e., connection, capability, counting, and courage) are another important facet of conceptualizing in Adlerian family play therapy (Lew & Bettner, 1998, 2000). Lew and Bettner posited that successful children have mastered the beliefs and skills necessary to be *connected* to others and feel a sense of family and community, are *capable* of taking care of themselves and believe they have skills, feel valued by others and know that they *count* and make a difference, and have *courage* when faced with challenges and new situations. When all family members have the vital protections provided by the Crucial Cs, they live in ways that are responsible, productive, cooperative, self-reliant, resilient, resourceful, contributing, and happy. During the first two phases of Adlerian family play therapy, the counselor observes the behavior of family members and asks questions with the goal of understanding whether they have mastered each of the Crucial Cs and incorporated each of these beliefs into their self-perceptions (Kottman, 1999). Based on this investigation, the counselor assesses which of the Crucial Cs could be considered an area of strength or weakness for each family member. Then the counselor plans play strategies designed to foster the Crucial Cs that are weaknesses and capitalize on the Crucial Cs that are strengths.

Lifestyle convictions are the person's basic beliefs about self, others, and the world/life (Kottman & Meany-Walen, in press). In many cases, these can be formulated through the counselor's imagining how family members would complete the following sentence:

I am . . .	I must be . . .	I should . . .
Others are . . .	Others must be . . .	
My relationships with others are . . .	My relationships with others must be . . .	
The world is . . .	The world should be . . .	
Life is . . .	Life should be . . .	
Based on these convictions, my behavior must be . . .		

Lifestyle convictions, which are usually out of clients' awareness, are a filter through which family members interpret everything that happens to them. Many lifestyle convictions are "mistaken beliefs" (inaccurate, faulty, or self-defeating convictions), but family members "act as if" they are all true. Because mistaken beliefs are discouraging, it is important for the counselor to develop strategies for helping family members reexamine their convictions and facilitate shifts in how they view self, others, and the world.

The purpose of the information gathering during Phase 2 is to help systematically conceptualize family members' lifestyles and plan intervention strategies for Phases 3 and 4. The counselor synthesizes the information about individual strengths and family assets, family constellation, family atmosphere, goals of misbehavior/purposes, personality priorities, Crucial Cs, lifestyle convictions, and mistaken beliefs into a lifestyle conceptualization for each member and for the family as a whole. Based on this systematic conceptualization, the counselor plans interventions for helping family members gain insight and learn new ways of coping with problems and interacting with one another. Building on the lifestyle conceptualization, the counselor decides on play, sand tray, and art strategies for (a) encouraging individual strengths and family assets, (b) shifting goals of misbehavior for both children and parents, (c) optimizing positive qualities and reducing negative aspects in helping family members to move toward healthier functioning within their personality priorities, (d) enhancing functioning at strong Crucial Cs and strengthening weaker ones, (e) adjusting mistaken beliefs and self-defeating behavior patterns, and (f) teaching skills family members need to learn.

Helping Family Members Gain Insight

In Phase 3, the counselor continues building the relationship with family members, adding techniques designed to help family members gain insight into the patterns. The tools used in the third phase are meta-communication (i.e., communicating about the nonverbal and verbal ways that communication occurs), metaphors, directive art activities, adventure therapy, and sand tray techniques. The counselor meta-communicates about family members' nonverbal communication, reactions, attitudes, and verbalizations, as well as about assets, lifestyle convictions, goals of misbehavior, Crucial Cs, personality priorities, lifestyle themes, family dynamics, and family interactional and communication patterns. It is also sometimes helpful to meta-communicate about the impact of family atmosphere or family constellation on members. By making interpretations in the form of a tentative hypothesis, the counselor can convey respect and invite family members to make corrections, adjustments, or other interpretations.

One way of meta-communicating is to "spit in the soup" of the family members about mistaken beliefs and self-defeating behaviors. The counselor can "spit in the client's soup" by pointing out (often with gentle humor) that the client is "acting as if" mistaken beliefs are actually true when they are not (e.g., "You always say no one in the family likes you, and yet when we are together everyone seems to want to connect with you"). This type of meta-communication can be about self-defeating behaviors or other patterns that are no longer working for family members (e.g., "You might have noticed that pouting never really gets the other people in the family to do what you want them to do"). It is important to use a light tone and avoid being judgmental or getting into a power struggle with the client about these thoughts or behavior; it is only necessary to make a brief comment about the fallacies inherent in them and quickly move on to something else.

The other primary technique used in the third phase involves metaphors—using client metaphors, creating metaphors for clients, and delivering metaphors to clients. Family members who are more comfortable with metaphoric communication than direct communication will often express and explore information in the form of stories about "a friend," stories in fantasy play, or stories acted out in the sand tray or art products. With these clients, the counselor always strives to use their metaphor rather than "breaking" the metaphor by suggesting the more direct interpretation. Role playing, puppet shows, storytelling, doll play, play with fantasy toys, and sand tray play therapy all create metaphoric ways for family members to communicate about what is happening in their lives. They give family members a vehicle to indirectly process thoughts, emotions, attitudes, perceptions, experiences, and relationships. The counselor can use stories as a mirror so family members can safely examine patterns in a way that feels safe and far enough removed from reality that it does not evoke a defensive or guilty reaction. The counselor can also use storytelling and/or bibliotherapy to help family members gain insight. By custom designing metaphoric stories or reading carefully selected books with family members, the counselor can allow family members to maintain a safe distance from emotionally evocative material and at the same time he or she can facilitate a deeper understanding of issues and patterns.

Art activities, sand trays, and adventure therapy are another way to help family members gain insight. The counselor may ask the family to draw an ideal family, do a sand tray on what their family would look like if they didn't have the current problem, change the way they move in and out of the family by changing the way they walk, or play a game in which they all hold hands in a certain pattern and then untangle themselves without letting go. The family counselor may implore his or her clients to create a sand picture or a mandala drawing to provide a projective means toward illuminating individual and familial dynamics. The selection of activities in this phase is open to imagination—any playful activity designed to help the members of the family understand themselves and one another better is acceptable. When family members gain a deepening grasp of family dynamics and the interaction of their individual lifestyles, the counselor moves toward the fourth phase of the therapy.

Reorienting and Reeducating

The agenda in Phase 4 of Adlerian family play therapy is to use play therapy tools to help family members learn and practice new ways of thinking about themselves and one another in the context of the family as well as more adaptive positive ways of interacting with one another. The counselor can reorient and reeducate family members by teaching them appropriate ways to get their needs met, new ways to communicate with one another, new ways to decide on family values and family rules, new ways to solve conflicts and solve problems, and new methods for establishing democratic practices in which parents are responsible for setting boundaries and limits in reasonable and respectful ways. It is often helpful to have several sessions with the parents by themselves, in order to teach them new parenting skills such as how to encourage the children and one another, how to identify goals of behavior (their own and the children's), how to set logical consequences, how to foster the Crucial Cs, and how to identify problem ownership. In these parent-only sessions, it is also appropriate to discuss personal issues that might be interfering with their ability to parent and other aspects of family relationships and possible marital issues that could be sabotaging optimal family functioning.

PRACTICAL INTERVENTIONS

In Adlerian family play therapy, there are a multitude of interventions, limited only by the counselor's imagination. Adlerians often use drawing to work with family members. In Phase 2, one practical intervention is the Family Art Assessment, which is used to explore family dynamics, Crucial Cs, personality priorities, and so forth (Landgarten, 1981). In this three-step procedure, the counselor asks each family member to select a different color of marker. Each person is to continue to use that same color throughout all three procedures in order to facilitate the counselor's observation of each person's contribution. In the first activity, the counselor asks the family members to divide into two teams. (They can use any method they wish to decide on the teams.) When they have decided on the teams, the counselor gives each team a large piece of paper and tells them that they are to draw something without talking to one another, signaling, or writing notes to one another when working on the art. When both teams are finished, they can talk as they generate a title for the artwork and write the name on the product somewhere.

In the second activity, the teams are dissolved, and the counselor gives the entire family one sheet of paper, asking them to draw something on the paper, again without communication. When they are finished with the artwork, they have permission to communicate as they choose a title and add it to the sheet of paper. For the third activity, the entire family works together to make a drawing, but this time they are allowed to communicate with one another. They must assign a title to the work and write it on the product.

As the family members work, the counselor observes them, watching for patterns in their interactions, considering questions such as:

- Who initiated the drawing and what was the process that led up to this person making the first mark on the page? In what order did the rest of the members participate?
- Which members' suggestions were used and which were ignored?
- What was the level of involvement on the part of each person?
- What was the symbolic content of each person's contribution?
- How much space did each person occupy?

- Was the family's working style cooperative, individualistic, or discordant?
- How did family members communicate support or encouragement to one another?

Another practical intervention that could be used in any phase of the family play therapy process would be a fun activity called "Hug Tag" (Ashby et al., 2008). This is a simple walking game of tag with a variation of how "base" (the place where participants are safe from being tagged as "it") is defined. The counselor explains to the family members that it is a walking game of tag and that the counselor will begin by being "it." When one family member gets tagged he or she is then "it" and needs to chase (while walking) other members and attempt to tag them so that they become "it." The important addition to a normal tag game is that family members are only safe from being tagged as "it" if they are hugging another member of the family or the counselor. Two people hugging are safe but if more than two people hug one another then none of them are safe. In order to keep everyone from simply hugging the entire game (though there might be some value in this too), the counselor clarifies that two people can only hug as long as they can hum. That is, at the beginning of their hug each person takes a breath and begins to hum. When they stop humming to take another breath, they are no longer safe and must move on. Once family member A has hugged family member B (for one hum), those two people cannot hug again until they have hugged someone else. In this way, they cannot simply take a breath and hug, then take a breath and hug the same person again.

Processing observations and questions for "Hug Tag" can include:

- Who was protected? Who was sacrificed?
- Which family members tended to gravitate toward/away from one another?
- Did family members appear comfortable or uncomfortable with this game?
- How did it feel when you were "it"?

CASE STUDY

The Luther (pseudonym) family came to therapy because of James's "out-of-control" behavior. James (8) was the youngest of three children, with an older brother, Caleb (10), and an older sister, Raquel (13). The parents, Karina and Malcolm, originally wanted to bring him to individual play therapy because of his behavior. They reported that he was disrespectful, disobedient, and "hyper." In talking with the parents in the initial intake session, Julian, the Adlerian play therapist, decided that the family might be better served by working in family play therapy. Julian assessed that the difficulty was more a system-wide struggle than an individual problem because Karina and Malcolm felt as though all three of their children were uncooperative and oppositional and they seemed overwhelmed by trying to parent them and maintain their own relationship. The parents described their family as having little structure, with yelling and threatening as the primary discipline strategies. They reported that these were the parenting techniques used by their own parents and “well, that is really all we know to do.”

Karina seemed to feel beleaguered by her need to “keep everybody happy” and wanted Malcolm to “stop being so judgmental and critical.” Malcolm wanted Karina to “get tougher” and support his discipline strategy. During that first session, as Julian worked to begin establishing a relationship with the parents by unconditionally listening to them describe family interactions, he formed the hypothesis that Karina’s primary personality priority was pleasing and Malcolm’s was control. He believed they were struggling with their inconsistent parenting styles and were having difficulty fostering the Crucial Cs in their children. He hypothesized that the main goal of the children’s misbehavior was power, with the occasional attention seeking. He wanted to observe the children and parents interacting and build relationships with each of the children in the next few sessions while he began to explore each family member’s lifestyle.

In the first full family session, Julian asked the members of the family to just play with one another. Chaos reigned. The children argued with one another and with the parents; the parents tried to impose some rules on the play, but were mostly unsuccessful. Karina worked hard to try to keep everyone happy, and Malcolm tried to get people to listen to him and do what he wanted. James, Caleb, and Raquel seemed discouraged and disgruntled. They occasionally ganged up on their mother, worked to press their father’s buttons, and were often rude to Julian. Despite this behavior, Julian made encouraging comments to all family members, pointing out assets, tracking behavior, reflecting feelings, returning responsibility, and setting several limits when the children threatened to break toys. In the second family session, Julian asked them to do the Family Art Assessment, observing their interaction. In the third family session, he asked them to each do a sand tray about the family. By the fourth family session, Julian had formulated a lifestyle conceptualization for each member and for the family as a whole. He developed a treatment plan in which he would help the family members gain insight into their intrapersonal and interpersonal dynamics.

As they moved into the third phase of the family play therapy process, Julian alternated free family play sessions, structured play, sand tray, and art activities. Julian wanted to help the children switch from the negative goal of power by allowing them to have age-appropriate power, but with developmentally responsive limits and consequences. He modeled how to use power sharing, limited choices, and logical consequences. He had parents-only sessions to teach more about sharing power, giving limited choices, and setting logical consequences. Then they had a family session so the parents could practice these strategies.

Since everyone in the family seemed to like to draw, he used activities such as quick draws—in which he gave family members two minutes to draw a series of feelings. He meta-communicated about the goals of the behavior he observed and about the way family members solved problems, communicated, and manifested their Crucial Cs and their personality priorities. Because he believed that all members of the family were discouraged, he made a concerted effort to make encouraging statements to all members. Julian made a rule that each person needed to make at least three encouraging comments to every other member of the family throughout the sessions. Because the family members were highly competitive, he actually kept score. He made up several stories about families that were struggling to understand and support one another. Throughout this phase, the family seemed to become more positive with one another and the children gradually became more cooperative.

In the fourth phase, Julian wanted to enhance the entire family's Crucial Cs—especially "connect" and "count." He wanted to help Karina shift from maladaptive pleasing to a more adaptive pleasing style by empowering her to set appropriate boundaries with the children. He wanted Malcolm to learn to share power, and to be more encouraging and use limited choices. He had a parent-only session to work on these things and gave them individually crafted homework assignments.

CONCLUSION

Adlerian family play therapy is an approach to working with families that honors Adler's philosophy about the roles of family members in creating and solving problems, and honors children's developmental capacities to express themselves and process information. The play and action part of the process allows the counselor to assess the interpersonal and intrapersonal dynamics of the family, in ways that self-report could not. Consistent with Adlerian theory, the counselor moves through the four phases of therapy—building relationships, exploring lifestyle, gaining insight, and reorienting/reeducating—by using custom and intentionally designed interventions for the family. As family members' lifestyles are revealed, family members can better understand how they interact with others and reasons for their family members' behaviors. The Adlerian family play therapist teaches, encourages, and models new and positive ways for family members to interact. This cultivation of the family improves individual, family, and social functioning, which is at the heart of all Adlerian counseling.

REFERENCES

Adler, A. (1979). *Superiority and social interest: A collection of later writings* (3rd rev.). New York, NY: Norton.

Ansbacher, H., & Ansbacher, R. (Eds.). (1956). *The individual psychology of Alfred Adler: A systematic presentation in selections from his writings*. San Francisco, CA: Harper & Row.

Ashby, J. S., Kottman, T., & DeGraaf, D. (2008). *Active interventions for kids and teens: Adding adventure and fun to counseling!* Alexandria, VA: American Counseling Association.

Bitter, J. (2014). *Theory and practice of family therapy and counseling* (2nd ed.). Belmont, CA: Brooks/Cole.

Bitter, J., & Byrd, R. (2011). Human conversations: Self-disclosure and storytelling in Adlerian family therapy. *The Journal of Individual Psychology, 67*, 305–323.

Bitter, J., Roberts, A., & Sonstegard, M. (2002). Adlerian family therapy. In J. Carlson & D. Kjos (Eds.), *Theories and strategies in family therapy* (pp. 41–79). Boston, MA: Allyn &on.

Carlson, J. D., & Robey, P. A. (2011). An integrative Adlerian approach to family counseling. *The Journal of Individual Psychology, 67*, 232–244.

Christensen, O. (Ed.). (2004). *Adlerian family counseling* (3rd ed.). Minneapolis, MN: Educational Media.

Czyszczon, G., Riviere, S., Lowman, D. K., & Stewart, A. L. (2015). Family play therapy: Practical techniques. In D. A. Crenshaw & A. L. Stewart (Eds.), *Play therapy: A comprehensive guide to theory and practice* (pp. 186–200). New York, NY: Guildford Press.

DeOrnellas, K., Kottman, T., & Millican, V. (1997). Drawing a family: Family art assessment in Adlerian therapy. *Individual Psychology, 51*(4), 451–460.

Dewey, E. (1973). Family atmosphere. In A. Nikelly (Ed.), *Techniques for behavior change* (pp. 41–47). Chicago: Alfred Adler Institute.

Dewey, E. (1978). *Basic applications of Adlerian psychology for self-understanding and human relationships*. Coral Spring, FL: CMI Press.

Dillman Taylor, D. (2013). *Confirming the constructs of the Adlerian personality priority assessment (APPA)* (Unpublished doctoral dissertation). University of North Texas, Denton, TX.

Dinkmeyer, D. (1997). Adlerian family therapy: An integrative therapy. In J. Carlson & S. Slavik (Eds.), *Techniques in Adlerian psychology* (pp. 456–465). Washington,DC: Accelerated Development.

Dreikurs, R., & Soltz, V. (1964). *Children: The challenge*. New York, NY: Hawthorn/Dutton.

Gladding, S. (2007). *Family therapy: History, theory and practice* (4th ed.). Upper Saddle River, NJ: Pearson.

Kfir, N. (2011). *Personality and priorities: A typology*. Bloomington, IN: Author House.

Kottman, T. (1999). Using the Crucial Cs in Adlerian play therapy. *Individual Psychology, 55*, 289–297.

Kottman, T., & Ashby, J. (1999). Using Adlerian personality priorities to custom-design consultation with parents of play therapy clients. *International Journal of Play Therapy, 8*(2), 77–92.

Kottman, T., & Ashby, J. (2015). Adlerian play therapy. In D. Crenshaw & A. Stewart (Eds.), *Play therapy: A comprehensive guide to theory and practice* (pp. 32–47). New York, NY: Guilford Press.

Kottman, T., Ashby, J., & DeGraaf, D. (2001). *Adventures in guidance: Integrating fun into your guidance program*. Alexandria, VA: American Counseling Association.

Kottman, T., & Meany-Walen, K. K. (in press). *Partners in play: An Adlerian approach to play therapy*. Alexandria, VA: American Counseling Association.

Landgarten, H. (1981). *Clinical art therapy: A comprehensive guide*. New York, NY: Brunner/Mazel.

Lew, A., & Bettner, B. L. (1998). *Responsibility in the classroom: A teacher's guide to understanding and motivating students*. Newton Centre, MA: Connexions Press.

Lew, A., & Bettner, B. L. (2000). *A parent's guide to understanding and motivating children*. Newton Centre, MA: Connexions Press.

Maniacci, M., Sackett-Maniacci, L., & Mosak, H. (2014). Adlerian psychotherapy. In D. Wedding & R. J. Corsini (Eds.), *Current psychotherapies* (10th ed., pp. 55–94). Belmont, CA: Thomson Brooks/Cole.

Meany-Walen, K. K., Bratton, S., & Kottman, T. (2014). Effects of Adlerian play therapy reducing students' disruptive behaviors. *Journal of Counseling and Development, 92*(1), 47–56. doi:10.1002/j.1556-6676.2014.00129.x

Meany-Walen, K. K., Bullis, Q., Kottman, T., & Dillman Taylor, D. (in press). Group Adlerian play therapy with children with off-task behavior. *Journal for Specialists in Group Work.*

Meany-Walen, K. K., Kottman, T., Bullis, Q., & Dillman Taylor, D. (in press). Adlerian play therapy with children with externalizing behaviors: Single case design. *Journal of Counseling & Development.*

Miller, W. (1994). Family play therapy: History, theory, and convergence. In C. Schaefer & L. Carey (Eds.), *Family play therapy* (pp. 3–20). Northvale, NJ: Jason Aronson.

Pew, W. (1976). The number one priority. In *Monograph of the International Association of Individual Psychology* (pp. 1–24). Munich, Germany: International Association of Individual Psychology.

Pfefferle, J., & Mansager, E. (2014). Applying the classical Adlerian family diagnostic process. *The Journal of Individual Psychology, 70*, 332–378.

Prochaska, J. O., & Norcross, J. C. (2010). *Systems of psychotherapy: A transtheoretical analysis* (7th ed.). Belmont, CA: Brooks/Cole.

Satir, V. (2006). *The Satir model: Family therapy and beyond*. New York, NY: Science Books.

Sherman, R. (1999). Family therapy: The art of integration. In R. Watts & J. Carlson (Eds.), *Interventions and strategies in counseling and psychotherapy* (pp. 101–134). Philadelphia, PA: Accelerated Development.

Sherman, R., & Dinkmeyer, D. (1987). *Systems of family therapy: An Adlerian integration*. New York, NY: Brunner/Mazel.

Sperry, L. (2011). Family therapy with personality-disordered individuals and families: Understanding and treating the borderline family. *The Journal of Individual Psychology, 67*, 222–231.

Sutherland, J. (2008). Adlerian family art therapy. In C. Kerr & J. Hoshino (Eds.), *Family art therapy: Foundations of theory and practice* (pp. 167–179). New York, NY: Routledge.

Sweeney, D., & Rocha, S. (2000). Using play therapy to assess family dynamics. In R. Watts (Ed.), *Techniques in marriage and family counseling* (vol. 1, pp. 33–48). Alexandria, VA: American Counseling Association.

Watts, R. E. (2010, June). *The innovative Adlerian: Past, present, future*. Invited keynote lecture presented at the North American Society for Adlerian Psychology Conference, Minneapolis, MN.

Yang, J., Milliren, A., & Blagen, M. (2010). *The psychology of courage: An Adlerian handbook for healthy social living*. New York, NY: Routledge.

II

Assessment and Clinical Applications

Chapter Six

Play-Based Family Assessment and Treatment Planning

Christine M. Koehler, Brittany Wilson, and Jennifer Baggerly

There is a dark, invisible workmanship that reconciles discordant elements and makes them move in one society. —William Wordsworth (1850, p. 18)

Wordsworth's words from *The Prelude* provide a metaphor that describes the mysteries of the family system. Families are like small societies that often contain some degree of discord, yet seek to function together. One purpose of family assessment is to illuminate the discordant elements by identifying and understanding dynamics that reconcile and move the family system toward better functioning.

Clinical assessment of children and families can be difficult to describe and understand because professionals from multiple disciplines (e.g., counseling, psychology, social work) and various theoretical orientations (e.g., family systems, humanistic, cognitive behavioral, developmental, etc.) assess children and families for various purposes using any number of methods. In addition, assessments are conducted to answer numerous questions set forth by families and professionals. Given these variables, the most effective assessment procedures are a combination of methods and sources of information (Whitcomb & Merrell, 2013).

The value of incorporating play into assessment has gained recognition for its utility and developmental appropriateness in working with families with young children (Brestan-Knight & Salamone, 2011; Gitlin-Weiner, Sandgrund, & Schaefer, 2000). However, little is known about using play-based assessment in the context of family counseling. By utilizing play in the assessment of a family, the counselor can access information that is otherwise unavailable through other means, measures, or processes. Additionally, information that is gathered through traditional methods such as self-report measures or clinical interviews can either be confirmed, complimented, or challenged through the results of family play-based assessments.

This chapter on family play-based assessment and treatment planning aims to narrow the gap for family counselors who would like to incorporate play into their initial and ongoing work with families, and for play therapists who would like to expand their work with the individual child to include the family. In this chapter, we will synthesize prominent literature related to play-based assessment, explain assessment protocol that informs treatment planning, provide practical assessment interventions, and describe a case study.

CURRENT RESEARCH AND THEORY

A synthesis of current literature can be categorized into two broad themes, specifically the history of and the rationale for family play-based assessments.

History of Play-Based Assessment

The history of play-based assessment is well documented across time. The first documented use of parent-child behavioral observations in a professional setting was discovered in a dairy dating back to 1787 (Brestan-Knight & Salamone, 2011). Since that time, parent-child observations of play have been recorded and utilized for psychotherapy purposes from the 1940s to current times. In the earlier years, such observations provided information regarding a child's development and early attachment styles. Yet, over time, the primary goals of play-based assessment have become evaluation to diagnose children, treatment planning, and treatment monitoring.

Historically, play-based assessments focused on assessment of the individual child. These assessments include, but are not limited to, the *Affect in Play Scale* (APS), the *Child-Initiated Pretend Play Assessment* (ChIPPA), the *Structured Play Assessment*, the *Test of Pretend Play* (ToPP), the *Children's Play Therapy Instrument* (CPTI), the *Play Therapy Observation Instrument* (PTOI), and the *Trauma Play Scale* (Kaugars, 2011). Other play-based assessments were specifically designed for children with autism and developmental disabilities such as the *Transdisciplinary Play-Based Assessment, Second Edition* (TPBA2) (Linder et al., 2008). These individual play-based assessments possess strong psychometrics and have demonstrated effectiveness with young children. In addition, research has shown a strong correlation between individual play-based assessments and traditional child assessments such as the *Bayley Scales of Infant Development-II* (Kelly-Vance, Needelman, Troia, & Ryalls, 1999).

As family systems approaches became more prominent within the last 30 years, counselors expanded their focus from just individual play-based assessments to family play-based assessments (Stollak, Barlev, & Kalogiros, 2000). This development has led to increased understanding of family dynamics and strengths. Research demonstrating the effectiveness of family play-based assessments has emerged (Brestan-Knight & Salamone, 2011; Gitlin-Weiner et al., 2000). For example, the *Dyadic Parent-Child Interaction Coding System* (DPICS) was found to correctly classify 94 percent of families as having either normal interactions or conduct problems between parent and child (Robinson & Eyberg, 1981). A recent derivative of DPICS, the *Parent Instruction-Giving Game for Youngsters* (PIGGY), also differentiated between two groups of noncompliant children and overactive parenting (Hupp, Reitman, Forde, Shriver, & Kelley, 2008).

Rationale for Family Play-Based Assessment

The literature reveals several clear rationales for using play in assessment. First, family self-report and social history is often insufficient to fully understand a family's functioning (Hanevold, 2005). Observations of family play interactions enhance and enrich the information gathered throughout the traditional data collection process of clinical interviews, self-report measures, or other means. Family play-based assessments provide counselors with increased clarity regarding the family's roles, communication patterns, approach to conflict resolution, and emotional resourcefulness (Landgarten, 1987).

Second, family play-based assessment is developmentally appropriate for children. Young children do not yet possess the cognitive capacities to communicate effectively through verbal communication. Instead, they communicate in a language that is most natural for them: play (Landreth, 2012; Ray, 2011; Stollak et al., 2000). Through play, children are better able to express their innermost feelings, wishes, fantasies, and perceptions. Counselors relying solely upon clinical family interviews may be in danger of hyperfocusing upon the adults' point of view and failing to acknowledge the child's perspective (Wilkinson, 2000). Yet, family play-based assessment allows the counselor to gain an understanding of children's perspectives.

Third, play-based family assessment facilitates rapport between a family and the counselor, which increases the family's trust, comfort, and motivation to participate further (Gil, 2015). Play may even help adults overcome feelings of self-consciousness and children's initial reluctance to participate. The enjoyment experienced between family members can provide needed hope for them to participate in the assessment and treatment process.

FAMILY PLAY-BASED ASSESSMENT PROTOCOL

While the assessment process is usually the first therapeutic opportunity to make psychological contact and create psychological safety, assessment is not therapy. In fact, for some counselors, it is preferable to schedule therapy clients and assessment clients on alternate days because it is difficult to alternate between roles. In therapy, the counselor's relational orientation facilitates the client's perception of nonjudgmental, unconditional regard, while in assessment the client may correctly perceive that the counselor's orientation is primarily evaluative.

In order to understand counselors' roles in family play-based assessment, it is helpful to consider the distinctive phases of the assessment process. Counselors will be gathering information and facilitating the process through the phases of pre-assessment, parent interview, assessment planning, assessment implementation, and treatment planning.

Pre-Assessment

The first contextual bit of information that a counselor can use to conceptualize the family is the tone and context of the initial contact by the family. The very way in which a parent connects with the counselor can hold meaningful data. At the time of the initial contact, the counselor should identify the following:

- Reason for referral, referral source, and context (i.e., what precipitating event led to the referral)
- Risk factors (e.g., trauma, family violence, suicidal ideation, substance abuse, Child Protective Services involvement)
- Family members (i.e., who lives in the household and who does not live in the household but is important), and non–family members (i.e., family friends, neighbors, boyfriends/girlfriends)
- Brief developmental history of children (e.g., developmental milestones, medical history, day care and school functioning, special needs, prior treatment)

This information guides the counselor in discerning the purpose and method of the assessment.

Parent Interview

It is helpful for counselors to conduct a semistructured interview to guide parents in the discussion and to gather and organize data. Some counselors prefer to have the parents complete an interview questionnaire before the first session to save time. The counselor can read the responses before the parent interview to prepare clarifying or follow-up questions. In order to prepare parents for a play-based approach, counselors can introduce some playful approaches such as asking them to select a toy or sand tray miniature that symbolizes each member of their family. For a thorough discussion and example format for the parent interview, refer to Patterson, Williams, Edwards, Chamow, and Grauf-Grounds (2009).

Assessment Planning

Once the preliminary interview has been conducted with the parents, the counselor can begin to select methods and activities based on the information collected and the referral question. Assessment planning varies based on the number of family members, ages, genders, and special needs in the family (e.g., sensory, fine or gross motor, attention, severe allergies) as well as cultural considerations such as spiritual or religious practices. The counselor selects an appropriate assessment activity (described below) based on the developmental level of the youngest family member. An alternative assessment is also selected just in case the first one does not work well.

Assessment planning also entails preparing or purchasing needed materials. The counselor should have a camera charged and ready to take pictures of drawings, paintings, sculptures, genograms, sand trays, or other creative work in order to preserve the data. The counselor prepares the therapy room, preferably a play therapy or activity therapy room, with needed materials and appropriate sitting space (e.g., carpet squares, beanbag chairs, couch, etc.).

Assessment Implementation

Several sessions may be required for assessment implementation. For example, a common agenda is as follows.

Session One

In order to assess the family as a whole, the counselor welcomes the entire family into the playroom with a statement such as "Welcome to our family playroom. This is a safe place where families can have fun and grow stronger." The counselor reiterates confidentiality with a statement such as "Just a reminder that what we say or do in here is private and confidential." Next, the counselor informs the family that they will have a set amount of time for free playtime (i.e., family-directed playtime). The counselor states, "You can play with all the toys and materials in most of the ways you would like." The counselor provides basic play therapy skills such as tracking play behaviors and family interactions as well as reflecting feelings. The counselor alerts the family when there are 5 minutes remaining in the free playtime.

During the family playtime, the counselor observes which family members initiate play and interactions, who plays with whom, the energy level of different family members, attachments between parents and children, responsiveness between family members, and overall cohesiveness. After the family playtime, the counselor conducts a brief family interview about what each member liked about the family playtime and makes general observations about the family's cohesiveness and strengths. For example, the counselor may say, "I noticed you all started off trying to play what Billy wanted but then you each spent most of the time doing your own thing. Jane, I noticed that you had a lot of energy, and Mom, you enjoyed watching her. Billy, I noticed that you stayed close to Dad, and Dad, you helped Billy when he asked."

Session Two

In order to observe the children's subsystem, the counselor invites only the children into the playroom for nondirective play followed by a structured activity and children's interview if developmentally appropriate. Parents need not be present during this time. The counselor provides structure by saying, "Today, you will have 25 minutes to play with all the toys in most of the ways you want and then we will do an activity that I will lead." While the children are playing, the counselor assesses play themes (e.g., good vs. bad, power, nurturing, aggression, etc.), metaphors, personality, and temperament.

After giving a 5-minute warning for the end of free play, the counselor states, "Please come sit over here so I can show you the activity I would like you to do." The counselor provides the materials and directions for a structured activity described below. Photographs are taken of artwork or creative activities. Based on observations in session two, the counselor confirms or rules out hypotheses about family dynamics that were made during session one. For example, if the counselor hypothesized in session one that the family is disengaged yet sees cohesion between the children, then the counselor modifies the hypothesis to be that the parents are disengaged but the children are connected.

Session Three

Further modifications in hypotheses are made by leading the entire family through two or three structured play activities with subsequent processing. For example, the counselor may say, "Today, I have planned some activities that I will lead the whole family through. Afterward, we will talk about what we learned about each other and the family." Again, the counselor records or photographs the activities or art products. Finally, the counselor confirms, rules out, and modifies hypotheses.

Session Four

In the final family play-based assessment, the counselor provides feedback to the family by sharing hypotheses and conceptualization in a tentative manner. For example, "In session one, I noticed Billy and Dad were connecting and Jane and Mom were connecting. Then in session two, I noticed that Billy and Jane were very connected." The counselor elicits feedback from the family via questions such as "Did anyone else notice that? Is that how it usually is at home?" Next, the counselor suggests treatment goals such as "I'm wondering if it may be helpful for us to plan ways for all family members to enjoy connection with each other."

The counselor collaborates with the family on the treatment approach and plan by allowing each family member to give input in order to increase commitment. For example, "I noticed that Jane enjoys drawing and that Billy enjoys working with clay. We could plan activities with drawing and clay. What other types of things would you enjoy?" After questions are raised and answered and approaches, goals, and plans are agreed upon by the counselor and family, then treatment can begin.

Treatment Planning

While assessment illuminates which needs will be addressed, treatment planning designates how it will be done. In treatment planning, the counselor must be clear in identifying the client. Depending on the context or the presenting problem, the client may be one or more parent, one or more children, or the entire family. The results of a family assessment may be used to (a) identify client and/or family goals, (b) recommend an overall treatment approach consisting of one or more modalities (e.g., individual, couples/marital, family, and/or group therapies), and (c) plan and facilitate session-specific interventions (e.g., guided relaxation, communication games, conflict resolution puppet show). As illustrated in session four above, the results of the assessment and recommendations should be shared with the family in a comprehensive feedback session.

Like assessment, treatment planning is a dynamic process. A counselor may design a treatment plan and soon after need to revise it. Additional assessment of the family at play would be appropriate in these cases. For example, when working with individual children in play therapy, a child will sometimes leave the session to seek out a parent in the waiting room. When the child is intent on showing the parent something about his play (e.g., handcuffing himself, painting his face, or destroying a particular object), the child is conveying "a message" to the parent (e.g., I feel trapped; I have a need to hide my true self; I feel enraged). When a child continues to "include" the parent in sessions in this way, the treatment plan may need to shift temporarily or long term from individual sessions to parent-child or family sessions. This shift may warrant gathering the family for a collaborative family drawing or other play-based assessment to explore or re-examine alternate directions for treatment.

Practical Interventions

The format of family play-based assessment interventions ranges from more structured and standardized approaches (Gehring & Page, 2000) to increasingly creative and informal approaches (Smith, 2000). Some have suggested the single most important factor to consider when selecting a play-based assessment is the presence or absence of a child's verbal skills as some activities require more or less verbal communication (Russ & Niec, 2011).

One structured family play-based assessment is the *Family Systems Test* (FAST) developed by Gehring and Page (2000). The FAST assesses relational structures of cohesion and hierarchy within the family by having each member place figures representing family members on a board (similar to a chessboard). The placement of figures on the board reveals each member's perception of the family as typical, ideal, or conflictual (Gitlin-Weiner et al., 2000). This assessment is normed for ages 6 and up and can be administered with one or several members present. While the directions to this assessment are straightforward and easy to follow, it may be challenging for young children to fully comprehend the directions. Nonetheless, this is a highly utilized assessment with strong psychometric properties and research support that provides many clinical implications and considerations.

The *Kinetic Family Drawing* (Burns & Kaufman, 1970) is a structured projective assessment in which family members are asked to draw each member of their family, including themselves, doing something. Then the counselor asks each family member to describe all the family members in the picture and say what they are doing. Subsequently, they can tell a story about the picture stating what happened immediately before and after as well as what they would like to change if they could. Extreme caution must be used by not overly interpreting the drawing. The drawing should not be used to determine abuse or predict behavior. It is only to be used for identifying individuals' perceptions of their family.

Dynamic Play is a specific, semistructured method of family assessment developed by Steve Harvey (2000). In Dynamic Play, families are given tasks centered on interpersonal interactions in a gamelike format and in the presence of a therapist. Variations in formats include art, movement, drama, and video expression (Harvey, 2000). Central to the Dynamic Play assessment process is the concept of creativity. Harvey suggested all family members have a way of creatively interacting with one another that influences the quality and meaning of interpersonal interactions and communications. The targeted gamelike prompts reveal ways in which families communicate and interact with each other.

Diagrammatic methods such as the family genogram, ecomap, and social network grid are less structured family play-based assessment approaches that visually depict the family system in a larger context or environment (Thomlinson, 2014). The counselor asks the family to create a genogram by selecting toys or sand tray miniatures for each family member that they place on a large piece of paper or in a sand tray. The counselor observes the type of toys selected for each person and prompts family members to draw or make a line indicating whether they are close or cut off.

The Family Art Assessment is another less structured family play-based assessment (Landgarten, 1987; Smith, 2000). This highly informative, interactive, and inclusive assessment involves three main steps: (a) every member of the family is instructed to choose a color and draw a picture together, which can be anything of their choosing, but without using any words; (b) next, the family is asked to complete a second drawing, again anything of their choosing, but this time they are permitted to use words; and (c) the family and the therapist then process this experience together (Landgarten, 1987; Smith, 2000). Due to the emphasis on family functioning, the Family Art Assessment is a highly valued assessment tool when working with families.

Providing expressive art activities is an informal family play-based assessment method. The counselor presents a continuum of art materials from least controlled to most controlled including lead pencils, colored pencils, felt markers, collage, oil pastels, watercolors, and wet clay (Landgarten, 1987). The counselor invites each family member to select an expressive art material that is comfortable for them. The counselor's directions can range from a structured suggestion such as "Make a family portrait using your selected art materials" to an unstructured suggestion of "Make anything you would like."

A family puppet interview is another informal family play-based assessment (Gil, 2015). In this approach, each family member is asked to (a) select two puppets, (b) give them a voice, (c) give them a name, and (d) interact with other family members' puppets in a puppet show they create that has a beginning, middle, and an end. Then the counselor interviews each puppet with questions such as "How did you feel when that happened" and "What do you wish would happen instead?" Family puppet interviews can provide counselors with information regarding the subjective views and beliefs of individuals within the family system.

A family drama is a variation on the family puppet play (Gil, 2015). The counselor provides a variety of costume props (e.g., white doctor's coat, black cape, police and firefighters' hats, witch's hat, military outfits, fancy dresses, cheerleader pom-poms, scarfs, necklaces, wigs, etc.) and asks the members to select some props. Then they are instructed to put on the props and walk around acting out the character they are pretending to be. For example, "I am a mean witch and I will turn you into a frog." Next, the family is asked to create a dramatic play with a beginning, middle, and an end in which each character takes part. After the family puts on the dramatic play, the counselor asks them the title of the play, the morale or message of the play, and what each member became aware of through the process. Finally, the counselor asks each member what they would like to change about the play.

Observation of various play-based family tasks is another informal assessment approach (Kinston & Loader, 1988; Stollak et al., 2000). Many tasks can be completed by families with even very young children. Tasks may be (a) primarily physical such as tug-of-war, blowing bubbles, or chase; (b) primarily dramatic such as role playing, dress up, or storytelling; or (c) primarily artistic such as drawing, painting, or sculpting (Harvey, 2000). Tasks may require or elicit problem solving, decision making, and/or conflict resolution (Keck & Sporakowski, 1982).

Observation of a family's nondirected play is the least structured play-based family assessment. Several aspects of functioning can be captured and assessed through the observation of a family's play. Stollak et al. (2000) compiled a list of family dimensions routinely utilized for evaluative purposes in family assessment. Although it was not originally created with play-based assessment in mind, the constructs can be used to gather meaningful data for descriptive and clinical utility. Additionally, Ray (2011) described themes routinely demonstrated by children through their play behaviors. Table 6.1 represents a blend of Stollak's list and Ray's play themes. The table presents commonly observed family dynamics, a short explanation of such dynamics, and commonly observed trends for each.

Aside from the different interventions available for the assessment and the domains that should be considered, the counselor has an additional, intuitive process to attend to during the family play-based assessment, specifically the therapist's own internal experience and countertransference. This internal experience and countertransference can be a powerful assessment in and of itself as it may reveal family dynamics that are unresolved in the counselor. Also, the counselor should be mindful of blind spots regarding subtle undercurrents such as unspoken rules of affect, behavior, or communication. In some cases it is advisable to consult with a supervisor in order to generate interpretations of the data that the assessing counselor did not detect.

Table 6.1. Commonly Observed Family Dynamics

Dynamic	***Explanation***	***Observed Trend/ Behavior***
Cohesion/Warmth	The degree of emotional bonding, closeness, and togetherness.	Family appears willing to help and support one another, a general sense of acceptance.
Flexibility/Adaptability	The degree to which family members are able to easily adapt to the changing needs of the family.	Family appears flexible and adaptable in their thinking and behaviors based on the needs of other family members.
Responsiveness/ Involvement	The extent to which family members are perceived to be interested, concerned, and valued by one another.	Family appears responsive to each other's physical and emotional needs.
Power/Control	The extent to which individuals attempt to dominate or control the family system or individual members within the family.	Family appears to function under the control of one person or alliance. This sense of control may even be debilitating to some members.
Conflict	The extent to which the family is in a state of conflict with one another. May be marked by habitual conflict.	Family members work together, or fail to work together, to solve conflict within the family.
Fairness/Justice	The extent to which a family operates based on a sense of fairness and equality.	Family members appear to be driven by what is "fair" or what is "right."
Anxiety	The degree of unease, worry, or apprehension within a family system.	Family members appear to be driven by a state of unease or nervousness with one another.

CASE STUDY OF FAMILY PLAY-BASED ASSESSMENT

There are times when no matter how much structure or planning goes into a family play-based assessment, all the clinician need do is "get out of the clients' way" and trust the process. Below is an example of a nondirective family play-based assessment that unfolded with little structure or protocol.

A family self-referred for treatment due to behavior problems with their son Zach (pseudonym), age 8. The parents had already taken him to another clinician but terminated prematurely because the father did not believe that therapy was "working" for his son. At the initial parent interview (not including the child), the parents reported that their son had phobias that were impacting his and the family's functioning. Upon further explanation, they described that he had difficulty separating from his parents and was unable to tolerate being alone to the degree he would not use the restroom alone at school. Many times at home, his mother or younger sister, age 6, was recruited to stand by the bathroom door while he showered or brushed his teeth. By report, all efforts to resolve his dependent behaviors generally resulted in explosive tantrums. The mother did not agree with her husband's perceptions, but from the father's point of view, Zach's phobias had caused him to become more and more manipulative. Additionally, he was routinely antagonistic and physically aggressive with his younger sister.

I (Koehler) advised the parents that I would begin individual play therapy with Zach as I had quickly noticed the division between the parents and the lack of a unified philosophy. It was my opinion that it would be more beneficial to work with the child. Over the next few sessions, we developed a warm and playful rapport. He loved the toys and the freedom of being in my office playroom, which contained a standard selection of play therapy toys and expressive materials. In one of his first sessions, Zach stated there was no place anywhere in the world like my office. Whenever I asked about his fear or worry directly, though, he became anxious or frustrated. Even if Zach was gently prompted about the subject, he became angry. If the intensity of his feelings became too much for him to tolerate, he ended sessions prematurely by walking out of the room without so much as a look over his shoulder. A child leaving a play session before it is over is important data. It can be a signal to the clinician that the intervention may need to include more than just the child. Thinking it could be possible with this case, I planned for the family to visit for a family play assessment. One week in advance, I communicated to the family that we would be having a session with all members. I planned two family activities.

When the time arrived, I greeted the family (all present except for the father, who was on a business trip) in the waiting room and invited everyone back into my room. The sister and mother stood to follow me and the boy began to protest loudly in the waiting room. He stated that he did not want to include his sister in the session. In order to better understand his reaction and evaluate his ability to redirect himself, I began giving him choices. I explained that he could choose to come into the session and participate or he could choose to come into the session and remain quiet, but that it was not his choice who else would come and participate. The choice of inviting his mother and sister had already been decided by me. He whined and protested while I reflected that it was hard for him but that we would be going into the session as our time had already started.

It took great strength to lead the family back to my office without him but as we three sat down, I stated that we were going to trust him to join us in his own time. Within less than five minutes, he entered the room very angry, but silent. His decision to join us was a great surprise to his mother and sister, while to me, it was a great relief. I acknowledged his choice to join us and stated that although it was not easy, he did it. He would not speak or make eye contact but he was clearly in distress by the expression on his face. He stomped over to a table, climbed on top, and laid across it holding his head in his hands.

We were all silent except for the sound of his agitated whimpering. All I could think to do was to narrate for him as he struggled with himself. I began reflecting, "You're feeling very upset, you're angry that you didn't get your own session." As his sister tried to speak to their mother, Zach sat up and went directly for the handcuffs. He began to put them on his mother and fastened them so tightly that it was visibly painful. I stated that he could choose to use the handcuffs but he did not get to choose how tight they were—and with that he loosened them. He then turned back to the toys and searched among the toy guns. All along, as I was quietly narrating, his sister was asking, "Zach, what are you doing? Why aren't you saying anything?"

I interpreted, "I think Zach is trying to tell us something without words." He found the toy gun that he was looking for and turned to hand it to his sister, who hesitated. She did not want to take it from him. She asked, "What am I supposed to do?" and he only nodded at the gun as he put it in her hands. As she took the gun he turned his back toward her, sunk to his knees and clasped his hands at the back of his head. He was enacting his own execution by his sister, with his mother in restraints. The intensity was so powerful and I knew I had to check in with Zach's mother. I turned to see her weeping. Zach turned and saw his mother's face as she wept and jumped to his feet and ran to her yelling, "Noooooo!" and he crumpled to the floor, now sobbing and begging her to stop crying. By now, his sister and I also had tears streaming down our cheeks and the family grabbed one another and hugged. Zach's mom hugged her children and rocked them as I sat with them in their pain and in my pain for them. I processed their sadness and their love and narrated as they held on to one another. After each person calmed down, I shared the importance of what had happened and how it would draw them closer.

When the session was over and I began to reflect and conceptualize, I remembered from my initial parent interview that Zach was not yet 2 years old when his sister was born and that it was a difficult time for him and his mother because he did not go to sleep well. When I followed up with his mother about his sleeping troubles, she shared that they had moved his room to the second story of their home when his sister was born. I do not think anyone in the family, including Zach, knew how deeply that had impacted him. From his perspective, he was banished, abandoned, replaced, and discarded when his sister was born. He carried both anger and resentment, and severe insecurity. At the center of it were his relationships with his mother and sister, whom he also dearly loves. With this new conceptualization, I revised the treatment plan to focus on strengthening his attachments and sense of self. Zach and his family responded well to this revised treatment approach as they reconciled the discordant elements and moved toward functioning better as a connected family.

REFERENCES

Brestan-Knight, E., & Salamone, C. A. (2011). Measuring parent-child interactions through play. In S. W. Russ & L. N. Niec (Eds.), *Play in clinical practice: Evidence-based approaches* (183–108). New York, NY: Guilford Press.

Burns, R. C., & Kaufman, S. H. (1970). *Kinetic family drawings (K-F-D): An introduction to understanding children through kinetic drawings*. Oxford, England: Brunner/Mazel.

Gehring, T. M., & Page, J. (2000). Family system test (FAST): A systemic approach for family evaluation in clinical practice and research. In K. Gitlin-Weiner, A. Sandgrund, & C. Schaefer (Eds.), *Play diagnosis and assessment* (pp. 419–445). New York, NY: John Wiley & Sons, Inc.

Gil, E. (2015). *Play in family therapy* (2nd ed.). New York, NY: Guilford Press.

Gitlin-Weiner, K., Sandgrund, A., & Schaefer, C. (2000). Family play assessments. In K. Gitlin-Weiner, A. Sandgrund, & C. Schaefer (Eds.), *Play diagnosis and assessment* (pp. 417–419). New York, NY: John Wiley & Sons, Inc.

Hanevold, W. (2005). Standards for Child and Family Assessment. Retrieved from http://www.odis.dhr.state.ga.us/.

Harvey, S. (2000). Dynamic play approaches in the observation of family relationships. In K. Gitlin-Weiner, A. Sandgrund, & C. Schaefer (Eds.), *Play diagnosis and assessment* (pp. 457–473). New York, NY: John Wiley & Sons, Inc.

Hupp, S. A., Reitman, D., Forde, D. A., Shriver, M. D., & Kelley, M. L. (2008). Advancing the assessment of parent-child interactions: Development of the Parent Instruction-Giving Game with Youngsters. *Behavior Therapy*, *39*(1), 91–106. doi:10.1016/j.beth.2007.05.004.

Kaugars, A. S. (2011). Assessment of pretend play. In S. W. Russ & L. N. Niec (Eds.), *Play in clinical practice: Evidence-based approaches* (pp. 51–82). New York, NY: Guilford Press.

Keck, S. E., & Sporakowski, M. J. (1982). Behavioral diagnosis and assessment in marital therapy. *Journal of Sex & Marital Therapy, 8*(2), 119–134.

Kelly-Vance, L., Needelman, H., Troia, K., & Ryalls, B. O. (1999). Early childhood assessment: A comparison of the Bayley Scales of Infant Development and play-based assessment in two-year-old at-risk children. *Developmental Disabilities Bulletin*, *27*(1), 1–15.

Kinston, W., & Loader, P. (1988). The family task interview: A tool for clinical research in family interaction. *Journal of Marital and Family Therapy, 14*(1), 67–87.

Landgarten, H. B. (1987). *Family art psychotherapy: A clinical guide and casebook.* New York, NY: Brunner/Mazel.

Landreth, G. L. (2012). *Play therapy: The art of the relationship* (3rd ed.). New York, NY: Routledge.

Linder, T., Anthony, T. Bundy, A., Charlifue-Smith, R., Hafer, J., Hancock, F., & Rooke, C. (2008). *Transdisciplinary play-based assessment* (2nd ed.). Baltimore, MD: Paul H. Brookes.

Patterson, J., Williams, L., Edwards, T. M., Chamow, L., & Grauf-Grounds, C. (2009). *Essential skills in family therapy: From the first interview to termination* (2nd ed.). New York, NY: Guilford Press.

Ray, D. (2011). *Advanced play therapy: Essential conditions, knowledge, and skills for child practice*. New York, NY: Routledge.

Robinson, E. A., & Eyberg, S. M. (1981). The dyadic parent–child interaction coding system: Standardization and validation. *Journal of Consulting and Clinical Psychology, 49*(2), 245–250. doi:10.1037/0022-006X.49.2.245.

Russ, S. W., & Niec, L. N. (2011). *Play in clinical practice: Evidence-based approaches*. New York, NY: Guilford Press.

Smith, G. (2000). Assessing family interaction by the collaborative drawing technique. In K. Gitlin-Weiner, A. Sandgrund, & C. Schaefer (Eds.), *Play diagnosis and assessment* (pp. 446–456). New York, NY: John Wiley & Sons, Inc.

Stollak, G. E., Barlev, A., & Kalogiros, I. (2000). Assessment of the child and family in play contexts. In K. Gitlin-Weiner, A. Sandgrund, C. Schaefer (Eds.), *Play diagnosis and assessment* (2nd ed., pp. 474–513). Hoboken, NJ: John Wiley & Sons, Inc.

Thomlinson, B. (2014). *Family assessment handbook: An introductory practice guide to family assessment* (3rd ed.). Boston, MA: Cengage Learning.

Whitcomb, S. A., & Merrell, K. W. (2013). *Behavioral, social, and emotional assessment of children and adolescents* (4th ed.). New York, NY: Routledge/Taylor & Francis Group.

Wilkinson, I. (2000). The Darlington Family Assessment System: Clinical guidelines for practitioners. *Journal of Family Therapy, 22*(2), 211–224. doi:10.1111/1467-6427.00147.

Wordsworth, W. (1850). *The prelude; Growth of a poet's mind*. New York, NY: D. Appleton & Company.

III

Clinical Applications for Psychosocial and Developmental Issues

Chapter Seven

Family Play Counseling with Children Affected by Autism

Robert Jason Grant

> Rather than talking about a child with special needs, we should talk about families with special needs, because when a child has uneven development—whether the cause is ASD or a severe language, motor, or other problem—the entire family has a challenge. —Greenspan and Wieder (2006, p. 163)

Parents and other family members play an important role in the emotional, psychological, and social development of children diagnosed with Autism Spectrum Disorder (ASD). Play is an interactive medium for parents and other family members to get to know their child diagnosed with ASD and build interpersonal connections (Hull, 2011). The process of including family members in treatment with their child diagnosed with ASD provides an opportunity for parents to become empowered in relating to and working with their child beyond which the play therapist is able to provide by working with the child in isolation.

Family members are typically present for a majority of the child's experiences and are the people in the child's life that remain constant, while mental health professionals are transient. This level of social and familial consistency provides opportunity for parents to become effective change agents for their child. MacDonald and Stoika (2007) stated that the best mechanism for children with ASD to learn language, relationship skills, social skills, and knowledge for everyday life is during their everyday life. There is no more meaningful time to teach language development, relationship skills, and social skills than while doing daily life together, and parents are typically the ones experiencing daily life with their child.

While various play therapy approaches have been gaining research acceptance as a treatment approach for children with ASD over the past decade

(Bromfield, 2005; Josefi & Ryan, 2004; Kenny & Winick, 2000; Lanyado, 2005; Simeone-Russell, 2011), treatment approaches involving parents and other family members have been a popular and beneficial model for treating ASD for many years. The merger of play therapy and family counseling as a protocol for treating children and their families affected by ASD not only supports treatment history and research but presents the most logical course for the lifelong challenges that can accompany an ASD diagnosis. VanFleet (2014) in her extensive work with Filial Therapy (a family play counseling approach) noted that family play counseling offers several potential benefits to families of children with ASD including the empowerment of parents and giving parents tools to understand and communicate with their child.

Established ASD treatments typically involve a parent training component where parents and/or other family members are taught how to implement a treatment approach at home with their child (Grant, 2014). Family play counseling provides the opportunity for a play therapist to involve and teach parents and other members of the family protocol and interventions that can be implemented in the home by the family. This type of approach not only creates valuable repetition of skill development for the child but equips family members with tools to address struggles in everyday life in the moment they are occurring. Further, it empowers parents in the lifelong process of providing support for their child with ASD.

CURRENT RESEARCH AND THEORY

Hull (2011) noted that research supports the need for therapists to work with parents who have a child with ASD and several benefits of working with parents that include the familiarity and consistency parents can provide, strengthening the parent/child relationship, and reducing parental stress. Many play-based ASD treatments exist that involve parents and other family members in the treatment process (Greenspan & Wieder, 2006; MacDonald & Stoika, 2007; Solomon, 2012). Reagon, Higbee, and Endicott (2006) proposed that professionals and parents can collaborate across home and school settings to incorporate multiple family members to teach pretend play that potentially achieves positive therapeutic outcomes for the family as well as the child with ASD. There have been several successfully implemented parent intervention protocols for children with ASD (Sofronoff, Leslie, & Brown, 2004; Sofronoff & Farbotko, 2002; Solomon, Ono, Timmer, & Goodlin-Jones, 2008).

Solomon et al. (2008) cited the benefits of incorporating parents when implementing Parent-Child Interaction Therapy (PCIT) with children with ASD. Solomon, Necheles, Ferch, and Bruckman (2007), who utilized the Developmental, Individual Difference, Relationship Based (DIR) model, found that parents were capable of interacting with their young children with ASD in a reciprocal and contingent manner and were rated as appropriately interactive. Furthermore, they recognized that parents could serve as their child's primary play partners and implement play-based interactions with their child with ASD to bring about positive psychological change.

Stoddart (1999) conducted several case studies looking at individual versus family therapy for children with ASD. He discovered several benefits to family therapy: parents gained a great knowledge about their child's ASD, parents were better able to educate other family members, parents increased understanding of their child's behavior issues, parents developed a closer relationship with their child, and parents demonstrated more effective parenting strategies. Krantz, MacDuff, and MacClannahan (1993) showed that parent-implemented home-based intervention for children with ASD produced increases in children's engagement and social initiations and decreases in disruptive behaviors.

Several studies involving parents in the treatment approach have yielded positive results due to parent or family involvement. Jocelyn, Casior, Beattie, Bow, and Kneisz (1998), looking at caregiver-based interventions, discovered that children with ASD improved language skills significantly and parents reported greater satisfaction when compared to the control group. Mahoney and Perales (2005), using a parent training model similar to the DIR protocol, found significant improvement in social reciprocity and language development in children with ASD. Dawson and Galpert (1990) showed that children ages 2 to 6 years old increased creative toy play and eye gaze with their mothers after participating in an imitative play study where mothers were taught the protocol to implement with their children. Solomon et al. (2007) highlighted the multiple benefits from several studies involving families in the treatment process. Among the noted benefits were development of joint attention and language, an increase in IQ, social skills improvement, advancement in school performance, and improvement in communication skills.

Greenspan and Wieder (1999) noted several benefits from including parents in treatment with children with ASD. They summarized that parents become the representative of what is outside the child and the foundation for reality. The parents' ability to enter the child's symbolic world becomes the critical vehicle for fostering emotional differentiation and higher levels of abstract and logical thinking. The benefits of including parents and other family members in a family treatment process reach across the system, influencing the child, the parents, and other family members in achieving individual and family goals in a true systemic process.

Several family play therapy approaches have shown success in treating children with ASD; most notably Filial Therapy (VanFleet, 2014), Theraplay® (Booth & Jernbeg, 2010), and AutPlay® Therapy (Grant, 2014). Family play therapy approaches provide a comprehensive treatment approach to working with the child and parent with goals designed to create healthy relationship connection, problem solving, behavior modification, and skill development (Grant, 2014; Green, 2012). Working with the whole family as opposed to the individual child with ASD provides opportunity for several areas of growth such as building connection between family members, increased understanding by family members of the child with ASD, providing socialization opportunities, and modeling important social and relationship skills (Hull, 2011).

VanFleet (2012) described Filial Therapy as a family play therapy approach where parents are taught how to conduct child-centered playtimes at home with their child and, in the process, become co–change agents with the therapist. VanFleet (2014) posited that the avenues for communication when verbal skills are not present, a greater connection between parents and child, a decrease in parents' stress levels, involvement of the whole family including siblings, and skill gain in parenting approaches are all potential benefits of using Filial Therapy with children with ASD and the benefits can apply across the spectrum to both low- and high-functioning children.

Theraplay is a directive approach that uses sensorimotor-based play to engage the child and counter autistic patterns. Parents are taught specific engaging and skill development interventions to play with their child. Parents are involved in each phase of Theraplay treatment and are empowered to become therapeutic partners with the therapist (Bundy-Myrow, 2012). Theraplay is uniquely designed for children with autism because it focuses on the common issues experienced by a child with ASD and works to improve communication, emotional regulation, social interactions, sensory issues, and parent/child relationship (Booth & Jernberg, 2010). Further, Simeone-Russell (2011) reported that Theraplay has been found to be very effective in developing engagement, interaction, communication, language, and social skills in children with ASD.

AutPlay Therapy is a family play therapy treatment approach that incorporates both nondirective and directive interventions for working with children with ASD. Parents and other family members are taught specific skill development techniques to implement at home with their child. Parents are trained in implementing the AutPlay protocol and become co–change agents in working with their child (Grant, 2014). AutPlay has been successfully used with both lower- and higher-functioning children on the autism spectrum to address and improve emotional regulation ability, social functioning, and relationship connection. Further, AutPlay research has shown that children with ASD also gain in sensory processing, anxiety reduction, and strengthening executive-functioning skills. The process of including parents and other family members in treatment with a child with ASD can take several forms and variations but the benefits of parent/family participation in the therapeutic process seem undeniable for both the child and his or her family.

Integrative Family Play Counseling Treatment Planning and Protocol

AutPlay Therapy is a family play therapy approach that is specifically designed for children with ASD. AutPlay interventions use a variety of integrative approaches to help children with ASD gain skill development. Expressive materials, games, toys, sensory-based materials, art, music, and movement are all components of directive play interventions designed to target and improve skill deficits.

In AutPlay Therapy, an extensive assessment is completed at the beginning of therapy that involves direct observation of the child and child and parent together as well as completion of AutPlay inventories by parents and other adults working with the child. A proper treatment plan begins with a thorough assessment, typically initiated at the beginning of therapy and lasting three to four sessions. Therapists can conduct observations of the child and/or observations of the child and parent together in a playroom setting along with providing parents specific assessment instruments to complete such as the AutPlay Social Skills Inventory and AutPlay Emotional Regulation Inventory. These tools assist clinicians in learning more about a particular child and his or her family. Therapists should focus on assessing social and emotional development and learning more about how the child's ASD manifests. Further, the therapist assesses for parenting strategies and parental attitudes/knowledge pertaining to ASD. The assessment component is essential, as each child on the autism spectrum will present differently in his or her functioning level and in what skills are possessed. The assessment component provides the therapist with a more complete picture of the child and the family that will assist in creating an individually tailored treatment plan.

Children with a diagnosis of ASD will typically present as being higher functioning or lower functioning (Green, 2012). Higher functioning typically refers to exhibiting fewer communication deficits and strong verbal abilities while lower functioning typically refers to exhibiting communication and verbal deficits along with social deficits—some to an extreme degree (Bundy-Myrow, 2012). AutPlay Therapy is designed to meet children at the level they present and work on advancement from that point. Once the assessment phase has been completed, it is time for the treatment phase, which can take one of two courses depending on the child's functioning level:

1. The therapist will begin to implement the AutPlay Follow Me Approach for children who present as lower functioning. The Follow Me Approach is implemented in a play therapy room by a therapist who

has been instructed in the Follow Me Approach protocol that involves following the child's lead while at the same time trying to engage, through play, with the child in whatever he or she is choosing to attend to or play. This approach utilizes toys, expressive art materials, and anything creative typically found in a play therapy room. The therapist focuses on improvement in relationship and engagement with the child while looking for opportunities for more reciprocal interaction that can lead to a more directive instructional approach.

2. The therapist will implement directive play interventions that target specific skill deficits for children who present as higher functioning. Directive play therapy interventions are chosen based on assessment materials that identify skills that the child needs to further develop. The therapist will implement and teach the child play therapy interventions during a session time and process with the child the skill being addressed. Play therapy interventions often incorporate art, music, movement, toys, and games. Therapists can choose from a variety of available AutPlay interventions or any play therapy interventions that are applicable for the child and address the targeted skill goals.

Parents will meet with the therapist in separate sessions, where parents learn how to implement either the Follow Me Approach or directive play interventions in the home setting. The therapist will have an established system for working with both child and parents and evaluating the home process. In AutPlay, the parents typically participate in therapy sessions with their child learning the intervention as the child does or sessions are divided with half of the session focused on the child and the other on the parents. This protocol continues until treatment goals have been meet. At that point, a termination phase is implemented that takes two to three sessions. During the termination phase, the therapist will want to celebrate the family's accomplishments and reinforce the skills that the child and parents have learned through therapy.

INTERVENTION: MUSIC AND MOVEMENT EMOTIONS

Music and Movement Emotions (Grant, 2014), designed for children and adolescents with ASD, increases emotional regulation ability and improves social skills. This intervention can be implemented in any setting and the therapist/parent will need a variety of musical instruments for the child to access. Many children with ASD respond positively to music and movement–based activities (Walworth, 2012). This intervention incorporates music and movement to address emotion identification and expression and the social construct of working and playing together to accomplish a task.

The child and therapist begin by choosing five feelings they are going to use in a music and movement performance that they will be creating. Once the feelings have been chosen, the child picks a musical instrument to accompany each feeling. The child and practitioner then decide on a movement to go along with each feeling and instrument. The child then decides the order of the performance (each feeling/instrument/movement should be performed one at a time). Once the order has been chosen, the performance is ready to begin. The child and therapist play the instruments and perform the movements together for each feeling in the order the child has chosen. For example: angry is chosen to be the first feeling, and drums are chosen to be the instrument to represent the feeling, and spinning around is chosen to be the movement to represent angry. The child and therapist announce the feeling (angry), then play the drums, and spin around for a few seconds. The second feeling/instrument/movement is then chosen and so forth until all five feelings have been performed. The following is an example of a performance outline:

1.	Feeling: Angry	Instrument: Drums	Movement: Spinning Around
2.	Feeling: Happy	Instrument: Flute	Movement: Hopping
3.	Feeling: Worried	Instrument: Shaker	Movement: Running Around Room
4.	Feeling: Proud	Instrument: Cymbals	Movement: Marching in Place
5.	Feeling: Sad	Instrument: Guitar	Movement: Shaking Hips

This intervention helps children increase emotional regulation ability, specifically identifying different emotions and how those emotions might feel. The music and movement elements provide an expressive outline to help the child better connect with the emotions that he or she is trying to identify. Further, the expressive piece provides an avenue to express emotions other than verbally and incorporates sensory elements that help the child feel more relaxed after expressing an emotion.

Music and Movement Emotions also increases social skills, specifically helping children to collaborate and implement a task with another person. The therapist can work with the whole family and teach the intervention to the family, and the family can create and perform together. The family should be instructed to create three to four performances at home between sessions. Each performance should try to incorporate different feelings and movements. Completing several performances at home provides the child with ASD the opportunity for repetition to help with skill development. Parents are taught to do this intervention at home and encouraged to role-play through negative feelings daily with their child.

CASE STUDIES

Case #1: Jenner

Jenner entered therapy as an 8-year-old male who had been diagnosed with ASD a few years prior by a neuropsychologist. He had recently transitioned from being in a private autism school to now being in second grade in a public school for the first time. Jenner had received an individualized educational plan (IEP) and participated in special education classes for the majority of his school time and in a few mainstream classes with the help of a paraprofessional. At the time Jenner and his family began play therapy, he was not participating in any other treatments related to his ASD diagnosis. Jenner's parents reported that he made substantial progress with his verbal and social skills during the time he participated in the private school.

Jenner's parents brought him to therapy due to transition difficulties with switching from the private school to the public school setting. He had been experiencing social skill struggles related to his divergent behaviors from other children. Jenner's parents stated that Jenner had begun to make statements such as, "I am different from everyone else," "I do not fit in," and "No one at my school or in my family is like me." Jenner's parents stated that they wanted help in learning how to talk with Jenner about his autism to help him better understand how it affects his behavior. They also requested help with improving his social skills and positive peer interactions.

Jenner lived with his biological mother and father and 6-year-old sister. Jenner's paternal grandparents were also actively involved in his life and assisted regularly in caring for Jenner and his sister. The family attended activities hosted by their church and participated in a local autism support group. Jenner participated with his family in various church-related events and activities but otherwise did not participate in any additional activities outside of school.

The first three sessions were primarily assessment-gathering sessions designed to gain more specific information about Jenner and designed to help Jenner and his family build rapport with the play therapist. Jenner participated in a child observation session, and the play therapist observed Jenner and his parents together in a child/parent interaction. Both observations were conducted in a play therapy room. Jenner's parents also completed two inventories: the AutPlay Social Skills Inventory and the AutPlay Assessment of Play Inventory. Both inventories were provided to identify skill strengths and deficits for Jenner in the areas of social skill and play functioning. Jenner's assessment sessions demonstrated that Jenner was able to participate at a limited level in directive instruction. Advanced instruction or activities beyond his limited skill level triggered discomfort resulting in Jenner refusing to participate.

After the assessment sessions were completed, the family would meet together, including Jenner's younger sister (whom Jenner seemed to interact with and respond to positively), with the therapist. Sessions would begin to address some of Jenner's social skill deficits through interactive structured play therapy interventions. Jenner and his family attended treatment once a week for approximately six months.

Implementation of Treatment

During the fourth session, the play therapist introduced the *Draw My Feeling Face* intervention to Jenner and his family. This intervention involves an adult making a face to the child and showing a feeling. The child then has to draw the face on a piece of paper and label the feeling. The child is then asked to make a face displaying a feeling, and then the adult draws the face and labels what feeling he or she thinks the child was showing. The play therapist chose this intervention for Jenner to help him begin to participate with, attune to, and reciprocally engage with others (all skills that may assist him in improving social interactions). The play therapist explained the intervention to Jenner and his family and instructed the family to observe as Jenner and the play therapist completed the intervention. Jenner had a difficult time engaging with the therapist. He was able to begin the intervention but seemed to become anxious about accomplishing the goal. He struggled with identifying the therapist's feeling face, struggled with drawing faces, and struggled with making a feeling face himself. It appeared that Jenner was concerned or preoccupied with accurately completing the activity without making mistakes.

After 15 minutes of working with Jenner, the play therapist suggested that Jenner and his younger sister try to complete the intervention together. Even though she was two years younger than Jenner, his sister was intellectually gifted and worked well with Jenner, often functioning more like an older sibling instead of a younger one. The idea to have Jenner and his sister complete the intervention was beneficial. They completed the intervention several times during the remainder of the session. Jenner's parents were instructed for Jenner and his sister to play the intervention several times at home before their next session and to try and play the intervention themselves with Jenner at least four to five times before their next session.

At the next session, Jenner's parents reported that Jenner and his sister played *Draw My Feeling Face* several times; they had also played the intervention with Jenner, and he responded positively each time. The play therapist played *Draw My Feeling Face* again with Jenner to assess if he would participate. Jenner completed several feeling faces with little to no struggle, a significant improvement from the previous session. The therapist decided to teach Jenner and his sister how to complete the play interventions instead of teaching them to Jenner only. This formula was successful for the entirety of treatment. The experience of learning something new and being challenged in skill areas was much more comfortable for Jenner to participate in with his sister first and then generalize to others.

During session five, the play therapist taught Jenner and his family two more play interventions: *Together Balloons* and *Progressive Balloon Game*. In *Together Balloons*, the family is instructed to pair up and place their hands forward in front of them while holding another person's hands. A balloon is thrown in the air, and the pair has to keep the balloon from hitting the ground while holding each other's hands. This play intervention was chosen to help Jenner learn to work together with another person, attune to another person, and facilitate secure attachment between Jenner and his other family members.

In *Progressive Balloon Game*, the family plays in pairs or as a whole group. There are four play levels with each becoming progressively difficult. The first level involves hitting the balloon back and forth and keeping it from hitting the ground (participants can use any body part, including hands, head, feet, and knees). After five minutes, the participants move to level two, which involves continuing to hit the balloon back and forth (keeping it in the air) with the dominant hand behind one's back. After five minutes of level two, the participants move to level three, which is the same goal only with both hands behind their back. After five minutes, the final level is played, which involves hitting the balloon with one's head only. The family is instructed beforehand that if the balloon hits the ground, to pick it up and keep going. This play intervention was chosen for Jenner and his family to help Jenner learn to participate prosocially in a group activity with others, help him with general self-regulation improvement, and provide his parents a tool to help Jenner practice social play skills. The play therapist taught both interventions to the family during the session. Both of Jenner's parents, his sister, and Jenner all participated, and the session was a success. Jenner's participation while teaching the interventions was somewhat reserved, but he remained present and tried to participate throughout the session. The family was instructed to try and play both interventions at home four to five times before the next weekly play session

In session six, the play therapist reviewed how the intervention playtimes were progressing at home with Jenner's parents. They reported playing both balloon interventions four times as a family since the last session. They reported that the playtimes had gone well, and Jenner seemed to enjoy them and appeared less anxious than he normally did when participating in activities with the family. They reported that family friends who have a neurotypical son close to Jenner's age visited them. They introduced the balloon games to the friend's son and Jenner to play together: the playtime went positively. In the past, when this family visited, Jenner would not engage with the other child. He might do some parallel play but nothing socially engaging. This time, however, Jenner played both balloon games with him for approximately 20 minutes and then reverted back to more isolated behavior. The family reported that they had not seen this type of play at this level from Jenner before, and they were pleased.

Outcome

The remainder of the play therapy sessions with Jenner and his family progressed in the same formula: checking in with Jenner's parents on interventions during home playtimes, discussing any questions and/or concerns Jenner's parents might have, and teaching Jenner and his family new play interventions to complete at home. At around the six-month mark of treatment, Jenner's father was transferred to another state, and the family relocated. At that point in therapy Jenner was engaging with other children in group play to a moderate extent and had demonstrated improvement in his social skill functioning. He also showed less dysregulation when entering new social situations. The social and play skill advancement improved Jenner's transition to the public school environment. He was participating with more children and had developed a couple of friends. Further, he seemed to display less anxiousness about going to school. Jenner's parents reported feeling more empowered to work with Jenner and stated that they felt they had several tools to help Jenner work on his social functioning and regulating ability. Overall, Jenner's treatment time appeared to be helpful.

Reflecting on Jenner's treatment, several components helped influence a successful treatment outcome. First, conducting a thorough assessment before entering treatment enabled the play therapist to make informed decisions for intervention selection. It was imperative that the play therapist first understand Jenner and his family before teaching play interventions. Second, incorporating Jenner's sister in the sessions proved to be a valuable tool. Third, teaching Jenner's parents to work with him at home between sessions provided opportunities to focus on skill development. It also empowered his parents to feel confident in working with Jenner throughout the day in multiple and diverse situations. Jenner's parents regularly reported being in a public situation with Jenner and referencing something they had been working on in one of their play interventions. Having tools to use in "real-life" situations in real moments was valuable to them and provided a practical application piece for Jenner.

Case #2: Kaily

Kaily was 3 years old when she first entered a playroom with her biological mother and father. Kaily had been diagnosed with ASD six months earlier through testing and evaluation conducted by an early intervention specialist.

Kaily was lower functioning with limited verbal skills. At the time Kaily began play therapy, she was participating in speech therapy, occupational therapy, music therapy, and on a waiting list for intensive in-home behavioral therapy. Kaily's parents sought play therapy to help them learn to play and interact more beneficially with Kaily and help Kaily gain social skills and play skills with peers and participate in group play with peers.

Kaily lived with her biological mother and father. Kaily had no siblings but was involved with other family members, specifically her maternal grandparents. Kaily's parents reported that they had family and community support systems in place and were active in various autism support groups. Kaily participated in several treatments throughout each week but was not involved in any social activities.

The first three play therapy sessions were designed to help Kaily build rapport and become more comfortable with the therapist and being in the playroom. The first three sessions were also used to further assess Kaily's skill functioning. The play therapist conducted a child observation session with Kaily and a parent/child observation session with Kaily and both her parents. Kaily's parents also completed four inventories: the Autism Evaluation Checklist, the AutPlay Social Skills Inventory, AutPlay Connection Inventory, and AutPlay Play Assessment Inventory. Kaily was observed in a playroom and was approximately 80 percent nonverbal. She periodically spoke words, but they were incomprehensible. She would occasionally say a word that was understandable and context appropriate, and she would occasionally provide an appropriate one-word response to a question. Most of the time, Kaily would not respond to the play therapist's presence in the playroom, she would not respond to any verbal prompting, and she seemed to not pay attention to the play therapist or his efforts at engagement. Kaily played with two to three toys repeatedly. After the assessment, the AutPlay Follow Me Approach was identified as the treatment paradigm. This approach was used due to Kaily's age, her inability to attend to or engage with another person, and her low verbal skills. Both Kaily and her parents would participate in treatment with the goal of teaching the AutPlay Follow Me Approach to Kaily's parents to implement in the home setting. Goals for treatment included increasing play interaction between Kaily and others, increasing engagement with another person, and increasing verbal skills. Further, it was discussed that the AutPlay Follow Me Approach would help Kaily gain skills to be able to participate in more directive play-based interventions designed to increase specific play skills, interventions that would require a greater level of attunement and engagement than she was currently displaying.

Implementation of Treatment

During the third session, the play therapist provided Kaily's parents an outline to review the AutPlay Follow Me Approach.

At the fourth session, the play therapist conducted an AutPlay Follow Me Approach session with Kaily as her parents observed from the corner of the playroom. The purpose of the session was to further assess Kaily's skill level and demonstrate a play session to her parents to help them begin to learn how to conduct play sessions at home. The play session lasted 20 minutes. The therapist demonstrated tracking and reflecting skills, letting Kaily lead the play and following her as she transitioned from between toys and made attempts to engage with her in her play. Kaily seemed to be comfortable with the play therapist's presence and attempts to engage her, although 90 percent of engagement attempts were not acknowledged. She did make eye contact during playtime with a toy car and answered a question posted by the therapist. This was the only overt engagement piece that occurred during the play session. At the end of the 20 minutes, the therapist reviewed the playtime with Kaily's parents and answered any questions they had about what they had observed. They were most curious about how often to try and engage Kaily and in what ways. The therapist discussed engagement attempts that were made and examples of other options that could have been attempted. Kaily's parents were instructed to review the written outline they had been given describing the AutPlay Follow Me Approach, and during the fifth session, they would observe the therapist demonstrating a playtime and have the opportunity to ask questions and clarify the process.

During the fifth session, Kaily's parents observed the play therapist conducting a play session with Kaily that lasted approximately 20 minutes. After the play session demonstration, the therapist processed the session with Kaily's parents and discussed any questions or observations they had. The session time progressed similarly to session four, except that Kaily seemed to attend to and play with a greater variety of toys. She also seemed to be making more attempts to communicate with the therapist verbally although much of what she was saying could not be understood. Kaily's parents were again instructed to review the written outline they were given describing the AutPlay Follow Me Approach and think about the observation they had watched. In thc next session, they would have the opportunity to practice the approach protocol.

During session six, the play therapist conducted a short demonstration of a playtime with Kaily and then worked with each parent separately in a different playroom, role playing and practiced the components of the AutPlay Follow Me Approach. Each role-playing time lasted approximately 15 minutes. Both parents seemed to understand the approach and successfully role-played through the session with the therapist acting as a child. Kaily's parents were instructed to practice the AutPlay Follow Me Approach at home with each other in a role-playing scenario, and during session seven, the therapist observed each of them having a play time with Kaily.

Session seven began with the father having playtime with Kaily while Mom and the play therapist observed from the corner of the playroom. Dad's session lasted approximately 15 minutes, and then Dad and Mom switched places, with Mom having a 15-minute playtime with Kaily and Dad observing. After Mom's playtime, the therapist processed through the experience with each parent giving them positive feedback as well as suggestions. Overall, both parents were efficient and seemed to have a solid grasp on how to have an AutPlay Follow Me Approach playtime. The feedback provided to them was to do fewer tracking statements and try to engage with Kaily in her play more frequently. The therapist also pointed out some examples of engaging they could attempt. Kaily's parents were instructed to continue to have some role-playing practice times at home with each other and the therapist would again observe them in the next session time.

During session eight, the mother was unable to attend, so the play therapist observed the dad having a playtime with Kaily. Their playtime lasted approximately 20 minutes. The remainder of the session was used to process the session with the father and review details for beginning the playtimes at home. This session with the father and Kaily had positive elements that had not been observed in previous sessions. Kaily moved around the playroom and played with a greater variety of toys than previous sessions. She also made several verbal comments to her dad and answered a few of his questions, sometimes with words that were not clear, but several times she was understood. The therapist encouraged him to make more reflective statements as Kaily seemed to be an expressive child, and there were several opportunities to reflect a feeling that Dad had been missing. He was also encouraged to look for opportunities to try and engage Kaily in her playtime. Overall, the play session was a success, and it was discussed that the parents could begin to have playtimes at home. The therapist instructed the dad to conduct a 20-minute playtime four times before the next session. He and the mother could have separate playtimes so each of them could try and have two playtimes before the next session. The therapist also discussed logistical issues of where the playtimes would be at home, what toys they would use, and when they would try to have the playtimes.

Session nine began by having each parent conduct a playtime with Kaily for about 10 minutes while the other parent and the play therapist observed. The therapist observed the two playtimes to be the most positive and productive to date. Both parents executed the protocol, and Kaily responded well to her parents. Kaily displayed more verbal interaction, and her parents attempted to engage with Kaily several times—the majority of those times Kaily reciprocated back. This reciprocal engagement was the most the play therapist had observed from Kaily to date. Both parent playtimes seemed to flow smoothly and naturally. Kaily's parents noticed the advancements and seemed pleased with how the playtimes were going. They reported four playtimes at home since the last session and were noticing an improvement in Kaily reciprocating play with them. They expressed that the playtimes at home had been successful. They had a question about how to set limits during the home playtime and how to handle going to the potty during a playtime as they were attempting to master potty training with Kaily. The therapist discussed and encouraged them to use redirection and set limits as little as possible. It was also discussed to leave the playtime to address potty issues and then return directly back and to remind Kaily they were continuing their playtime.

Outcome

Sessions 10–20 continued with Kaily's parents having four to five playtimes between sessions and processing home playtimes during session times. The session times also included short play sessions with Kaily conducted by the play therapist or Kaily's parents. Kaily continued to progress in becoming more engaging during her playtimes. Her parents reported each session improvement in engaging with them, acknowledging and attuning to them, and some increase in verbal statements. Kaily's parents regularly reported they were having playtimes with their child that felt more natural and enjoyable. Around session 16, Kaily's parents introduced games to Kaily to play such as hitting a balloon back and forth or blowing and popping bubbles. The games were simple connection/participation games. Kaily responded to the introduction of the games and participated with her parents. In session 16, Kaily's parents were instructed to teach the AutPlay Follow Me Approach playtime to Kaily's grandparents and ask them to begin having a playtime with Kaily once a week. By session 20, Kaily was having playtimes once a week with her grandparents, and displayed the same skills she was displaying during parent playtimes. During session 21, original treatment goals were reevaluated, and new goals were established for Kaily and her family that were more directive in targeting specific skills and implementing specific play based interventions to work on improving identified skill deficits. By session 21, Kaily was able to participate in more directive approaches focusing on specific interventions designed to improve skill levels whereas this was not possible for her at the beginning of treatment.

CONCLUSION

Family play counseling offers many benefits to children and their families affected by ASD. Research demonstrates the importance of including parents and other family members in the treatment process when working with children with ASD (Solomon, Ono, Timmer, & Goodlin-Jones, 2008). Further, a growing amount of research supports a play-based approach when working with children with ASD (Gallo-Lopez & Rubin, 2012). This highlights the benefits that family play therapy contributes to treating children with ASD by combining both play and the family in the treatment process.

Family play therapy approaches such as Theraplay, Filial Therapy, and AutPlay Therapy demonstrate success with children and their families affected by ASD. AutPlay Therapy in particular mirrors working with families in ways that match established autism treatments and also includes a play therapy base that is naturally engaging to the child with autism. Further, AutPlay Therapy provides the therapist with a comprehensive family play therapy protocol for working with these families. Although more research needs to be presented to fully explore the benefits of family play counseling, the evidence is growing and more and more therapists seem to be finding positive results when implementing family play counseling approaches with their clients with autism.

REFERENCES

Booth, P. B., & Jernberg, A. M. (2010). *Theraplay*. San Francisco, CA: Jossey-Bass.

Bromfield, R. (2005). Psychodynamic play therapy with a high functioning autistic child. In G. L. Landreth, D. S. Sweeney, D. C. Ray, L. E. Homeyer, & G. Glover (Eds.), *Play therapy interventions with children's problems: Case studies with DSM-IV-R diagnoses* (pp. 51–53). Lanham, MD: Rowman & Littlefield Publishing Group.

Bundy-Myrow, S. (2012). Family Theraplay: Connecting with children in the autism spectrum. In L. Gallo-Lopez, & L. C. Rubin (Eds.), *Play-based interventions for children and adolescents with autism spectrum disorders* (pp. 73–96). New York, NY: Routledge.

Dawson, G., & Galpert, L. (1990). Mothers use of imitative play for facilitating social responsiveness and toy play in young autistic children. *Journal of Development and Psychopathology, 2*, 151–162.

Gallo-Lopez, L., & Rubin, L. C. (2012). *Play-based interventions for children and adolescents with autism spectrum disorders*. New York, NY: Routledge.

Grant, R. J. (2014). *AutPlay® therapy handbook*. Springfield, MO: RJG Publishing.

Grant, R. J. (2014). *Play based interventions for autism, ADHD, neurodevelopmental disorders, and developmental disabilities*. Springfield, MO: RJG Publishing.

Green, E. J. (2012). The Narcissus myth, resplendent reflections and self-healing: A contemporary Jungian perspective on counseling high-functioning Autistic children. In L. Gallo-Lopez, & L. Rubin (Eds.), *Play based interventions for children and adolescents with Autism spectrum disorders* (pp. 177–192). New York, NY: Routledge.

Greenspan, S., & Wieder, S. (1999). A functional developmental approach to autistic spectrum disorders. *Journal of the Association for Persons with Severe Handicaps, 24*(3), 147–161.

Greenspan, S., & Wieder, S. (2006). *Engaging autism*. Cambridge, MA: Da Capo Press.

Hull, K. (2011). *Play therapy and Asperger's syndrome*. Lanham, MD: Jason Aronson.

Jocelyn, L. J., Casiro, O. G., Beattie, D., Bow, J., & Kneisz, J. (1998). Treatment of children with autism: A randomized controlled trail to evaluate a caregiver-based intervention program in community day-care centers. *Journal of Developmental and Behavioral Pediatrics 19*(5), 326–334.

Josefi, O., & Ryan, Y. (2004). Non-directive play therapy for young children with autism: A case study. *Clinical Child Psychology and Psychiatry, 9*, 533–551.

Kenny, M. C., & Winick, C. B. (2000). An integrative approach to play therapy with an autistic girl. *International Journal of Play Therapy, 9*(1), 11–33.

Krantz, P. J., MacDuff, M. T., & McClannahan, L. E. (1993). Programming participation in family activities for children with autism: Parents' use of photographic activity schedules. *Journal of Applied Behavioral Analysis, 26*(1), 137–138.

Lanyado, M. (2005). Treating autism with psychoanalytic play therapy. In G. L. Landreth, D. S. Sweeney, D. C. Ray, L. Homeyer, & G. Glover (Eds.), *Play therapy interventions with children's problems: Case studies with DSM-IV-R diagnoses* (pp. 51–53). Lanham, MD: Rowman & Littlefield Publishing Group.

MacDonald, J., & Stoika, P. (2007). *Play to talk: A practical guide to help your late-talking child join the conversation*. Madison, WI: Kiddo Publishing.

Mahoney, G., & Perales, F. (2005). Relationship-focused early intervention with children with pervasive developmental disorders and other disabilities: A comparative study. *Journal of Developmental and Behavioral Pediatrics, 26*(2), 77–85.

Reagon, K. A., Higbee, T. S., & Endicott, K. (2006). Teaching pretend play skills to a student with autism using video modeling with a sibling as model and play partner. *Education and Treatment of Children, 25*, 517–528.

Simeone-Russell, R. (2011). A practical approach to implementing Theraplay for children with autism spectrum disorder. *International Journal of Play Therapy, 20*(4), 224–235.

Sofronoff, K., & Farbotko, M. (2002). The effectiveness of parent management training to increase self-efficacy in parents of children with Asperger's syndrome. *Autism, 6*(3), 271–286.

Sofronoff, K., Leslie, A., & Brown, W. (2004). Parent management training and Asperger's syndrome: A randomized controlled trial to evaluate a parent based intervention. *Autism, 8*(3), 301–317.

Solomon, M., Ono, M., Timmer, S., & Goodlin-Jones, B. (2008). The effectiveness of parent-child interaction therapy for families of children on the autism spectrum. *Journal of Autism and Developmental Disorders, 38*, 1767–1776.

Solomon, R. (2012). The play project: A train-the-trainer model of early intervention for children with autism spectrum disorder. In L. Gallo-Lopez & L. C. Rubin (Eds.), *Play-based interventions for children and adolescents with autism spectrum disorders* (pp. 249–269). New York, NY: Routledge.

Solomon, R., Necheles, J., Ferch, C., & Bruckman, D. (2007). Pilot study of a parent training program for young children with autism: A play project home consultation program. *Autism, 11*(3), 205–224.

Stoddart, K. P. (1999). Adolescents with Asperger's syndrome: Three case studies of individual and family therapy. *Autism, 3*(3), 255–271.

VanFleet, R. (2012). Communication and connection: Filial Therapy with families of children with ASD. In L. Gallo-Lopez & L. C. Rubin (Eds.), *Play-based interventions for children and adolescents with autism spectrum disorders* (pp. 193–208). New York, NY: Routledge.

VanFleet, R. (2014). *Filial Therapy: Strengthening parent-child relationships through play* (3rd ed.). Sarasota, FL: Professional Resource Press.

Walworth, D. (2012). Music Therapy interventions for social, communication, and emotional development for children and adolescents with ASD. In L. Gallo-Lopez & L. C. Rubin (Eds.), *Play-based interventions for children and adolescents with autism spectrum disorders* (pp. 317–332). New York, NY: Routledge.

Chapter Eight

Play-Based Family Counseling for Children in Divorced or Blended Families

Jennifer Baggerly and Eric Green

> Divorce is like two lions in a den attacking each other. You know somebody is going to get hurt real bad. All kids can do is sit behind a window and watch it happen. —Nine-year-old boy
>
> Daddy left. Will Mommy leave me too? What will happen to me? —Eight-year-old girl[1]

Divorce is the most probable, disrupting family event children experience. Approximately half of all marriages end in divorce. In 2009, over 1,100,000 U.S. children lived with a parent who experienced divorce in the last year (Elliott & Simmons, 2011). Up to one-third of these children will live in a stepfamily sometime between birth and age 18 (Copen, Daniels, Vespa, & Mosher, 2012). An estimated 60 percent of divorces involve children under the age of 6 (Rogers, 2004).

Children whose parents divorce tend to experience more behavioral, academic, and psychological problems than those whose parents remain married (Anthony, DiPerna, & Amato, 2014; Johnston, Roseby, & Kuehnle, 2009; Weaver & Schofield, 2015). Children in stepfamilies tend to experience frequent and intense conflicts with stepparents about family roles and with stepsiblings about boundaries (Pace, Shafer, Jensen, & Larson, 2015). The impact of divorce can be seen in the play of children as girls express their pain through verbal aggression and boys express theirs through physical aggression (Hipwell, Murray, Ducournau, & Stein, 2005).

Family counselors need strategies to help parents and children mitigate the negative consequences of divorce. This chapter will prepare family counselors to work with parents and children after a divorce by (a) reviewing current research and theory, (b) discussing play-based family counseling treatment plans and protocols, (c) describing practical interventions, (d) applying the treatment plan and protocol to a case study, and (e) providing a summary and future directions.

CURRENT RESEARCH AND THEORY

Children's response to parental divorce ranges from quiet adjustment to noisy aggression (Lansford, 2009). Each child's individual reaction depends on a multitude of factors including parent attachment, developmental stage, risk and protective factors, and interventions received (Harvey & Fine, 2010).

Attachment

The emotional toll of divorce can impact the parent-child attachment. In a 25-year longitudinal study of mother-child attachment after divorce, Wallerstein, Lewis, and Packer Rosenthal (2013) found that over half of mothers were significantly less available and responsive to their children due to pursuit of other intimate relationships and/or education. These researchers concluded that even years after the divorce the mother-child attachment can suffer due to diminished attention to parenting. "Following divorce, the mother is faced with the enormous task of compartmentalizing her anger, hurt, and disappointment in the failed marriage, and of maintaining that cauldron of feelings separate from her parenting" (Wallerstein et al., p. 169).

However, if a stable co-parental relationship exists after the divorce, children are more likely to maintain a secure working model to predict their parents' behavior, which helps them shape future attachment behaviors (Roberson, Sabo, & Wickel, 2011). In contrast, if the co-parental relationship is conflicted or cut off, then children are more likely to have an avoidant working model, which can diminish future attachment behaviors. Therefore, Roberson et al. recommend counselors begin treatment by (a) promoting emotional safety for parents through empathy and a nonjudgmental stance, (b) coaching parents to have a businesslike relationship with each other and consistent rules for children, and (c) fostering effective communication regarding their children.

Developmental Stage

Divorce can destabilize children's developmental process because their sense of safety, which is needed for normal development, has been disrupted. Piemont (2009) asserts that "the marital container protects the child by maintaining an emotional refuge from the outside world along with at least some protection from the internal storms of normal development" (p. 99). Divorce can erode this secure container, which slows children's ability to resolve typical psychosocial developmental crises described by Erikson (1963) (e.g., basic trust vs. mistrust in infancy; autonomy vs. shame in early childhood; initiative vs. guilt in preschool age; industry vs. inferiority in school age; identity vs. confusion in adolescents).

Behavior problems after a divorce can be predicted by children's developmental stage (Lamb & Lewis, 2011; Wallerstein, 1986). Preschool children are likely to show regression, intensified fears, sleep disturbances, fear of abandonment, aggression, and separation anxiety. Children ages 5–8 often show open grieving, worry and longing for the departed parent, fear of being replaced, and fantasy that their parents will reunite. Children ages 9–12 tend to express intense anger at one or both parents for causing the divorce; experience grief, anxiety, loneliness, and humiliation of their own powerlessness; and view one parent as "good" and the other as "bad." Adolescents may experience depression, suicidal preoccupation, intense anger, aggression, anxiety about their own future marriage, and identification with one parent while they battle against the other.

Risk and Protective Factors

Children's adjustment after divorce is mitigated by numerous complex protective factors. Kushner (2009) identified key protective factors as regular involvement with the nonresidential parent, diminished parental conflict following the divorce, and positive parenting. In addition, Weaver and Schofield (2015) found that key protective factors included higher family incomes before the divorce, more maternal sensitivity prior to the divorce, higher child IQ, more supportive environments, and less maternal depression. Children who had these protective factors experienced a more positive trajectory of fewer internalizing and externalizing behavior problems. "This finding indicates that divorce itself may not be as detrimental for children as the circumstances that accompany it and suggests a possible avenue for intervention—helping divorced parents provide a supportive and stimulating home environment" (Weaver & Schofield, p. 8).

In their study of 560 stepfamilies, Pace et al. (2015) found that clear-sending communication can mediate stepfamily satisfaction and stability. These researchers define clear-sending communication as "frequent, open, easily understood communication about problems, positive aspects of the relationship, and even mundane daily experiences" (Pace et al., 2015, p. 29). They recommend an emotionally focused approach of restructuring interactions to accommodate attachment needs.

Clearly, many protective factors such as economic status and child IQ are beyond the influence of counselors. However, counselors can provide interventions to facilitate supportive environments, clear-sending communication, and decreased maternal depression, all of which lead to children's coping efficacy after a divorce.

Interventions

The plethora of interventions for divorced parents and their children can be categorized into (a) group interventions without play or expressive arts, (b) group interventions with play or expressive arts, (c) individual play therapy, (d) filial therapy, and (e) play-based family counseling. Rigorous research studies have been conducted on group interventions without play or expressive arts. In their randomized control study of 240 divorced families with children 9–12 years old, Vélez, Wolchik, Tein, and Sandler (2011) found that social learning and cognitive behavioral interventions delivered in a mothers' group and a children's group improved mother-child relationship quality, coping efficacy, and active coping in children at their 6-month and 6-year follow-up.

Other evidence-based group interventions for children of divorce include the community-based Children's Support Group (Pedro-Carroll, 2005) and the school-based Children of Divorce Intervention Program. Both of these approaches were children's group interventions that focused on expressing feelings, clarifying divorce-related misconceptions, and increasing communication and problem solving. Although these programs read stories to children, they did not use play or expressive arts as the primary intervention.

Children's group interventions that do use play and expressive arts have been shown to be effective as well. In their 8-week program, Rich, Molloy, Hart, Ginsberg, and Mulvey (2007) provided children group interventions to normalize the divorce experience, increase understanding of their emotions, accept revised family roles, and improve interpersonal skills. Children were prompted to express their perceptions of divorce by drawing pictures, writing poetry, or creating rap songs. Simultaneously, parents met in a separate group to increase understanding of their children's experience, improve parenting skills through psychoeducation, and provide emotional support.

Individual play therapy with children who experienced divorce has been described as beneficial to children (Hecker & Sori, 2006; Siegel, 2007). Individual play therapy allows children to express their experience of the divorce through play without worrying about hurting their parents' feelings.

For example, children may play out a scene in which baby farm animals yell "I hate you" to adult farm animals that are then thrown out of the sandbox. Individual play therapy provides a safe, confidential space for children to process these intense feelings.

Child-Parent Relationship Therapy (CPRT) has been found to reduce parenting stress and child behavior problems and increase child-parent connection in divorced parents and their children (Dillman Taylor, Purswell, Lindo, Jayne, & Fernando, 2011). CPRT is a 10-session manualized method of teaching parents Child-Centered Play Therapy (CCPT) procedures and skills so they can conduct play sessions with their own children. After several didactic and experiential sessions, parents videotape their 30-minute play sessions at home with their children and then receive supervision in subsequent CPRT sessions.

In contrast to the approaches described above, play-based family counseling (described below) offers several benefits. First and foremost, play-based family counseling promotes young children's participation in the counseling process, enhances the child-therapist relationship, builds positive emotional experiences between parent and child, and directly addresses divorce-related issues (Willis, Walters, & Crane, 2014). As opposed to children's group interventions, play-based family counseling provides immediate positive parent-child interactions regarding the divorce (Bowers, 2013; Lowenstein, 2010). In contrast to cognitive behavioral therapy, play-based family counseling helps parents enter their children's world through play. According to Panksepp (2010), play is an instinctual action that creates social joy when people are connected to significant others. Kestly (2014) describes play as the neurobiological glue for a secure relationship between parent and child. As opposed to CPRT, play-based family counseling provides more direct therapeutic support to help grieving parents who may not have the emotional strength to implement therapeutic skills. It also explicitly addresses divorce-related concerns by helping them process the divorce and create new family routines.

PLAY-BASED FAMILY COUNSELING TREATMENT PLANNING AND PROTOCOL

Goals

Emery (2012) identifies several important goals for parents and children in and after divorce. These goals include managing anger, grieving the loss of previous family structure, renegotiating power boundaries, providing reassurance and consistency, maintaining discipline, allowing loyalties, solidifying decision-making processes, establishing children's schedules, and communicating respectfully. These goals are needed because "relationships do not end in a divorce: they are transformed, dramatically" (Emery, 2012, p. 3). A cumulative list of recommended goals and play-based family counseling interventions is presented in Table 8.1.

Intervention Framework

A play-based family counseling intervention framework for divorced and blended families integrates family counseling, CCPT, expressive arts, and psychoeducation (Gil, 2015; Siegel, 2007). Play-based family counseling engages parents and children in fun-filled activities that move them physically and emotionally. "Adults and children alike are invited to participate in whole-brain and body activities that awaken and mobilize inner resources that may be otherwise dormant or inaccessible for whatever reason" (Gil, 2015, p. xi). Play-based family counseling is implemented with the parent seeking counseling and his or her children. However, counselors should contact the other parent to offer separate sessions for him or her and the children.

Each play-based family counseling session begins with 25 minutes of CCPT in which children lead the play (Landreth, 2012). The family counselor provides carefully selected toys as well as therapeutic skills of tracking play behavior, reflecting feelings, building self-esteem, facilitating understanding, and setting therapeutic limits. The family counselor coaches the parent to follow his or her child's lead in the play by using the whisper technique of "what should I do?" The purposes of beginning with CCPT include honoring the child's need to play, helping the parent to understand the child's world, facilitating a secure attachment between parent and child, and opening emotional receptivity. After 20 minutes of play, the counselor tells the parent and child, "In 5 minutes, we will be doing another activity together."

At the end of the 25 minutes of CCPT, the family counselor asks the parent and child to sit in a circle for expressive arts activities. A list of activities to facilitate specific goals is provided in Table 8.1. For example, to accomplish the goal of expressing feelings about the divorce, parents and children are asked to draw their perception of the divorce. Some children have drawn divorce as a war scene or a big blob that haunts the family (Rich et al., 2007). An alternative to drawing is to ask parents and children to write a rap song to identify and express their emotions about the divorce (Delucia-Waack & Gellman, 2007). These creative and expressive arts activities help children and parents enhance their attachment while they process the pain together (Malchiodi, 2014).

Psychoeducation for divorced and blended families begins with the development of effective coping skills such as regulated breathing, positive self-talk, exercise, and regularly scheduled family fun time. Once these coping skills have been developed, family counselors can help parents and children

Table 8.1. Goals, Objectives, and Play-Based Family Therapy Interventions after Divorce

Objectives	*Interventions*
Goal 1: Establish a secure attachment between parent and child	
• (1). Parent will create a safe and supportive home environment.	• Counselor provides warm environment with home-style decorations (e.g., heart-shaped wreath, candles, photos of happy parent and child) and child-centered environment (some child-size furniture, carefully selected toys, and bright colors). • Counselor demonstrates warm, accepting, nonjudgmental attitude toward all family members (including parent who is not present). • Counselor facilitates family drawing or sandplay of their home and discusses what makes it safe and supportive. • Counselor uses toy animals to facilitate a discussion of strategies to maintain a safe and supportive home.
• (2). Parent will demonstrate sensitivity to and acceptance of children's experiences and feelings.	• Counselor demonstrates child-centered play therapy skills of tracking play behavior, reflecting feelings, encouragement, and setting therapeutic limits while parent joins child in child-directed play • Counselor provides parent with handout describing Child-centered play therapy skills and informs parent of future option of CPRT.
• (3). Parent will demonstrate nurturing and engaging behaviors toward child.	• Counselor will prompt parent in specific nurturing activities with child (e.g., putting hand lotion on child, tossing marshmallows into child's mouth, singing song to child, or other Theraplay activities).

Objectives	*Interventions*
• (4). Parent will provide reassurance and consistency to child	• Counselor prompts parent to reassure child of her or his love and dedication to child's well-being by drawing a heart and writing messages of "since I love you, I will . . . . (e.g., sing to you every day, tickle you, cook you dinner, etc.)." • Counselor prompts parent and child in drawing or using sand miniatures to create genogram and social resource map to highlight support available to child.
Goal 2: Demonstrate positive, effective coping strategies.	
• (1). Parent and child will identify family's positive, effective and negative, ineffective coping strategies.	• Counselor leads family in a game of coping charades (silently acting out a coping strategy while other person guesses what it is). • Counselor helps family distinguish between positive, effective coping strategy and negative, ineffective coping strategy. • Counselor leads family in art project of creating a family crest (i.e., protective shield) with symbols of their coping strategies.
• (2). Parent and child will demonstrate positive, effective coping strategies.	• Counselor prompts child into teaching parent how to do each positive, effective coping strategy (i.e. regulated breathing, thought stopping, prayer, exercise). • Counselor prompts child and parent to play basketball and when they miss then they demonstrate a coping strategy.
Goal 3: Express and modulate feelings related to divorce.	

Objectives	*Interventions*
• (1). Parent and child will express and modulate feelings (e.g. anger, guilt, sadness, loneliness).	• Counselor asks parent and child to each draw a picture of the divorce as if were something. As an alternative, they could write a rap song about the divorce. • Counselor provides a drawing of "feelings thermometers." Each family member selects a color to represent a particular feeling (e.g., red for anger, black for sadness) and draws in how much of that feeling they have. Counselor provides outline of a person and asks each family member to draw in where in their body they feel each feeling. • Counselor helps family identify strategies to modulate (e.g. decrease intensity of) each feeling and asks members to add a modulating color (e.g., white or yellow) to each color on their previous drawings). • In order to demonstrate how family members can help each other carry burdens, counselor gives family challenge of moving one family member to the opposite side of the room without the person walking.

Objectives	*Interventions*
• (2). Express and modulate grief and loss of previous family structure.	• Counselor asks family to put on a puppet show to demonstrate grief related to divorce. Then counselor interviews each puppet to ask how they prefer to be comforted. • Counselor asks the family to find a toy, sand tray miniature, or draw and cut out a figure to represent each family member. Then counselor asks family members to place each family member in a sand tray in a way that represents how they were before the divorce. Counselor asks what the feelings and thoughts were of each family member. Then, counselor asks the family to move family members in a way that represents how there are now. Counselor asks what the feelings and thoughts are of each family member now. • Counselor asks the family to write a goodbye letter to the previous family structure and a welcome letter to the current family structures.
Goal 4: Develop and integrate an accurate understanding of divorce.	
• (1). Parent and child will express age-appropriate, nonjudgmental explanations of family changes.	• Counselor asks family to use expressive arts (e.g., clay and/or drawings) to create a timeline of major family events including marriage, births, difficulties, divorce, and new starts. • Counselor asks family to play a game of "truth or trash" in which counselor poses reasons (e.g., one silly or preposterous reason and one appropriate reason) for each major event in the timeline and they guess if it is true or trash. For example, your parents got divorced because (a) an elephant sneezed so loud it separated them or (b) they tried their best but could not solve their adult problems.

Objectives	*Interventions*
• (2). Parent will correct child's divorce-related misconceptions.	• Counselor continues game of "truth or trash" in which counselor poses beliefs children have about divorce. Family members have to decide if it is truth or trash. For example, ask, "Is this truth or trash—your parents could not get along with each other so when your mom yells at you, she might leave you too." Explain that while some children worry about this, it will not happen and that parents need to reassure children that they are secure.
• (3). Parent and child will express a restorative narrative of family changes related to the divorce.	• Counselor leads family in creating a family storybook that depicts a restorative narrative of family changes before, during, and after the divorce. A metaphor of bridges made from twisted colored pipe cleaners can be used to represent transitions from one place to another.
• (4). Parent will allow loyalties to other parent and child will enjoy freedom to love both parents.	• Counselor leads children in making a Passport with their picture and one page for each parent that lists things they like about that parent. On the last page of the passport, list children's rights to be love each parent, be happy with each parent, and not hear bad things about the other parent.
Goal 5: Strengthen new family structure, rules, and routine.	
• (1). Parent and child will identify appropriate family roles.	• Counselor asks family members to find a puppet to represent self and to put on a puppet show that shows a typical day from beginning to end.
• (2). Parent will renegotiate power boundaries and personal boundaries.	• Continuing with puppet show, counselor asks each puppet who should be in charge of what. Counselor asks each puppet what they can change to make their family get along better. Counselor asserts that parent is in charge. • Counselor asks family to draw a map of their home with different colors representing boundaries for each person. Counselor leads discussion of rules to respect others' space, privacy, and things.

Objectives	*Interventions*
• (3). Parent will maintain adult authority, a predictable routine, clear rules, and facilitate regular contact with other parent.	• Counselor leads family in using art material to make a schedule of routines; a list of household rules, responsibilities, and rewards (e.g., trip to the park, family games, watching movies); a calendar of regular contact with other parent; and fun back up plans if contact with other parent does not occur.
• (4). Parent will respond to children's behavioral challenges (e.g., sleep disturbances, separation anxiety, aggression) and maintain appropriate discipline.	• In a private sessions with the parent, counselor consults with parent on appropriate strategies in responding to and resolving children's behavioral challenges. Counselor provided guidance on appropriate prevention and discipline.
• (5). Parent will manage own depression and/or anxiety.	• In a private session with the parent, counselor provides parent with resources and referrals to manage and resolve depression and/or anxiety.
Goal 6: Demonstrate effective communication and problem solving strategies.	
• (1). Family will demonstrate effective communication between parent and child.	• Counselor asks family members to use puppets to demonstrate how to use a respectful tone to ask for someone's attention (e.g., "Mom, I want to tell you something.), state how they feel (e.g., I feel angry when you call dad names), and ask for what they need (e.g., I need to not hear that). Counselors pose different scenarios for family members to practice.
• (2). Parent will demonstrate effective communication between self and other parent.	• Continuing with puppet play, counselor prompts parent on how to communicate in a business-like manner with a nonjudgmental stance. Counselor asks parent to pose different scenarios and role models how to respond. Then, parent is asked to respond to the same scenario.

Objectives	*Interventions*
• (3). Parent and child will demonstrate problem-solving strategies and decision making processes.	• Counselor asks family members to collaboratively draw or create pictures of their common problems as if they were silly-looking monsters. Ask the family to name the monster (e.g., the Loch-Messy Room Monster). Cut the picture into 8 puzzle pieces. On the back of each piece, write one part of the problem that needs to be solved and how to solve it. Then reassemble the monster puzzle pieces with the solution side showing. Discuss how you were able to manage your monster.

develop an accurate understanding of their divorce-related experiences (Lebow & Rekart, 2007). For example, when parents negatively interpret their children's upset as a result of the other parent's bad behavior, family counselors help parents consider an alternative narrative. "They reframe a new narrative suggesting other sources for children's distress, such as their powerful feelings about separation, the natural difficulties in learning to live in two households, or memories of old events" (Lebow & Rekart, 2007, p. 85).

Psychoeducation is also needed to strengthen the new family structure, rules, and routine. When one parent leaves the home, families experience a disequilibrium in the family structure, which causes insecurity in children. A sense of security can be reestablished by clearly communicating that the remaining parent is in charge and will implement rules and routines. Family counselors teach families communication skills and problem-solving strategies to help them renegotiate these new rules and routines.

PRACTICAL INTERVENTION

Family puppet play is a practical intervention that allows each family member a safe distance to project personal thoughts and feelings about the divorce onto the puppets (Gil, 2015). This activity can be used to achieve numerous goals listed in Table 8.1. For example, goal 3, objective 2 is to "express and modulate grief and loss of previous family structure." Family counselors help parent and children achieve this goal by stating the following to family members:

1. "Today, we will do a family activity of using puppets to share thoughts and feelings about the divorce. There are numerous puppets on the shelf. Please take some time to select a few that interest you."
2. "Please give each of your puppets a name and a voice. Have the puppet say its name and something about itself."
3. "Now that we know each puppet, I will give you some time to create a story about how the puppets felt before the divorce and after the divorce. Please let me know when you are ready."
4. "I am eager to see your puppet show. Begin whenever you are ready. Rather than narrating the story, be sure to have each puppet speak for itself."
5. "Thank you for sharing your puppet show with me. I have a question for the puppet named ____. You said you missed your dad. When does this happen? What do you need from others to help you feel better? Now I have a question for the puppet named ____. You said you feel lonely. What is the loneliness teaching you? What do you do for yourself to feel better?"
6. "You can put the puppets down now. If you were to give a title to your puppet show, what would it be? What are some lessons that you and others can learn from your story? What did you learn about yourself and your family members from this activity?"
7. "Thank you for sharing. It took a lot of courage to do that. I learned that in the middle of your grieving process, you can still have fun, stick together, and grow stronger."

CASE STUDY

In order to protect confidential information, the following case study is a composite of children who have received play-based family counseling. Maria is a 35-year-old Mexican-American woman who sought counseling for herself, her 6-year-old son, Jose, and her 4-year-old daughter, Sonya, due to a high conflict divorce from her husband of 9 years. During the parent-only intake, the mother reported her son showed more aggression toward her, and her daughter had separation anxiety. The mother reported several incidents of violence in the home prior to the divorce as well as her own depression.

During child-centered sibling play therapy (i.e., a modality in which children/siblings lead the play and the counselor follows) in the initial session, Jose repeatedly punched the bop bag Bobo doll with intensity while Sonya sat near her mother rocking the baby doll. The counselor tracked (or verbally reinforced) play behavior by saying, "Jose, you are punching that with all your strength, and Sonya, you are rocking the baby doll." After Jose replied, "Yeah, I'm the man protecting my family," the counselor reflected feelings and enlarged the meaning with, "You're feeling strong and believe it is your job to protect your family." After that, Sonya said, "The baby needs to hide." The counselor reflected feelings and enlarged the meaning with, "The baby is scared, and you're trying to help her be safe. That's what moms do."

After the 25 minutes of CCPT, the counselor then moved into a more integrative stance (i.e., combining elements of non-directive or child-centered play therapy with more directive perspectives in which the counselor suggests or directs activities of the play and/or introduces interventions) by continuing to work on the goal of establishing a secure attachment between the mother and her children with specific suggestions. The counselor prompted the mother to provide nurturing activities to her children of rubbing hand lotion on them, tossing marshmallows in their mouths, and singing their family-favorite religious song to them. Then, the counselor asked the family to work together to draw a social resource map of all the people and places (e.g., school, church, community center) that helped them feel safe and happy. The counselor emphasized that the mother had several important people (e.g., aunt, co-workers, neighbors) to support her and the children.

To help achieve the goal of expressing and modulating feelings related to the divorce, the counselor asked the mother and children to draw a picture of the divorce as if it were something. Jose drew a picture of a large red T-rex dinosaur yelling at a smaller yellow Stegosaurus dinosaur. Sonya drew a picture of rain clouds with a sun that had a frown. The mother drew a picture of a tornado destroying a house. When asked what feeling their pictures showed, Jose said "anger," Sonya said "sadness," and the mother said "terror and helplessness." The counselor asked them to add something to their picture to make the feeling be a little less big. Jose added a flying Pterodactyl dinosaur that was dropping food for both dinosaurs. With guidance, Sonya added growing flowers that were smiling because of the rain. The mother added a storm shelter with her and the children holding hands. The counselor recommended that each day they continue to look for ways to add something to their day to help them feel less angry, sad, terrified, and helpless.

To facilitate the goal of developing and integrating an accurate understanding of the divorce, the counselor asked the mother and children to make a timeline of events before, during, and after the divorce. Noting that the children seemed to believe that the divorce was because their mother was angry at their father for taking them to an amusement park, the counselor played a game of "truth or trash" with them. The counselor read a card that said "taking children to an amusement park can cause a divorce" and asked them to discuss if this was "truth or trash." The counselor clarified that parents get divorced because they have lots of big adult problems that cannot be solved, not because of one small thing.

To promote the goal of effective communication and problem solving, the counselor helped Jose say, "Mom, I feel angry that we can't pay for me to be on the soccer team anymore." They were able to create a solution that his mother would arrange for his cousins to play soccer with him twice a week. The counselor helped Sonya say, "Mom, I feel sad that you don't spend as much time with me because of work." They were able to problem solve by having Sonya help her mom in the kitchen followed by 15 minutes of play.

As a result of 10 sessions of family counseling, the mother reported that she felt more hopeful, Jose showed less aggression, and Sonya showed less separation anxiety. The counselor observed a more secure attachment between the mother and children. In addition, they were able to talk about the divorce with less anxiety and about their future with more hope.

SUMMARY AND FUTURE DIRECTIONS

Approximately half of all marriages will end in divorce. Children whose parents divorce may experience behavioral, academic, and psychological problems. Divorce can negatively impact parent-child attachment, children's normal development, and maternal mental health. Stepfamilies tend to experience frequent and intense conflict. These deleterious effects of divorce may be mitigated by play-based family counseling that integrates CCPT, expressive arts, and psychoeducation. Overall, intervention goals include (1) establish a secure attachment between parent and child; (2) demonstrate positive, effective coping strategies; (3) express and modulate feelings related to divorce; (4) develop and integrate an accurate understanding of divorce; (5) strengthen new family structure, rules, and routine; and (6) demonstrate effective communication and problem-solving strategies. One practical expressive arts intervention is a family puppet show to help families modulate feelings and develop problem-solving skills.

Future directions in play-based family counseling include qualitative and quantitative research. Using a qualitative approach, researchers could interview parents and children about their perceptions of the experience. Using a quantitative approach, researchers could compare pre- and post-test behavior checklists and parenting stress scores of play-based family counseling and traditional family counseling. Such research will guide counselors in strengthening divorced families in the most effective and efficient way possible.

Textbox 8.1. Resources for Children of Divorce

http://www.nasponline.org/resources/parenting/divorce_ho.aspx
http://www.helpguide.org/articles/family-divorce/children-and-divorce.htm

NOTE

1. Opening quotes were retrieved from http://www.divorceandkids.com/Kids%20 QuotesDrawings/kids_quotes.htm.

REFERENCES

Amato, P. R. (2010). Research on divorce: Continuing trends and new developments. *Journal of Marriage and Family, 72*, 650–666. http://dx.doi.org/10.1111/j.1741-3737.2010.00723.x

Anthony, C. J., DiPerna, J. C., & Amato, P. R. (2014). Divorce, approaches to learning, and children's academic achievement: A longitudinal analysis of mediated and moderated effects. *Journal of School Psychology, 52*(3), 249–261. doi:10.1016/j.jsp.2014.03.003.

Bowers, N. R. (2013). *Play therapy with families: A collaborative approach to healing*. Lanham, MD: Jason Aronson.

Copen, C. E., Daniels, K., Vespa, J., & Mosher, W. D. (2012). *First marriage in the United States: Data from the 2006–2010 national survey of family growth*. Atlanta, GA: U.S. Department of Health and Human Services.

Delucia-Waack, J. L., & Gellman, R. A. (2007). The efficacy of using music in children of divorce groups: Impact on anxiety, depression, and irrational beliefs about divorce. *Group Dynamics: Theory, Research, and Practice, 11*(4), 272–282. doi:10.1037/1089-2699 .11.4.272.

Dillman Taylor, D., Purswell, K., Lindo, N., Jayne, K., & Fernando, D. (2011). The impact of child parent relationship therapy on child behavior and parent-child relationships: An examination of parental divorce. *International Journal of Play Therapy, 20*(3), 124–137. doi:10.1037/a0024469.

Elliott, D. R., & Simmons, T. (2011). *Marital events of Americans: 2009. American Community Survey Reports*. Washington, DC: United States Census Bureau. Available at http:// www.census.gov/prod/2011pubs/acs-13.pdf.

Emery, R. E. (2012). *Renegotiating family relationships: Divorce, child custody, and mediation* (2nd ed.). New York, NY: Guilford Press.

Erikson, E. H. (1963). *Childhood and Society*. (2nd ed.). New York: Norton.

Gil, E. (2015). *Play in Family Therapy* (2nd ed.). New York, NY: Guilford Press.

Johnston, J., Roseby, V., & Kuehnle, K. (2009). *In the name of the child*. New York, NY: Springer.

Harvey, J. H., & Fine, M. A. (2010). *Children of divorce: Stories of loss and growth* (2nd ed.). New York, NY: Routledge.

Hecker, L. L., & Sori, C. F. (2006). Divorce and stepfamily issues. In C. F. Sori (Ed.), *Engaging children in family therapy: Creative approaches to integrating theory and research in clinical practice* (pp. 177–204). New York, NY: Routledge/Taylor & Francis Group.

Hipwell, A. E., Murray, L., Ducournau, P., & Stein, A. (2005). The effects of maternal depression and parental conflict on children's peer play. *Child: Care, Health and Development, 31*(1), 11–23. doi:10.1111/j.1365-2214.2005.00448.x.

Kestly, T. A. (2014). *The interpersonal neurobiology of play: Brain-building interventions for emotional well-being*. New York, NY: W. W. Norton & Company.

Kushner, M. A. (2009). A review of the empirical literature about child development and adjustment postseparation. *Journal of Divorce & Remarriage, 50*(7), 496–516. doi:10.1080/ 10502550902970595.

Lamb, M. E., & Lewis, C. (2011). The role of parent-child relationships in child development. In M. E. Lamb, M. H. Bornstein (Eds.), *Social and personality development: An advanced textbook* (pp. 259–307). New York, NY: Psychology Press.

Landreth, G. (2012). *Play therapy: The art of the relationship* (3rd ed.). New York, NY: Taylor & Francis.

Lansford, J. E. (2009). Parental divorce and children's adjustment. *Perspectives on Psychological Science*, *4*, 140–152. http://dx.doi.org/10.1111/j.1745-6924.2009.01114.x.

Lebow, J., & Rekart, K. N. (2007). Integrative family therapy for high-conflict divorce with disputes Over child custody and visitation. *Family Process*, *46*(1), 79–91. doi:10.1111/j.1545-5300.2006.00193.x.

Lowenstein, L. (Ed.). (2010). *Creative family therapy techniques: Play, art, and expressive activities to engage children in family sessions*. Toronto, Canada: Champion Press.

Malchiodi, C. (2014). Art therapy, attachment, and parent-child dyads. In C. A. Malchiodi & D. A. Crenshaw (Eds.), *Creative arts and play therapy for attachment problems* (pp. 52–66). New York, NY: Guilford Press.

Pace, G. T., Shafer, K., Jensen, T. M., & Larson, J. H. (2015). Stepparenting issues and relationship quality: The role of clear communication. *Journal of Social Work, 15*(1), 24–44. doi:10.1177/1468017313504508.

Panksepp, J. (2010). Science of the brain as a gateway to understanding play: An interview with Jaak Panksepp. *American Journal of Play, 2*(3), 245–277.

Pedro-Carroll, J. L. (2005). Fostering resilience in the aftermath of divorce: The role of evidence-based programs for children, *Family Court Review, 43*(1), 52–64.

Piemont, L. (2009). The epigenesis of psychopathology in children of divorce. *Modern Psychoanalysis, 34*(2), 97–115.

Rich, B. W., Molloy, P., Hart, B., Ginsberg, S., & Mulvey, T. (2007). Conducting a children's divorce group: One approach. *Journal of Child and Adolescent Psychiatric Nursing, 20*(3), 163–175. doi:10.1111/j.1744-6171.2007.00107.x

Roberson, P. E., Sabo, M., & Wickel, K. (2011). Internal working models of attachment and postdivorce coparent relationships. *Journal of Divorce & Remarriage, 52*(3), 187–201. doi:10.1080/10502556.2011.569442

Rogers, K. N. (2004). A theoretical review of risk and protective factors related to post-divorce adjustment in young children. *Journal of Divorce & Remarriage*, *40*, 3–4.

Siegel, J. P. (2007). The enduring crisis of divorce for children and their parents. In N. B. Webb (Ed.), *Play therapy with children in crisis: Individual, group, and family treatment* (3rd ed., pp. 133–151). New York, NY: Guilford Press.

Vélez, C. E., Wolchik, S. A., Tein, J., & Sandler, I. (2011). Protecting children from the consequences of divorce: A longitudinal study of the effects of parenting on children's coping processes. *Child Development*, *82*(1), 244–257. doi:10.1111/j.1467-8624.2010.01553.x.

Wallerstein, J. S. (1986). Child of divorce: An overview. *Behavioral Sciences & the Law*, *4*(2), 105–118. doi:10.1002/bsl.2370040202.

Wallerstein, J., Lewis, J., & Packer Rosenthal, S. (2013). Mothers and their children after divorce: Report from a 25-year longitudinal study. *Psychoanalytic Psychology*, *30*(2), 167–184. doi:10.1037/a0032511

Weaver, J. M., & Schofield, T. J. (2015). Mediation and moderation of divorce effects on children's behavior problems. *Journal of Family Psychology*, *29*(1), 39–48. doi:10.1037/fam0000043.

Willis, A. B., Walters, L. H., & Crane, D. R. (2014). Assessing play-based activities, child talk, and single session outcome in family therapy with young children. *Journal Of Marital and Family Therapy*, *40*(3), 287–301. doi:10.1111/jmft.12048.

Chapter Nine

Integrative Family Play Therapy with Children Affected by Sexual Trauma

Sueann Kenney-Noziska

> Nobody can go back and start a new beginning, but anyone can start today and make a new ending. —Maria Robinson[1]

Sexual trauma is all too frequent for children and adolescents. Although statistics vary depending upon the definition and methodologies used, the sexual victimization of children is recognized as a worldwide problem. Current prevalence rates suggest approximately 1 in 7 girls and 1 in 25 boys will be sexually abused before they turn 18 (Townsend & Rheingold, 2013). However, the impact of sexual trauma is not confined to the victim. It also impacts the victim's family and should be conceptualized as a family system issue. This chapter will focus on employing an integrative play therapy approach to address sexual trauma from a family system perspective.

CURRENT RESEARCH AND THEORY

There are many forms of sexual trauma including both contact and noncontact activities (Goodyear-Brown, Fath, & Myers, 2012; Hall & Hall, 2011; Saunders, 2012). Sexual trauma includes such things as intrafamilial sexual abuse (i.e., incest), extrafamilial sexual abuse, rape, date rape, statutory rape, voyeurism, exposure to pornographic material, child pornography, and other forms of sexual exploitation. Activities that fall into this broad categorization can include genital fondling, oral acts, penetration, and exhibitionism (Goodyear-Brown et al., 2012).

Although not all victims of sexual trauma experience clinical levels of distress, the overall short- and long-term impact of sexual trauma is well documented in the literature. The Adverse Childhood Experience (ACE) study, an ongoing, longitudinal examination of the childhood origins of our leading health and social problems, suggests that sexual trauma during childhood and adolescence leads to an increased risk of unhealthy behaviors, risk of violence or revictimization, disease, disability, and premature mortality (Anda, Butchart, Felitti, & Brown, 2010). More specifically, the most common negative outcomes of childhood sexual abuse are post-traumatic stress disorder symptoms, externalizing problems, and internalizing problems (Trask, Walsh, & DiLillo, 2011).

Long-term effects and symptoms associated with childhood sexual abuse include depression, guilt, shame, self-blame, eating disorders, somatic complaints, anxiety, dissociative patterns, repression, denial, sexual problems, and relationship problems (Hall & Hall, 2011). Finkelhor and Browne (1986) further expand understanding of the sequelae of sexual abuse to include symptomatology resulting in (a) traumatic sexualization, (b) betrayal, (c) stigmatization, and (d) powerlessness. Based on the abundance of scientific literature, it is evident that sexual trauma is not an experience that is short-lived or clinically insignificant.

Although often conceptualized as a single population, sexually traumatized children and adolescents are a heterogeneous group with no clear victim profile (Sánchez-Meca, Rosa-Alcázar, & López-Soler, 2011; Saunders, 2012; Sawyer & Hansen, 2014). A major challenge for clinicians working with victims of sexual trauma is the heterogeneity of symptoms, including both the severity and type of symptoms presented (Sawyer & Hansen, 2014). Sexually traumatized youth span a continuum from those with severe trauma to those with subclinical impairment. Recent literature suggests that even the subclinical population may benefit from treatment for improvement in overall psychological well-being and to avoid long-term consequences (Sawyer & Hansen, 2014).

Regardless of whether sexual trauma is the identified problem, polyvictimization is common for victims of sexual abuse, and, as such, practitioners should not err by viewing the child exclusively as a victim of sexual trauma and underattend to other potentially traumatic experiences (Saunders, 2012). Similarly, comorbidity is common for individuals with sexual trauma (Trask et al., 2011). Sexual trauma should be conceptualized as creating an increased risk for mental health problems versus resulting in a certain disorder or diagnosis (Saunders, 2012).

Given the heterogeneity of symptoms and the complexities of this population, treatment must be informed by a thorough, ongoing assessment. Common themes in the assessment of sexual trauma include (a) clinical interviews and standardized assessment measures, (b) multi-informant assessment, (c) broadband and abuse-specific assessment tools, and (d) trauma exposure, posttraumatic stress disorder, depression, anxiety, and sexual behavior (Van Eys & Truss, 2012).

Many factors influence the efficacy of treatment for victims of sexual trauma (Hetzel-Riggin, Brausch, & Montgomery, 2007; Sánchez-Meca et al., 2011; Saunders, 2012; Trask et al., 2011). Treatment for sexual trauma is influenced by victim characteristics (e.g., age, gender), offender characteristics (e.g., relationship to the victim, age), characteristics of the sexual assault (e.g., types of sexual acts, duration), and treatment characteristics (e.g., theoretical approach, modality).

Treatment Targets

During the past two decades, sexual victimization of children and adolescents has been studied extensively with efforts toward understanding the treatment needs of this population and defining common treatment targets. The evidence-based practice movement has aided in this effort and provides clinicians with scientifically researched, manualized protocols that have empirical support for being effective in treatment of sexual trauma.

Definitions of what qualifies an approach as evidence-based vary and evidence-based protocols span a continuum from those that have been rigorously evaluated to those which are considered promising practices or emerging. The National Child Traumatic Stress Network (NCTSN), the California Evidence-Based Clearinghouse for Child Welfare (CEBC), and Blueprints for Healthy Youth Development each provide a registry of various evidence-based programs for working with children and adolescents, including those impacted by sexual trauma. Readers are encouraged to seek additional information regarding these best practice approaches for consideration in their work with victims of sexual trauma. Protocols should be examined based on their level of evidence, appropriateness for the community and target population, training requirements, feasibility of adoption and implementation, and potential for sustainability (NCTSN, 2015).

Many evidence-based, trauma-focused treatments have overlap in intervention objectives and practice elements. These commonalities provide benchmarks and treatment targets for practitioners. Recently, Strand, Hansen, and Courtney (2013) conducted a qualitative content analysis of eight trauma treatment manuals. The analysis identified 35 intervention objectives and 59 practice elements that were then organized into nine domains:

- Trauma assessment
- Safety
- Engagement
- Attachment/strengthening relationships
- Core treatment interventions

- Attention to social context
- Trauma processing
- Consolidation/posttraumatic growth
- Therapist self-care

For the play therapist working with sexually traumatized children and adolescents, these areas can serve as potential treatment targets for victims and their families.

Overall, treatment as a whole is reported to be effective in reducing the negative outcomes of sexual trauma, with victims reporting significant symptom reduction posttreatment as compared to pretreatment scores or control groups (Trask et al., 2011) as well as no treatment (Hetzel-Riggin et al., 2007). Trauma-focused cognitive behavioral approaches combined with supportive therapy and a psychodynamic element (e.g., play therapy) appear to show the best results (Sánchez-Meca et al., 2011). The most appropriate treatment elements should be based on the victim's particular symptoms (Sánchez-Meca et al., 2011) and the main presenting secondary problem (Hetzel-Riggin et al., 2007). Best practice includes individually oriented treatment which is responsive to the victim (Saunders, 2012; Sawyer & Hansen, 2014).

FAMILY PLAY THERAPY TREATMENT PLANNING AND PROTOCOL

There is a growing body of literature that indicates that sexual trauma is a family system issue. Caregivers and nonvictimized siblings are not immune to the impact of sexual trauma. They can experience systemic trauma as a result of the family's involvement with multiple agencies (e.g., Child Protective Services, legal system), emotional distress and mental health symptoms, and relational, financial, vocational, and residential difficulties (Dyb, Holen, Steinberg, Rodriguez, & Pynoos, 2003).

Within the family context, members may experience substantial emotional distress including shock, betrayal, anger, worry, fear, powerlessness, self-blame, guilt, shame, and sadness as a result of a family member's sexual trauma. The family's daily life can be negatively impacted. Family members may lack accurate information about the sexual trauma and may experience cognitive distortions regarding the trauma. Additionally, family members may be unaware of how to provide support to the victim and can be at a loss for effective coping mechanisms. As such, family members should be viewed as secondary victims in cases of sexual trauma.

Parents of sexually traumatized children and adolescents may struggle with negative perceptions of themselves and their parenting abilities (Johnson, Wolfteich, & Harrell, 2014) and may feel increasingly overwhelmed. Siblings experience postdisclosure changes and can suffer psychological distress, increased risk of sexual victimization, isolation, stigmatization, and shame.

Dysfunctional family system issues may have existed prior to the sexual trauma and may have even contributed to the victimization. Addressing family system issues such as communication patterns, boundaries, relational patterns, and parenting strategies should be considered a part of the victim's treatment.

Therefore, treatment for sexual trauma should be based not only on the client's needs, but also on the wider family system's needs. Effective treatment for sexual trauma includes the short- and long-term functioning of the family regardless of the primary treatment modality. Family and parental issues should be identified and treated with facilitation of parental support in the earliest stages of treatment (Kilroy, Egan, Maliszewska, & Sarma, 2014).

Family Play Therapy

Family play therapy is the convergence of play therapy and family systems theories to create an approach that brings the power of play to the family system (Czyszczon, Riviere, Lowman, & Stewart, 2015; Gil, 2011). The involvement of the family is especially important for victims of sexual abuse as child sexual abuse creates significant mental health risks to nonoffending family members (Tavkar & Hansen, 2011). Consistent with the body of clinical and scientific research on sexual victimization, integrating family play therapy as part of sexual trauma treatment allows comprehensive treatment in the context of the whole family.

Given that addressing sexual victimization requires elements of safety and distancing, the use of family play therapy and other expressive media is a natural fit. Play, art, sand, and other expressive modalities should be thoughtfully woven into the overall treatment plan with treatment targets guided by the individual client's needs and the broad family context.

Treatment of intrafamilial sexual abuse always includes family therapy when reconciliation, reparation, and reunification occur. Although these needs can present in clinical practice, they are beyond the scope of this chapter. The reader is encouraged to obtain additional information and training to address these complicated factors.

However, not all families impacted by sexual trauma are candidates for the use of integrative family play therapy. It is the responsibility of the play therapist to assess each family's physical and psychological safety and readiness (Czyszczon et al., 2015).

PRACTICAL INTERVENTIONS

Trauma-focused play therapy interventions can be invaluable when working with children and adolescents who have suffered sexual victimization. Play therapy and other expressive activities allow clinical attention to be directed toward pertinent treatment targets in a developmentally appropriate, non-threatening manner. A variety of practical interventions are available to professionals who are properly trained in their application. Below are some practical techniques.

Enhancing Emotional Regulation

Following traumatic events, interventions for facilitating emotional regulation are a well-supported treatment component. *Revealing Your Feelings* (Kenney-Noziska, 2008) is a play therapy technique in which participants take turns revealing "hidden" feeling words using Color Switcher markers from Crayola. The feelings targeted in the activity can be determined by the therapist or collaboratively between the therapist and the child. This intervention can be utilized during the beginning stage of treatment to explore the generality of emotions, during the working stage of treatment to process emotions directly connected with the sexual trauma, and during the termination stage of treatment to process feelings regarding the end of therapy. The intervention allows flexibility in the feelings selected to be processed based on the specific needs of the child and family and can be used during individual, group, or family sessions.

Additional play therapy interventions useful in facilitating emotional expression after sexual trauma include *Where I Hurt* (Crisci, Lay, & Lowenstein, 1998), *Feeling Puppets* (Cavett, 2010), and *Feeling Word Squares* (Lowenstein, 2014).

Trauma Processing

Trauma organization and processing, a cornerstone of trauma treatment, allows desensitization to trauma reminders, facilitates a coherent life narrative, and allows interhemispheric integration. *Putting the Pieces Back Together* (Goodyear-Brown, 2010) is designed to access, explore, and integrate sensory memories related to trauma and provides a structured approach to do so. A puzzle of a face is assembled and somatosensory memories are identified as pieces are connected (e.g., nose, eyes). Additional expressive interventions for trauma narration include *Trigger Box Game* (Crisci et al., 1998) and *Unpacking My Baggage*.

Further support for the use of play therapy and other expressive modalities for trauma processing can be found in emerging neuroscientific research that suggests that traumatic memories are stored iconically in the right hemisphere of the brain. These memories are best accessed using expressive approaches. The uncovering and understanding of the neurodevelopmental mechanisms underlying trauma support the use of play therapy and other expressive modalities (Chapman, 2014; Crenshaw & Tillman, 2015; Gil, 2010; Malchiodi, 2015; van der Kolk, 2014).

CASE EXAMPLE: SABRINA (AGE 7)

Referral Information

Sabrina, age 7, was referred to treatment by her parents due to sexual abuse by her 16-year-old half brother, John. The sexual abuse was ongoing for a period of 2 years and included voyeurism, genital fondling, oral copulation of Sabrina by John, oral copulation of John by Sabrina, and vaginal penetration of Sabrina. Presenting symptoms included anxiety, bouts of crying, nightmares, poor concentration, and withdrawal.

Sabrina resides with her father, Michael, mother, Monica, and older sister, Emma (age 10). John, the half brother who perpetrated the sexual abuse, was from Michael's previous marriage. The abuse was disclosed 2 months after John and his mother moved to another state. During the sexual abuse, John lived 50 percent of the time with Sabrina and her family.

A comprehensive assessment, which included completion of psychosocial assessment paperwork, completion of standardized clinical measures, a clinical interview with Sabrina's mother, and a record review pertaining to the investigation of sexual victimization, was conducted. Following the intake with Sabrina's mother, a play-based assessment using both directive and nondirective interventions was conducted with Sabrina.

Clinical impressions and observations suggested that Sabrina was suffering from clinical levels of anxiety and associated symptoms related to her sexual trauma. Sabrina was developmentally on track, in good physical health, had no other reported history of trauma, and did not have a prior history of mental health treatment.

Case Conceptualization

Given the availability of evidence-based treatment components and practice standards which indicate treatment of sexual trauma should be individually tailored based on client symptoms and secondary problems, an integrative approach to therapy was employed with an emphasis on technical eclecticism using play therapy and other creative interventions to address salient individual and family needs. Utilizing components identified by the NCTSN (2015), core treatment targets for Sabrina included psychoeducation, emotional regulation, coping strategies including anxiety management skills, and trauma narration and organization.

Treatment consisted of weekly individual therapy for Sabrina, collateral sessions with Monica, and family sessions with Michael, Monica, Emma, and Sabrina every four to five weeks. Monica was both supportive and protective of Sabrina post-disclosure. As such, she was an integral part of treatment from the onset. Among other roles, Monica served as a co-regulator of affect, an additional container for Sabrina's trauma content, and co-creator of the trauma narrative (Goodyear-Brown, 2010). Monica was often "invited" at the end of directive play sessions to "learn" the skill Sabrina was working on.

On the other hand, Michael struggled to negotiate his role as a parent to both the victim and the adolescent who perpetrated the sexual trauma. Although he believed Sabrina's disclosure, Michael was torn in how to support both Sabrina and John. Regardless, the family system was ideal for an integrative family play therapy approach.

Sabrina's Individual Therapy

Prior to her initial session, Monica explained to Sabrina that the therapist was a "special helper" for children who had been sexually abused and gave Sabrina "permission" to talk about her feelings and what she had experienced. Individual sessions were divided into half—with the first part of the session being directive play therapy interventions and the second part of the session dedicated to child-led thematic play.

Directive interventions were employed to target specific areas salient in sexual trauma. *Brave Bart: A Story for Traumatized and Grieving Children* (Sheppard, 1998), which explores, normalizes, and validates common post-traumatic reactions, was read during the initial stages of treatment to provide psychoeducation regarding the impact of trauma.

Interventions that focused on emotional expression highlighted Sabrina's confusion not only about the sexual abuse itself but also about why John "picked" her, what caused the abuse to happen, and if it was okay that she "missed" her brother despite what he did to her. She also identified confusion about being believed and supported by her father since he continued to have contact with John. Interventions supporting the development and use of coping strategies and anxiety management were intertwined with interventions emphasizing emotional expression. *Tin Man, Rag Doll*; deep breathing via play-based interventions involving bubble blowing; *Four Square Breathing*; and *I Spy the Here and Now* were utilized to facilitate relaxation and active coping skills. Cognitive coping was introduced via *I Think I Can, Putting a Positive Spin on It* (Goodyear-Brown, 2010), and *Good Coach, Bad Coach* (J. Shelby, personal communication, March 4, 2015). Adaptive thoughts to reduce anxiety and promote a more restful sleep pattern included "It's not my fault," "I did the right thing (by telling)," and "I should've been able to trust him."

Once psychoeducation, emotional expression, coping, and anxiety management were conducted, play therapy began to target trauma processing including identifying reminders and trauma triggers, recalling memories of the chronic sexual victimization, and integration of the sexual abuse into Sabrina's life narrative. *Up the Ladder* was utilized to create a hierarchy of reminders related to Sabrina's sexual abuse. Family system reminders, such as photographs which included John, paternal grandparents visiting, and Emma mentioning John, became treatment targets for family sessions. *Unpacking My Baggage* allowed the sorting of feelings, thoughts, causality, meaning, and memories related to the sexual abuse to be processed from Sabrina's perspective. This intervention, which takes several sessions, revealed distortions regarding who was responsible for the abuse and the impact of the abuse. For example, in regard to what caused the sexual abuse to happen, Sabrina responded, "Because I didn't say no" and "Because he [John] loved me."

These types of distortions were directly targeted in future sessions using directive cognitive-behavioral interventions such as *Twisted Thinking* (Kenney-Noziska, 2008), an intervention which provides reframes for common distortions that occur during sexual abuse; *Don't Lose Your Marbles*; and *Healing the Hurt*. The latter two interventions involved a collaborative reframing of cognitive distortions in which the therapist and Sabrina co-created adaptive ways to appraise the abuse. For example, "I didn't say no" was challenged and reframed to become "I couldn't say no because he was older than me."

During the child-led portion of the session, play themes were assessed using Finkelhor and Browne's Traumagenic Dynamic Model (1986). Initial therapeutic responding remained surface level with an emphasis on tracking the content of the play and reflecting back statements made by Sabrina. As play themes became richer and better understood by the therapist, deeper therapeutic responding occurred with an emphasis on labeling affect, identifying coping, identifying elements of sexual trauma, reframing distortions, and introducing components of healing and recovery.

A primary play theme involved the dollhouse; people figurines; and two horses, a larger horse and a smaller horse. Play focused on the horses being "best friends" (Sabrina's words) while being cared for by the family. However, when alone in the barn, stable, or pastures, the larger horse would victimize the smaller horse in some manner. The larger horse kicked the smaller horse, ate the smaller horse's food, excluded the smaller horse from playing with the other animals, "bayed" at the small horse in mean and threatening ways, and would not allow the smaller horse to gallop.

Although no sexual content was depicted, thematic play was rich with elements of chronic sexual abuse—secrecy, isolation, helplessness, distortions about cause and effect. While maintaining the metaphor, the therapist highlighted these dynamics and a reworking of the dynamics of sexual trauma occurred via play.

Family Counseling Sessions

Given that family involvement is well-documented as an important component for treatment of sexual trauma, family therapy was an intentional component of Sabrina's treatment plan. Similar to individual sessions, family therapy assumed a technically eclectic approach with treatment targets defined by clinical research, evidence-based components, client needs, and family needs using expressive modalities. As issues and dynamics prevalent to sexual trauma surfaced during individual sessions, these issues were considered as potential targets for family play therapy sessions.

As is the case with family play therapy, the "process" was the salient focus; a means to facilitate support for Sabrina, provide healing for the family, and process the sexual abuse from a family perspective. The therapist observed family dynamics, communication patterns, and family relationships. Structurally, the tension between Michael and Monica was evident. It was difficult for them to talk directly to each other and make eye contact with each other during family sessions. Similarly, eye contact from Michael to both children appeared to be a struggle. Eventually, through the course of family therapy, Michael was able to speak directly with the girls about the guilt he experienced as a result of John sexually abusing Sabrina.

During early phases of family sessions, the need for psychoeducation emerged as a prevalent family system issue. Subsequently, *Figuring out the Puzzle*, a play-based intervention that explores myths and facts about sexual trauma, was employed. Family members took turns selecting a piece of the puzzle, discussing the statement as a family, and identifying the statement as either a true statement about sexual abuse or a false statement. False statements were tossed aside and true statements were kept. After the entire puzzle pieces had been delineated as either true or false, the family attempted to assemble a puzzle. The family intervention would only be successful if they had identified statements that were accurate. The intervention provided information on family members' perceptions and appraisals of sexual abuse and provided an opportunity for the family to have a safe environment to acquire accurate information about sexual trauma.

The *Family Puppet Interview* (Gil, 1994), during which family members create their own puppet show, provided rich insight into family dynamics. As the family engaged in the process of creating their show, conflict arose between the siblings with the culmination being Emma shouting, "Fine! Then I don't want to play. It's Sabrina's fault we're here anyway. Let her decide!" This was processed during the session using the puppets the family had already selected for their show. The therapist normalized feelings of anger, emphasized that the family was in therapy because John sexually abused Sabrina, reframed Sabrina's disclosure as an act of bravery, and acknowledged that the sexual abuse impacted the entire family, not just Sabrina.

At this juncture, Monica cried openly and shared her perception that everyone in the family was suffering because of John and the sexual trauma. She provided support to both girls—reassuring Sabrina that none of "this" was her fault and encouraging Emma to talk more about her thoughts and feelings. Michael even suggested that Emma receive individual therapy if she needed her own place to talk about her perceptions.

The next family session, the *Family Puppet Interview* (Gil, 1994) was continued. The family created a story in which a small horse (played by Sabrina) saved the other animals in the forest from a forest fire. During the puppet interviews, puppets talked about the fire occurring because of a careless camper, that none of the animals were to blame, and that the horse was brave to risk her life to save the other animals. The metaphors were rich for family system perspectives related to Sabrina's sexual trauma.

Following completion of Sabrina's trauma narrative, which was done individually and processed with her parents, a modified version of *Unpacking My Baggage* was employed in family sessions. The category "memories" was replaced with "impact" (of the sexual abuse). This allowed each family member to share their thoughts, feelings, and perceptions of the sexual abuse, the meaning of the abuse, and how it impacted them as a family. This activity, which took several family therapy sessions, helped the family process the sexual abuse as a system and allowed for creation of a family trauma narrative.

During the end stages of treatment, *The Ripple Effect*, a play-based technique emphasizing healing, recovery, and posttraumatic growth, helped Sabrina and her family explore the impact of the sexual abuse and facilitated closure for the family system. The intervention conceptualized sexual trauma as creating a "ripple" throughout a family. For this intervention, the family gathered in a circle, a large rock was placed in the middle of the circle to represent the sexual abuse, and family members took turns pulling streamers from a paper bag. If a yellow streamer was pulled, the family member identified an area of growth for the family as they recovered from the sexual trauma, and if a red streamer was pulled, a difficult change was identified. Streamers were arranged as "ripples" around the rock of sexual trauma. Positive changes included being stronger, feeling safe, and not having secrets. Difficult changes included sadness, betrayal, and the family never being the same again.

Adjunctive Services

During the initial assessment, Monica disclosed that she was the victim of stranger rape in her early 20s. Although Monica had previously received therapy, Sabrina's sexual abuse triggered Monica and she began to struggle beyond what could be addressed in collateral sessions or family sessions. During the early phase of Sabrina's treatment, a referral was made for Monica to receive individual therapy with a different provider to rework her history of sexual victimization.

Additionally, during the middle phase of treatment when trauma processing was facilitated, the marital stress between Michael and Monica reached a boiling point and a referral for marriage therapy was given. At one point, the couple temporarily separated and Michael moved out of the house. However, he continued to participate in family sessions to support Sabrina's treatment. Eventually, the couple reconciled and Michael moved back home.

Conclusion of the Case

The integration of individual and family play therapy slowly provided the support and healing Sabrina and her family needed and deserved. Sabrina's anxiety became manageable as she grew to understand her sexual trauma, identified feelings associated with the abuse, developed coping strategies to manage distress, reprocessed her traumatic experience, and received support from her family. Sessions were gradually tapered until therapy was completed. During the final family session, *Family Puppet Interview* was employed a final time with the family creating a public service announcement (PSA) about sexual abuse and sexual abuse recovery.

CONCLUSION

As illustrated by Sabrina's case, treatment of sexual trauma is complex and challenging. Reactions to sexual trauma vary and are influenced by contextual factors including family system issues. Work with victims of sexual trauma should include an integrative approach involving evidence-based information, client needs and preferences, and the family system. Ongoing research regarding the impact of sexual trauma and treatment approaches for those impacted by sexual trauma is needed to better understand the sequelae of this victimization and the mechanisms which lead to better prognosis and treatment outcomes. Play therapists will be challenged to utilize this emerging information to provide quality care to children, adolescents, and their families.

NOTE

1. Robinson, Maria, *From Birth to One* © 2003. Reproduced with the kind permission of Open University Press. All rights reserved.

REFERENCES

Anda, R. F., Butchart, A., Felitti, V. J., & Brown, D. W. (2010). Building a framework for global surveillance of the public health implications of adverse childhood experiences. *American Journal of Preventative Medicine, 39*(1), 93–98.

Cavett, A. (2010). *Structured play-based interventions for engaging children in therapy*. West Conshohocken, PA: Infinity Publishing.

Chapman, L. (2014). *Neurobiologically informed trauma therapy with children and adolescents*. New York, NY: W.W. Norton & Company, Inc.

Crenshaw, D. A., & Tillman, K. S. (2015). Trauma narratives with children in foster care: Individual and group play therapy. In D. A. Crenshaw & A. L. Stewart (Eds.), *Play therapy: A comprehensive guide to theory and practice* (pp. 262–275). New York, NY: Guilford Press.

Crisci, G., Lay, M., & Lowenstein, L. (1998). *Paper dolls and paper airplanes: Therapeutic activities for sexually traumatized children*. Charlotte, NC: Kidsrights.

Czyszczon, G., Riviere, S., Lowman, D. K., & Stewart, A. L. (2015). Family play therapy: Practical techniques. In D. A. Crenshaw & A. L. Stewart (Eds.), *Play therapy: A comprehensive guide to theory and practice* (pp. 149-160). New York, NY: Guilford.

Dyb, G., Holen, A., Steinberg, A. M., Rodriguez, N., & Pynoos, R. S. (2003). Alleged sexual abuse at a daycare center: Impact on parents. *Child Abuse & Neglect, 27*(8), 939–950.

Finkelhor, D., & Browne, A. (1986). The traumatic impact of child sexual abuse: A conceptualization. *American Journal of Orthopsychiatry, 55*(4), 530–541.

Gil, E. (1994). *Play in family therapy*. New York, NY: Guilford Press.

Gil, E. (2010). Children's self-initiated gradual exposure: The wonders of posttraumatic play and behavioral reenactments. In E. Gil (Ed.), *Working with children to heal interpersonal trauma: The power of play* (pp. 44–63). New York, NY: Guilford Press.

Gil, E. (2011). Family play therapy: Igniting creative energy, valuing metaphors, and making change from the inside out. In C.E. Schaefer (Ed.), *Foundations of play therapy* (2nd ed., pp. 207–226). New York, NY: John Wiley and Sons, Inc.

Goodyear-Brown, P. (2010). *Play therapy with traumatized children: A prescriptive approach*. Hoboken, NJ: John Wiley & Sons, Inc.

Goodyear-Brown, P., Fath, A., & Myers, L. (2012). Child sexual abuse: The scope of the problem. In P. Goodyear-Brown (Ed.), *Handbook of childhood sexual abuse: Identification, assessment, and treatment* (pp. 3–28). Hoboken, NJ: John Wiley & Sons, Inc.

Hall, M., & Hall, J. (2011). *The long-term effects of childhood sexual abuse: Counseling implications*. Retrieved February 16, 2015, from http://www.counseling.org/docs/disaster-and-trauma_sexual-abuse/long-term-effects-of-childhood-sexual-abuse.pdf?sfvrsn=2

Hetzel-Riggin, M. D., Brausch, A. M., & Montgomery, B. S. (2007). A meta-analytic investigation of therapy modality outcomes for sexually abused children and adolescents: An exploratory study. *Child Abuse & Neglect, 31*, 125–141.

Johnson, E. L., Wolfteich, P. M., & Harrell, T. H. (2014). Difference in caregiver self-efficacy and satisfaction related to sexual abuse of offspring. *Journal of Child Sexual Abuse, 23*, 504–518.

Kenney-Noziska, S. (2008). *Techniques-techniques-techniques: Play-based activities for children, adolescents, and families*. West Conshohocken, PA: Infinity Publishing.

Kilroy, S. J., Egan, J., Maliszewska, A., & Sarma, K.M. (2014). "Systemic trauma": The impact on parents whose children have experienced sexual abuse. *Journal of Child Sexual Abuse, 23*, 481–503.

Lowenstein, L. (2014). *Cory helps kids cope with sexual abuse: Playful activities for traumatized children*. Toronto, ON: Champion Press.

Malchiodi, C. A. (2015). Neurobiology, creative interventions, and childhood trauma. In C. A. Malchiodi (Ed.), *Creative interventions with traumatized children* (2nd ed., pp. 3–23). New York, NY: Guilford Press.

National Child Traumatic Stress Network. (2015). *National child traumatic stress network empirically supported treatments and promising practices.* Retrieved February 15, 2015, from http://www.nctsn.org/resources/topics/treatments-that-work/promising-practices

Sánchez-Meca, J., Rosa-Alcázar, A. I., & López-Soler, C. (2011). The psychological treatment of sexual abuse in children and adolescents: A meta-analysis. *International Journal of Clinical & Health Psychology, 11,* 67–93.

Saunders, B. E. (2012). Determining best practice for treating sexually victimized children. In P. Goodyear-Brown (Ed.), *Handbook of childhood sexual abuse: Identification, assessment, and treatment* (pp. 173–197). Hoboken, NJ: John Wiley & Sons, Inc.

Sawyer, G. K., & Hansen, D. J. (2014). Heterogeneous symptom patterns of sexually abused children in treatment: Understanding the complexity of the problem. *Journal of Child Sexual Abuse, 23,* 900–917.

Sheppard, C. H. (1998). *Brave Bart: A story for traumatized and grieving children.* Albion, MI: The Institute for Trauma and Loss in Children.

Strand, V. C., Hansen, S., & Courtney, D. (2013). Common elements across evidence-based trauma treatment: Discovery and implications. *Advances in Social Work, 14*(2), 334–354.

Tavkar, P., & Hansen, D. J. (2011). Interventions for families victimized by child sexual abuse: Clinical issues and approaches for child advocacy center–based services. *Aggression and Violent Behavior, 16*(3), 188–199.

Townsend, C., & Rheingold, A. A. (2013). *Estimating a child sexual abuse prevalence rate for practitioners: A review of child sexual abuse prevalence studies.* Charleston, SC: Darkness to Light.

Trask, E. V., Walsh, K., & DiLillo, D. (2011). Treatment effects for common outcomes of child sexual abuse: A current meta-analysis. *Aggression and Violent Behavior, 16*(1), 6–19.

van der Kolk, B. A. (2014). *The body keeps the score: Brain, mind, & body in the healing of trauma.* New York, NY: Viking.

Van Eys, P., & Truss, A. (2012). Comprehensive and therapeutic assessment of child sexual abuse. In P. Goodyear-Brown (Ed.), *Handbook of childhood sexual abuse: Identification, assessment, and treatment* (pp. 143–170). Hoboken, NJ: John Wiley & Sons, Inc.

IV

Ethics and Self-Care

Chapter Ten

Supervision of Play Therapists Conducting Family Counseling

Linda E. Homeyer and Marshall Lyles

> Family therapists and play therapists share a noble trait: They are by far the most creative and dynamic therapists in existence. Family therapists . . . engage the family's participation in a dynamic way, either by intensifying or replacing verbal communication. —Eliana Gil

Clinical supervision is critical for the professional development of mental health professions, the ethical care of clients, and protection of the public. All mental health disciplines require supervision at various stages: throughout graduate programs, while post-graduate pre-licensure, and when learning a new specialty or area of counseling.

Play therapy is a psychotherapy specialty practiced by a wide variety of licensed mental health professionals, including (but not limited to) counselors, social workers, psychologists, and family therapists. Play therapists believe in the therapeutic powers of play as the means through which the client (child, adolescent, or adult) makes contact with the play therapist. The meaning and symbolism of play, themes in the play, and the play process are all part of therapeutic interventions. How play is used therapeutically is based on the approach of the individual play therapist. Mental health professionals who purport themselves as a play therapist should have training and supervision in this specialty, as supported by all disciplines' ethical codes. Licensed mental health professionals may also obtain the Registered Play Therapist (RPT) or Registered Play Therapist-Supervisor (RPT-S) designation by meeting specific education, training, and supervision experience requirements as established by the Association for Play Therapy (2015).

Recognized as a core discipline in mental health by the U.S. government, marriage and family therapy (MFT) exists as a professional license in all 50 states. The field of MFT considers the family to be the client and this systemic lens exists as the primary distinguishing characteristic of MFT. Though family systems serve as a guiding principle among MFT clinical theories, it is not a clinical theory itself. Many clinical approaches fit under the MFT umbrella, and when it comes to developing a child-focused approach, these various systems-informed models often define family therapy or family counseling differently. One MFT theory may consider working with parents alone as a family approach while other theories believe having the child in the room to be a necessary component of family therapy. For the purposes of this chapter, family counseling will refer to the involvement of children as the focus of the therapeutic target, incorporating both play and family work. Even though clinicians from an MFT background often identify as therapists and not counselors, family counseling will be the chosen vernacular in an attempt to apply these concepts to multiple mental health disciplines.

Play therapists conducting family counseling need to select an appropriate supervisor. Research by VanderGast, Culbreth, and Flowers (2010) found 86 percent of play therapy supervisees preferred their supervisor have a professional identity as a play therapist and 90 percent preferred a Registered Play Therapist-Supervisor (RPT-S). This was regardless of the supervisor's mental health discipline. Only 29 percent of those participating in the research preferred a supervisor with the professional identity of a marriage and family therapist.

The intent of this chapter is to promote an integrated professional identity of play therapists and family therapists, particularly when developing proficiency to work with the family unit. First, we will synthesize prominent literature on play therapy supervision and family therapy supervision. Second, we will discuss supervision planning and approaches to integrating supervision followed by practical supervision experiential activities. Third, we will present a case study of an integrative supervision approach. Finally, we will discuss ethics in integrative supervision.

PLAY THERAPY SUPERVISION

As with other specialties, play therapy supervision differs from supervision for traditional talk psychotherapy with adults (Allen, Folger, & Pehrsson, 2007; Deering, 1994; Metcalf, 2003; Neill, 2006; Ray, 2004). Neill (2006) articulates the multiple and unique issues the supervisor of child therapists and play therapists encounter. A play therapy supervisor should have knowledge of play therapy literature, theory, and research; have well-developed play therapy skills; and advanced understanding and experience of the multiple systems involved with the treatment of children and adolescents (Neill, 2006; Ray, 2006, 2011). Additionally, supervisors must be aware that play therapists often experience the evoking of intense emotions when working with children (Neill, Holloway, & Kaak, 2006), countertransference issues from the play therapist's own childhood (Metcalf, 2003), and increased experience of the parallel process (Deering, 1994).

There is no generally accepted supervision model specifically for the specialty of play therapy. It is generally agreed that supervisors, regardless of the area of psychotherapy, must have the ability to assess a basic knowledge base, evaluate skill development, and promote clear case conceptualization. The supervisory skills of teacher, counselor, and consultant found in many models (Bernard, Williams, Hess, Holloway, & Carroll, cited in Bernard & Goodyear, 2004) are also seen as necessary for the play therapy supervisor. Holloway (1995) adds the development of the supervisee's professional role, emotional awareness, and ability to self-evaluate. The Integrated Developmental Model of supervision (Stoltenberg, McNeill, & Delworth, 1998) is frequently identified as appropriate for supervising the variety of supervisees, from students to novice and experienced mental health professionals, who are adding the play therapy specialty to their practice.

Allen et al. (2007) describe a three-stage developmental model for the supervision of play therapy students by non–play therapy supervisors in graduate-program settings. Their Client-Centered theory-based model builds on the conceptual structure of students' clinical skills, bridging adult and play therapy communication skills. In contrast, Ray (2011) writes about the Child-Centered Play Therapy (CCPT) supervision process. Ray indicates play therapy supervisors should have extensive play therapy clinical experience, as well as knowledge and skills of the theory or approach of play therapy. Additionally, the supervisor should have a working knowledge in play behavior, parent education and consultation, and group dynamics. Ray states a "therapist who would engage children in play must be grounded in child development, attentive to the child's unique perceptions and experiences, and ready to function nonverbally or verbally in the experiential and symbolic work of childhood" (p. 90). Ray does not purport a CCPT supervision model, but the components of CCPT which must be addressed, including many general areas, as noted above.

Seymour and Crenshaw (2015) discuss the supervisor's use of reflective practice in play therapy supervision. This ability to be more self-reflective and self-aware assists the play therapist in becoming more fully integrated and congruent. Modeling reflective practice to supervisees is an important dynamic for the play therapist's own self-care and optimal client care. Based in Seymour and Crenshaw's own clinical experiences they identify eight essential internal disciplines for the reflective play therapist: empathy, wholeheartedness, vulnerability, genuineness, courage, self-care, humility, and compassion (p. 486). Other authors have offered specific forms to assist in play therapy supervision. Ray (2004, 2011) offers a play therapy skill checklist; Garza, Falls, and Bruhn (2009) provide a discrimination scale for developing deeper-level responses. A time-intensive supervision model suggested by Bratton, Landreth, and Homeyer (1993) is used in university settings. However, addressing the issue of assisting play therapists to integrate their work with a family systems approach has not yet occurred.

FAMILY COUNSELING SUPERVISION

Supervision of family counseling (therapy) is guided by the AAMFT's supervision standards (2014). While many standards are consistent with other mental health disciplines, there are other factors more unique to family counseling supervision: ability to apply systemic thinking and ability to simultaneously attend to many relationships. In addition, these supervisors must be able to assist supervisees' ability to identify relevant contextual case factors.

Determining essential knowledge and skills needed for family counseling proficiency serves as an outline for the goals of effective family counseling supervision. Celano, Smith, and Kaslow (2010) discuss developing a systemic formulation, forging a systemic therapeutic alliance, reframing, managing negative interactions, building cohesion, restructuring parenting, and understanding and applying evidence-based couple and family therapy models. Highlighting the benefits and risks that accompany intergenerational work, these authors assert the importance for building supervisees' awareness and confidence in managing problematic family patterns that emerge in the therapy room.

The traditional approach to family counseling supervision involved the application of separate family counseling clinical theories to supervision and counselor education (Morgan & Sprenkle, 2007). Each clinical model would describe the supervisory process through its theoretical lens, creating as many family counseling supervision models as there are clinical models. The common factors and core competencies approaches, in contrast, provide opportunities for supervisors and supervisees to establish an effective working relationship even if they subscribe to different clinical theories (Sprenkle, 1999). Common factors in the literature emphasize solid relational development in supervision as fundamental (Morgan & Sprenkle, 2007). Hill (2009) uses an attachment paradigm to elevate the importance of this relationship as a safe place from which supervisees can embrace the anxiety inherent in developing competency.

In another relationally sensitive approach consistent with the field's postmodern trends, MacKay and Brown (2013) advocate for integrating a directive approach (Bowenian in their example) with a collaborative approach. This is advantageous as supervisees are directly *taught* when circumstances require quick and assertive action, but supervisees are more *collaboratively* included in their processing and growth when urgency is not present. Shaw (2013) adds that the movement toward collaboration in supervision assists in establishing the relational environment, particularly when the supervisory relationship is well contracted, but notes that supervision cannot be merely collaborative. The supervisor must be evaluative and acknowledge the power differential without misusing it.

Family counseling supervision often achieves this balancing act by employing a reflective means of feedback in supervision. Being reflective as client issues are processed through case presentation is common across mental health disciplines, but attempting reflective supervision during the act of therapy itself has become a common family counseling practice with the use of the reflecting team (Davis, 2012). The reflecting team can consist of fellow supervisees, students, advanced clinicians, teachers, and the client, as these combinations of observers and participants comment on the therapy so that therapist and client can hear those reflective statements and observations. This type of systemic reflection honors the multirelational nature of family counseling and provides immediate opportunities for the reflection experience.

Senediak (2013) describes all reflective aspects of supervision, referencing the intervention categories of "reflection-on-practice" and "reflection-in-action," as helpful to supervisee development. She posits that both forms have a positive influence on developing family counselors' inner awareness, adding that such insight is vital given the increased possibility of countertransference due to more people being involved in family therapy than individual therapy. Other ways reflective thought is incorporated into family counseling supervision is by family-of-origin work through person-of-the-therapist exploration (Kate et al., 2013; Senediak, 2013).

Rigazio-DiGilio's (2002) view of integrative supervision concludes that integration offers flexibility in meeting a variety of supervisees' needs by including the diverse perspectives among family counseling schools of thought. She believes multiple reference points from an integrative approach maximizes options for growth.

SUPERVISION PLANNING AND AGREEMENT

When arranging a supervisory relationship to integrate the two areas of play therapy and family counseling, it is critical to develop an agreement regarding the specific needs of the supervisee in a clearly written supervision plan prior to beginning the relationship. This will assist in clarifying the unique context for integrative work and identifying the professional developmental level of the supervisee in both play therapy and family counseling. The plan would identify the supervisee's area of current experience through the following questions: What coursework and/or trainings has the supervisee pursued in the two areas? Is there licensure as a marriage and family therapist? Or another mental health discipline license? What is the amount of clinical experience in play therapy and in family counseling? Already met criteria as a registered play therapist? Seeking concurrent licensure and registration supervision?

It is recommended that the supervision agreement clearly document this assessment. It can simply be done with a list of such options with notations for each, documenting the area of supervision being agreed upon. Clear expectations regarding frequency of supervision sessions should also be written into the agreement. For example, an already licensed mental health professional may be provided a more flexible schedule of supervisory sessions. Supervisees are also encouraged to know what areas of expertise they are seeking in a supervisor. This discussion is critical to be sure expectations are reasonable and able to be met. The use of a Professional Disclosure for Supervision and an Informed Consent for Supervision, both clearly identifying these issues and other appropriate areas, should be a standard of practice.

INTEGRATING SUPERVISION APPROACHES

When developing the supervision approach for family-based play therapists, many unique factors must be considered. First, the initial approach is usually shaped by the role the supervisor takes during the development of the supervisory relationship. Second, the approach must be informed by methodology and practices inherent to effective and existing supervision models. Third, an appropriate integrative supervision approach should focus on several guiding key concepts, specifically developmental stages, experiential process, systemic perspective, and reflective practice.

Developmental Stages

Many prevalent and well-supported supervision models focus on professional developmental stages through which supervisees move during their growth as therapists (Loganbill, Hardy, & Delworth, 1982). These developmental models support the supervisor's ability to create an environment that facilitates the supervisee's ongoing development of clinical competence and confidence.

Stoltenberg et al. (1998) focus on three levels of supervisee development that are defined by the amount of motivation, autonomy, and awareness the supervisee possesses. As supervisees develop, their increased autonomy and awareness alters their needs from the supervision process. This perspective provides an ease of applicability for a supervisee who may have experience in one area, but is adding clinical competence in another. The practicality and broad use of this model makes it a strong choice for using in an integrative supervision approach.

Experiential Process

The play therapy aspect of supervision requires an experiential playful process. Play therapy requires a specific skill set for being with children and families in the play therapy room. As the developmentally appropriate therapeutic intervention for children, play therapy is based in the premise that children use play as their language and toys as their words (Ginott, 1960). The supervisee, whether initially a play therapist or a family counselor, needs to know the language of play. One of the most effective ways to do so is to experience the language itself, play. Several authors have written about a wide variety of experiential activities which are adapted from clinical to supervisor use (Bratton, Ceballos, & Sheely, 2008; Casado-Kehoe & Ybanez, 2010; Drewes & Mullen, 2008; Morrison & Homeyer, 2008; Mullen, Luke, & Drewes, 2007; Purswell & Stulmaker, in press). These activities, some of which are described below, can facilitate skill building within the supervisory experience and raise self-awareness for the supervisee.

Anekstein, Joskins, Astramovich, Garner, and Terry (2014) developed a model of supervision to assist, in part, in the development of the supervisee's self-awareness. Anekstein et al. (2014) integrated sand tray therapy as described by Homeyer and Sweeney (2011) with Bernard's (1979) Discrimination Model of supervision. Since sand tray can quickly access deeper emotional issues, Anekstein et al. used it as an experiential activity in supervision to highlight the supervisee's parallel process. When using this approach, the supervisor must be careful not to take on the role of counselor but rather refer supervisees to their own personal counselor when deeper issues need to be explored.

Systemic Perspective

Family counseling supervision requires cultivating a systemic lens for content and process (Celano, Oyeshiku, Smith, & Kaslow, 2010). Many authors (Celano et al., 2010; Nutt & Stanton, 2008) reference the various aspects that define a systemic frame of reference including attending to multiple relationships, considering contextual factors, looking at the purposes behind symptomatic behaviors, and examining family-of-origin dynamics. Supervision must parallel the inherently systemic nature of family counseling.

Another systemic dynamic involves the relational complexities that exist with having a family as the client. Supervising family therapists requires monitoring their awareness of the family system and their own involvement in that system. In addition to monitoring this, the supervisor must remember and attend to his or her role in the system. Albeit invisible, supervisors may influence the family system of their supervisees' clients. Thinking systemically allows a supervisor to remain aware of these processes.

A paradigm that balances the complexities of tasks and functions within the supervisory relationship comes from the social roles supervision models. These approaches have a supervisor conceptualize the number of relational roles a supervisor plays with a supervisee. In Internal Family Systems language (Mojta, Falconier, & Huebner, 2014), a supervisor has many "parts" that influence the supervisee's development. The art of supervision is revealed as a supervisor chooses which role to play during certain supervisory moments. Family counseling supervisors, then, choose to highlight a task or role based on what the system's context demands.

Reflective Practice

Parlakian (2001) refers to three building blocks for reflective practice in supervision: reflection, collaboration, and regularity. Reflection allows for supervisors to return responsibility to supervisees by encouraging them to search within themselves for answers. Collaboration requires sharing of power between supervisee and supervisor through open dialogue. Regularity is consistently spending time to cultivating the relationship.

Relationship remains at the center of reflective supervision. Remaining present and mindful with supervisees models this behavior for their own work with clients and serves as an effective method for empowering supervisees to build the mental processes necessary for clinical work. Reflective experiential moments allow supervisees to process therapeutic experiences as their clients do, building a systemic lens which supervisees can use from multiple points of view.

Admittedly, this sort of processing can become complex. However, play-based family counseling is complex and play therapists must develop an increasing capacity to monitor everything that is occurring in the therapy room. The reflective and experiential perspective allows a supervisee to appropriately narrow focus to understand and connect with the needs of a single family member, especially a child. The reflective and systemic work pulls focus back to experience that perspective in the context of the family. In this, a supervisor acts like a camera zoom function for the supervisee, narrowing and broadening the perspective for a supervisee, as needed, while the reflective posture ensures the supervisee is the one looking through the lens. This is especially helpful for the therapist who is integrating play therapy and family because it increases the ability to see where learning, skill building, and competence needs to occur.

An Integrated Approach

Our integrated approach builds on the four key concepts previously described: developmental stages, experiential process, systemic perspective, and reflective practice. This provides for the creativity and flexibility needed to supervise the integration of the work of play therapists and family counselors.

Determining the professional developmental stage of the supervisee (in both play therapy and family counseling) during the planning and agreement phase informs the direction of supervision. Some supervisees may be novice in both play therapy and family counseling, while others may be experienced in one area and inexperienced in the other. These differing presentations impact the course of professional development for the supervisee, which, in turn, affects the course of supervision. The following developmental levels are adapted from Stoltenberg et al. (1998):

- Level One: As supervisees initially enter into working with clients, their motivation is high, but their autonomy is low. Supervisors tend to be more directive, often in a teacher role, as supervisees require more instruction. Supervisors must remember to think systemically, experientially, and reflectively while operating in level one mode. Modeling helps to "teach" while remaining experience based.
- Level Two: At this level, supervisees have moved into working stages with clients and can begin to feel frustrated with clients and themselves, often causing motivation to wane. They may have mastered basic skills, but advanced skills are often more challenging. Self-awareness can become an added difficulty if frustrations are preventing supervisees from noticing their own countertransference. Therefore, supervision interventions are based in the tasks related to monitoring and supporting (with some teaching added as necessary).
- Level Three: Supervisees at this level are preparing for their launch into autonomous practice. They should possess enough motivation and awareness to seek out help when needed, but do not expect simplistic answers. This helps to mitigate frustration as the process of supervision emphasizes consulting interactions, encouraging supervisees to seek out their own solutions while remaining in a supportive environment.

In most developmental supervision models, supervisors' roles are often determined by the supervisees' needs at a particular stage of growth. When supervising the integration of two clinical areas, a supervisor may need to address seemingly conflicting developmental tasks. For the advanced play therapist that is new to family counseling, the supervisor may want to emphasize the competence in play therapy by assuming a consultant role. However, the supervisor may simultaneously need to be more directive with family-related teaching moments. This integrative approach expects a supervisor to evaluate the option of offering different roles when a supervisee's play therapy development differs from his family counseling level.

Regardless of the developmental stage, the reflective task of supervision remains constant. Even when inexperienced therapists require directive guidance and occasional teaching moments, supervision should promote a supervisee's ability to conceptualize on his own. Furthermore, all roles a supervisor may play require that the supervisor remain mindful and self-aware. Following are some strategies to reflectively implement supervisor roles for both experiential/play-based moments and systemic/family-based moments.

Teaching

The role of teacher is quite directive, but can be implemented reflectively when recursive questioning and other related techniques are used. This role is typically required when therapists are most novice in a clinical area or when new situations arise in familiar scenarios. An effective teacher-supervisor possesses sufficient advanced knowledge to offer supervisee-students and remains open to learning from them as well.

Modeling

Modeling is experiential by nature and, again, can be a directive intervention, especially when overtly scripted. However, some modeling moments occur more covertly as when a supervisor subtly engages in a process she hopes the supervisee will learn to replicate by internalization. Either way, modeling is a vital supervisory role; it builds on learning theory constructs that tell us sometimes a skill needs to be experienced or witnessed in order to be understood.

Supporting

The task of supporting may be referred to as the counselor or therapist role in some supervision models. As supervisors, there is a delicate balance between exposing personal situations that might impact a supervisee's clinical skills development and engaging in personal therapy (which is inappropriate). Nonetheless, truly reflective relational work with a supervisee will need to enter personal arenas so that self-awareness is promoted. This may result in uncovering areas for which the supervisee will be referred for counseling to adequately deal with a personal issue which could impact ability to counsel with competency.

Consulting

Consulting may be the least directive task a supervisee engages in with a supervisee. This role usually comes with advanced development as a supervisee is moving toward more autonomy and confidence. Consultation typically occurs between peers as one professional lends a listening ear to another's processing of therapeutic moments; therefore, this is an effective role to take on when launching a supervisee into his own professional role.

Monitoring or Evaluating

Though sometimes uncomfortable, we have chosen to include the role of evaluator for ethical reasons. Supervisors are the gatekeepers of the profession, charged with monitoring the emergence of only prepared and qualified mental health providers into the professional community. Therefore, supervisors need to embrace the duty of evaluating progress and levels of competence in supervisees. When performed reflectively, though, a supervisee develops the ability to self-monitor. This is an invaluable trait for any therapist or counselor, supervisor, or supervisee.

PRACTICAL SUPERVISION EXPERIENTIAL ACTIVITIES

Selection of supervision interventions requires the supervisor's awareness of the supervisees' specific need at the moment. From this integrative perspective, this includes:

- Level of professional experience in play therapy and family counseling;
- Guiding key concepts of developmental stage, experiential process, systemic perspective, and reflective practice;
- Stoltenberg stage (motivation, autonomy, awareness); and,
- Appropriate supervisory role of teaching, modeling, supporting, or consulting.

An initial experiential activity assists the supervisee in reflecting on the professional developmental areas of play therapy and family systems. One play-based strategy is to ask the supervisee to build a scene in the sand tray that symbolizes her strengths and weaknesses in each of the two areas. Discussion and processing provides the building awareness, for both supervisee and supervisor. This also helps develop the supervisor relationship.

On a teaching level, play therapists without whole-family experience may need to be instructed on understanding systemic dynamics in the therapy room. However, a supervisor need not sacrifice playfulness or reflectiveness in order to offer necessary instruction. Supervisors can use a play-based strategy of asking the supervisee to imagine the client family as a mobile with the parent(s) at the top and children hanging below them. The supervisee is asked to draw this mobile in a way that reflects the presenting issues as well as the out-of-balance family system. Then the supervisee makes adjustments needed by various family members to get the system back in balance. As the case is processed, the supervisor can refer the supervisee back to the drawn mobile to underscore how all relationships are interconnected in a system and that behavior of one affects all the others.

Conversely, family counselors without the play therapy experience can be introduced to play through creating a play genogram. The instructions are to ask the supervisee to draw the genogram of a client family on a large sheet of paper and then add miniature items (from a sand tray collection) to represent each family member. This can be used as a teaching experience of how to use a play technique with families while also serving as a reflective experience on understanding a family's issues. The supervisor can ask the therapist to add a self-symbol to help raise self-awareness of the therapist's role within the system.

With the increased opportunity for countertransference, supervisees may or may not be aware of their own internal reactions that are becoming a part of the greater system. From a supporting role, the supervisor may need to intervene in order to bring mindfulness into the process and this can be accomplished by asking the supervisee to create a sand tray. The prompt can be as simple as creating the clients' family system on one side of the tray and the supervisee's family system on the other side. The tray can be processed with the goal of examining possible similarities and differences and how these can be assets or liabilities.

Play therapists shifting from parent consultations to working more directly with the entire family system may need heightened self-awareness of alliance with one or more family members, impacting the ability to engage with all members. A playful strategy to address this is to ask the supervisee to select one miniature to symbolize self and place it in a center position on a table or in a sand tray. Then the supervisee selects a miniature which symbolizes how he *feels* about each family member. These figures are then placed around the play therapist figure, near or far, reflective of the therapeutic relationship with each. In a supportive role, the supervisor leads the supervisee in processing the results by focusing on self-awareness and building ongoing reflective skills.

CASE STUDY

Sara, an advanced play therapy intern, recently began to work at a family-based site. Though she was educated in the basics of family therapy, her actual experience in working with parents and children simultaneously is limited. The supervisory relationship has existed for several months and mutual respect has been established.

Developmentally, Sara has achieved high autonomy in her play therapy skills and her motivation for continued growth in this specialty remains. According to Stoltenberg, these factors contribute to Sara being assessed at the highest level of supervisee growth. However, the lack of familiarity with family therapy has created a crisis of confidence. Sara has reverted to a state of dependence on the supervisor; consequently, her motivation levels are fluctuating and she frequently feels anxious about sessions. This complicates the developmental assessment as she is functioning at a lower level for family therapy.

One of Sara's family clients has created even more personal struggle for her than the others. One month ago, Sara conducted a parent intake session with a single mother who was struggling with managing her eight-year-old son's behavior. Sara felt connected to the mother and was initially excited to work with this family. However, three family sessions later, she had become overwhelmed by the son's out-of-control behaviors in the room and the mother's oscillation between permissive parenting and disciplining in anger.

If these had been play therapy sessions with only the boy, Sara would have felt effective at setting limits and intervening on the child's developmental level. However, managing the parenting dynamics simultaneously was proving challenging. Sara was hesitant to infringe on the mother's parenting territory, but was also feeling frustrated by the mother. When Sara presents for supervision, she discusses this case and states she needs help with treatment planning.

It would have been a legitimate choice for a supervisor to step into a teaching role, focusing on skill development with family systems. However, this supervisor strongly sensed that the parenting dynamic had personally triggered Sara and this should be addressed before Sara would be able to effectively implement any family-based treatment strategy. The supervisor needs to select a supervision technique that supports and models the tasks that need to be executed. Since this will be a sensitive subject matter, maintaining a safe relationship and a reflective tone will be paramount.

Sara was asked to complete a sand tray activity that would help with personal insight and case conceptualization. On one side of the tray, Sara was directed to create the client family's genogram from miniatures. She was encouraged to be metaphorical in her selection of miniatures to allow for increased safety. Before processing, Sara was then prompted to create her own genogram on the other side of the sand tray, capturing her family structure at age eight (same as the child client) while being as metaphorical as possible.

When beginning to process, Sara was informed that the purpose of this activity was not personal counseling and if any internal struggles appeared then it would be advisable to follow up with her therapist. The goal was to observe influencing factors that create relational dynamics in families and to identify any connections between the clients' story and her own. Sara began to reflect on her client's genogram and was struck by the three generations of trauma that contributed to single parenting in each generation. With this insight, Sara astutely connected her personal frustration with the overwhelmed feelings her own single mother would exhibit. When the supervisor modeled how to gently interrupt nonproductive patterns, Sara was able to experience the skill she needed to practice with her clients. In addition, she realized that an important treatment goal is modeling mindful parenting for the mother (so that the mother did not choose to continue unpredictable behavior rooted in stress).

In future sessions, Sara reported she had been able to individually teach the mother effective reflection of emotions and limit setting and was able to model these skills in the therapy room. In time, the family sessions became manageable and Sara was able to design a treatment plan that promoted relational connection between mother and son while also healing unresolved emotional pain.

ETHICS IN INTEGRATIVE SUPERVISION

Ethics is core to the public trust placed in mental health practitioners. The facets of ethical considerations in supervision are multiple and beyond the scope of this section of this chapter. With this acknowledgment, the reader is encouraged to seek additional readings for a more comprehensive understanding of all areas which make up ethical supervision. With this understanding, therefore, those areas of concerns related uniquely to the integration of play therapy with family counseling will be addressed here. The supervisor must not only be aware of the ethical considerations in the supervisory relationship but also monitor the ethical behavior of the supervisee with clients.

Already mentioned in this chapter is the sensitive nature of using experiential activities with the supervisee. Both authors of this chapter believe such experiences are foundational to becoming a competent play therapist who conducts family counseling. Even the teaching of activities for use with clients can result in bringing up personal issues within the supervisee. Certainly those experiences designed to increase supervisees' self-awareness and self-reflection are likely to bring up sensitive, personal issues. Some of these can be appropriately handled with care within the supervisory relationship. Others will require careful assessment on the part of the supervisor to know when to refer the supervisee to personal counseling. Since the supervisor is also part of the systemic process, he or she must be vigilant for his or her own need for personal counseling.

Another ethical concern is the management of the supervisee's strong emotional connection and reaction to the child client (Clark & Croney, 2006). Play therapy, like family counseling, is about relationships and relationships can be complicated. Supervisees may be unaware of critical information which they should be sharing with the supervisor (Clark & Croney, 2006). The supervisor must be mindful of such possibilities and require the supervisee to present videotapes of clients' sessions for review during supervision sessions.

Work with minors necessitates special ethical considerations. Confidentiality is typically "held" by the parent, rather than the child, since most states consider the parent the legal client. Information from custody agreements, court documents, and foster care systems must be reviewed carefully to determine who may provide consent for treatment and who may have access to the clinical record. The play therapist, who may see only the child, typically works carefully with the caregiver to protect the privacy of the child-client while keeping the caregiver informed. Yet, when working with families, more stakeholders are involved. Disclosure of information forms may be needed to communicate with key stakeholders such as teachers, courts, welfare agencies, hospitals, other mental health professionals, medical doctors, etc. (Clark & Croney, 2006, p. 57). The supervisor must assist the family therapist, new to working with minors, to carefully manage all the interdependent relationships in an ethical and legal manner.

CONCLUSION

Supervision of play therapists conducting family counseling is complex due to the layers of multiple relationships within the system of supervisor-supervisee, supervisee-family, supervisee-child, and parent-child. Further complexity occurs when play therapy is integrated with family counseling. The proposed integrative supervision model synthesizes key components of play therapy supervision and family counseling supervision. Supervision planning and agreement as well as the integrative supervision approach uses key guiding concepts of developmental stages, experiential process, systemic perspective, and reflective practice. The supervisory roles of teaching, modeling, supporting, consulting, and monitoring/evaluating can be facilitated through play-based supervision strategies of creating sand tray scenes, play genograms with miniatures, and family mobiles. Due to the complexity of supervising play therapists conducting family counseling, ethical procedures must be closely monitored.

REFERENCES

Allen, V., Folger, W., & Pehrsson, D. (2007). Reflective process in play therapy: A practical model for supervising counseling students. *Education, 127*(4), 472–479.

American Association for Marriage and Family Therapy. (n.d.). *About marriage and family therapists*. Retrieved January 8, 2015, from http://www.aamft.org/iMIS15/AAMFT/Press/MFT_Qualifications/Content/About_AAMFT/Qualifications.aspx?hkey=00f76834-705e-4dd9-9dfe-46e6467eb7ca.

American Association for Marriage and Family Therapy. (2014). *Approved supervision designation: Standards handbook*. Alexandria, VA: Author.

Anekstein, A., Joskins, W., Astramovich, R., Garner, D., & Terry, J. (2014). "Sandtray Supervision": Integrating models and sandtray therapy. *Journal of Creativity in Mental Health, (9)*(1), 122–134. doi:10.1080/15401383.2014.876885.

Association for Play Therapy. (2015). *Credentialing guide*. Retrieved February 25, 2015, from http://c.ymcdn.com/sites/www.a4pt.org/resource/resmgr/RPT_and_RPT-S_Credentials/RPTS_Guide.pdf.

Bernard, J. M. (1979). Supervision training: A discrimination model. *Counselor Education and Supervision, 19*, 60–68. doi:10.1002/j.1556-6978.1979.tb00906.x.

Bernard, J., & Goodyear, R. (2004). *Fundamentals of clinical supervision* (3rd ed.). New York: Pearson Education.

Bratton, S., Ceballos, P., & Sheely, A. (2008). Expressive arts in a humanistic approach to play therapy supervision: Facilitating therapist self-awareness. In A. Drewes, & J. A. Mullen (Eds.), *Supervision can be playful: Techniques for child and play therapist supervisors* (pp. 211–232). Lanham, MD: Jason Aronson.

Bratton, S., Landreth, G., & Homeyer, L. (1993). An intensive three day play therapy supervision/training model. *International Journal of Play Therapy, 2*(2), 61–79. doi:10.1037/h0089366.

Casado-Kehoe, M., & Ybanez, K. (2010). Clinical supervision. In S. Degges-White and N. Davis (Eds.), *Integrating the expressive arts into counseling practice: Theory-based interventions* (pp. 219–254). New York: Springer.

Celano, M. P., Oyeshiku, K., Smith, C. O., & Kaslow, N. J. (2010). A competency-based approach to couple and family therapy supervision. *Psychotherapy (Chicago, Ill.), 47*(1), 35–44. doi:10.1037/a0018845

Clark, J. J., & Croney, E. L. (2006). Ethics and accountability in supervision of child psychotherapy. In T. K. Neill (Ed.), *Helping others help children: Clinical supervision of child psychotherapy* (pp. 51–72). Washington, DC: American Psychological Association.

Davis, J. (2012). The golden pig, reflections as ancestral blessings: The reflecting process in teaching family therapy. *Family Process, 51*(3), 405–419. doi:10.1111/j.1545-5300.2012.01405.x

Deering, C. G. (1994). Parallel process in the supervision of child psychotherapy, *American Journal of Psychotherapy, 48*(1), 102–110.

Drewes, A., & Mullen, J. A. (2008). *Supervision can be playful: Techniques for child and play therapist supervisors.* Lanham, MD: Jason Aronson.

Garza, Y., Falls, L., & Bruhn, R. (2009). Measuring deeper meaning responses: A discrimination scale for play therapists in training. *International Journal of Play Therapy, 18*(3), 147–161. dx.doi.org/10.1037/a0015548

Gil, E. (1994). *Play in family therapy*. New York, NY: Guilford Press.

Ginott, H. (1960). A rationale for selecting toys in play therapy. *Journal of Consulting Psychology, 24*, 243–246. dx.doi.org/10.1037/h0043980

Hill, E. W. (2009). Confronting anxiety in couple and family therapy supervision: A developmental supervisory model based on attachment theory. *Australian & New Zealand Journal of Family Therapy, 30*(1), 1–14. doi:10.1375/anft.30.1.1

Holloway, E. (1995). *Clinical supervision: A systems approach.* Thousand Oaks, CA: Sage.

Homeyer, L., & Sweeney, D. (2011). *Sandtray therapy: A practical manual.* New York, NY: Routledge.

Kate, R., Paul, R., Jenny, B., Donnelly, M., Donnelly, H., Gosbee, M., et al. (2013). Family of origin coaching for clinicians in a child and adolescent mental health service. *Contemporary Family Therapy: An International Journal, 35*(4), 684–697. doi:10.1007/s10591-013-9244-8.

Loganbill, C., Hardy, E., & Delworth, U. (1982). Supervision: A conceptual model. *The Counseling Psychologist, 10*(1), 3–42. dx.doi.org/10.1177/0011000082101002.

MacKay, L., & Brown, J. (2013). Collaborative approaches to family systems supervision: Differentiation of self. *Australian & New Zealand Journal of Family Therapy, 34*(4), 325–337. doi:10.1002/anzf.1036.

Metcalf, L. M. (2003). Countertransference among play therapists: Implications for therapist development and supervision. *International Journal of Play Therapy, 12*(2), 31–48. dx.doi.org/10.1037/h0088877.

Mojta, C., Falconier, M. K., & Huebner, A. J. (2014). Fostering self-awareness in novice therapists using internal family systems therapy. *American Journal of Family Therapy, 42*(1), 67–78. doi:10.1080/01926187.2013.772870.

Morgan, M. M., & Sprenkle, D. H. (2007). Toward a common-factors approach to supervision. *Journal of Marital and Family Therapy, 33*(1), 1–17. doi:10.1111/j.1752-0606.2007.00001.x

Morrison, M., & Homeyer, L. (2008). Supervision in the sand. In A. Drews & J. Mullen (Eds.), *Supervision can be playful: Techniques for child and play therapist supervisors* (pp. 233–249). Lanham, MD: Jason Aronson.

Mullen, J., Luke, M., & Drewes, A. (2007). Supervision can be playful, too: Play therapy techniques that enhance supervision. *International Journal of Play Therapy, 16*(1), 69–85. dx.doi.org/10.1037/1555-6824.16.1.69.

Neill, T. K. (Ed.). (2006). *Helping others help children: Clinical supervision of child psychotherapy*. Washington, DC: American Psychological Association.

Neill, T. K., Holloway, E., & Kaak, H. O. (2006). A systems approach to supervision of child psychotherapy. In T. K. Neill (Ed.), *Helping others help children: Clinical supervision of child psychotherapy* (pp. 89–108). Washington, DC: American Psychological Association.

Nutt, R. L., & Stanton, M. (2008). Family psychology specialty practice. *Professional Psychology: Research and Practice, 39*(5), 519–528. doi:10.1037/0735-7028.39.5.519

Parlakian, R. (2001). *Look, listen, and learn: Reflective supervision and relationship-based work*. Washington, DC: Zero to Three.

Purswell, K., & Stulmaker, H. (in press). Expressive arts in supervision: Choosing developmentally appropriate interventions. *International Journal of Play Therapy.*

Ray, D. (2004). Supervision of basic and advanced skills in play therapy. *Journal of Professional Counseling, 32*(2), 28–41.

Ray, D. (2006). Supervision in play and filial therapy. In T. K. Neill (Ed.), *Helping others help children: Clinical supervision of child psychotherapy* (pp. 89–108). Washington, DC: American Psychological Association.

Ray, D. (2011). *Advanced play therapy: Essential conditions, knowledge, and skills for child practice*. New York: Taylor & Francis.

Rigazio-DiGilio, S. A. (2002). Integrative supervision: Approaches to tailoring the supervisory process. In T. C. Todd & C. L. Storm (Eds.), *The complete systemic supervisor: Context, philosophy, and pragmatics* (pp. 195–216). Lincoln, NE: IUniverse.

Senediak, C. (2013). Integrating reflective practice in family therapy supervision. *Australian & New Zealand Journal of Family Therapy, 34*(4), 338–351. doi:10.1002/anzf.1035.

Seymour, J., & Crenshaw, D. (2015). Reflective practice in play therapy and supervision. In D. Crenshaw and A. Stewart (Eds.), *Play therapy: Comprehensive guide to theory and practice* (pp. 483–495). New York, NY: Guilford Press.

Shaw, E. (2013). Mentoring or monitoring: Formulating a balance in systemic supervision. *Australian & New Zealand Journal of Family Therapy, 34*(4), 296–310. doi:10.1002/anzf.1034

Sprenkle, D. H. (1999). Toward a general model of family therapy supervision: Comment on Roberts, Winek, and Mulgrew. *Contemporary Family Therapy: An International Journal, 21*(3), 309–315. dx.doi.org/10.1023/A:102195621459.

Stoltenberg, C., McNeill, B., & Delworth, U. (1998). *IDM supervision: An integrated developmental model for supervising counselors and therapists*. San Francisco, CA: Jossey-Bass.
VanderGast, T., Culbreth, J., & Flowers, C. (2010). An exploration of experiences and preferences in clinical supervision with play therapists. *International Journal of Play Therapy, 19*(3), 174–185. doi:10.1037/a0018882.

Chapter Eleven

Tempered in the Fire

Self-Care and Mindfulness in Preventing Clinical Burnout

Rosalind Heiko

> It is not your responsibility to finish the work [of repairing the world], but you are not free to desist from it either. . . . —Pirke Avot, Sayings of the Jewish Fathers, 2:16, Third Century, C.E.

Tempering is an ancient heat treatment technique that involves the rapid cooling of metal to transform it into its hardest state. Through this process, stability is achieved. Similarly, mechanisms to temper, or reduce, the level of perceived and actual stress can be utilized by family play counselors who feel "burned out" by vicarious trauma, exhaustion, and stressful cases. The term "burnout" distinguishes therapists who exhibit " . . . chronic exhaustion, cynicism, and a lack of personal accomplishment" (Bakker & Costa, 2014, p. 112) from those who are merely overly stressed and overworked.

The Pirke Avot (2005) quote at the beginning of this chapter refers to the understanding that there will never be enough resources, time, person power, or energy to accomplish everything in one lifetime. Additionally, family play counselors observe many challenges and stressors, including poverty, financial stress, high-conflict divorce, insecure attachments, neglect, rage, and meanness that attack and deplete the capabilities, resources, and spirit of families and children. Over time, they witness disrespect, mistakes, and destructive failings of parents, adults, and trusted companions within families they serve, as well as interference from bureaucratic structures. In addition to their large caseloads, family play counselors are challenged to manage increasing administrative demands, diminishing reimbursements from insurance companies, extended work hours, and stringent HIPAA-compliant requirements.

Although it is not up to family counselors to repair all of their individual clients' wounds or suffering, it is common that they feel feel overwhelmed at the enormity of the task. Among the many challenges they face, they assist family members in remaining intact and gaining mastery of communication skills. Throughout sessions, counselors "absorb and contain" complex thoughts, feelings, and experiences of their clients (Green, 2014), and burnout can result from the protracted and effortful emotional effects of this demanding career. Researchers have noted that over time, therapists can experience feelings of negative self-worth, despair, helplessness, changed energy levels, chronic fatigue, and a sense of being trapped (Sorgaard, Ryan, Hill, & Dawson, 2007). Therefore, it is imperative that family play counselors be able to hold compassion for themselves and accept their own weaknesses and shortcomings, taking time to reflect on what it is that they can and cannot do. Careful preparation, a deep understanding of the journey of professional development, and mindfulness can assist family counselors in managing the feelings of burnout that accompany work with individuals and families. As the birch tree demonstrates rapid adaptation and regrowth following forest fires or disasters, so too can family play counselors experience feelings of regeneration and hopefulness, even amid the most difficult therapeutic work.

THE JOURNEY OF PROFESSIONAL DEVELOPMENT

Family play counselors' professional development can be viewed as a progression through archetypes, or matrices from which human experience is derived (Hollis, 2005; Pearson, 2012). Although this is not a linear, hierarchical model, the process often unfolds through two archetypes: (1) the *Seeker,* and (2) the *Fool*. The Seeker encompasses the scholar who enjoys the learning process, manifests independent thinking and problem solving, and aspires to capture the essence of what is valuable to the practice of family play counseling. The Fool, on the other hand, is able to lighten the atmosphere in intense family interactions in a manner that invokes an alliance. He is the one who speaks up authentically to exhort individuals to trust themselves in the moment, enriching their interactions in family counseling. Play is the province of the Fool; thus, he welcomes fun, mischief, and playfulness, prerequisites for engaging in family play counseling.

The *Innocent* is an archetype that represents the earliest stage of professional development, perhaps during graduate studies as an intern, or in beginning practice as a family counselor. Family counselors must learn how to juggle the beliefs of systems, both family and business/agencies, with their development and presentation of a professional persona. The Innocent can be optimistic, sometimes to the extreme, idealizing and trusting blindly in the authority of the training/theoretical models of practice. "Beginner's Mind" characterizes this stage of development, at which time many family play counselors might expect to change the world of clients and "the system" into a much better place. These early career stage counselors may want to say or do the correct thing at all times. As a result, they might deny the negative, the weaknesses, or difficulties they observe in themselves and their clients. Self-awareness and self-reflection are important in this early stage. Play counselors who are not yet comfortable in confronting "darker" emotions may subsequently blame themselves (or others) in new, potentially threatening family therapy experiences. Using supervision, consultation, and some of the other reflective strategies mentioned below may prove beneficial.

In the next stage of professional development, the *Hero/Warrior* has more experience in crafting interventions, navigating challenging family experiences, and exposure to varied client populations. Family counselors demonstrate courage and discipline, often imposing high standards of practice on themselves. They use their strength and determination to overcome obstacles in the path of healthy family communication, harmony, and health. Heroic counselors strive to bring meaning and cooperative understanding to their undertakings with families; however, they may struggle to choose which battles to fight, which to walk away from, and which to engage with at a later time. Counselors at this stage of professional development may fear vulnerability, and having high standards for oneself and others can be a burden. Counselors risk feeling hopeless, discouraged, and burnt out when they do not believe they have lived up to their potentiality as a helper. Counselors must be aware of times to back off, and resist the urge to "push through" at any cost in order to conserve personal resources and energy.

The middle of the family play counselor's professional journey is contained within the *Caregiver* and *Ruler* archetypes. Caregivers choose to use compassion and compelling maternal/paternal nurturing abilities to help families heal and learn coping skills. Rulers organizing principles and beliefs in structure and responsibility are among the best skills that a family play counselor "brings to the table." Many counselors experience depletion of time, energy, and resources when they sacrifice self-nurturing for the primary activity of protecting and caring for others. Meanwhile, the Ruler archetype attempts to maintain control and may sacrifice innovative, creative interventions, and interests in building new therapeutic interventions. It is important for counselors at this stage of development to remember that the best Rulers in the kingdom look to the good of the entire kingdom (e.g., the systems of family and individual needs, as well as the interface of therapist goals and resources), but also realize that each individual is responsible for her own life. At times during this period of professional development, the stress of juggling client, personal, and professional demands can begin to override counselors' abilities to focus on self-care activities. It is crucial to continue to evaluate core beliefs and return to rebalancing goals and priorities as a family counselor.

In the final stage of professional development, the *Sage* counselor has mastered the crafting of creative and targeted family play interventions and engagement with the various family, community, and therapeutic systems, despite fears and vulnerabilities. A family counselor who has reached this place in her professional and personal life has the courage to be authentic and finds freedom in seeing the larger landscape of practice opportunities and limitations. Sages have the capacity to work in balance, but must be careful not to be overly critical of, irritable with, or judgmental about other professionals who are still learning mastery, or with her clients who experience suffering and trauma. They must also recognize when their needs and interests lead them in other directions and toward closure of their family counseling career. With integrity and dignity, they gather the strength to walk away from the work to which they have dedicated themselves, armed with gratitude and "compassionate acceptance" (Arrien, 2006, p. 168).

MINDFULNESS AND SELF-CARE IN FAMILY PLAY COUNSELING WORK

Just as family counselors often ask clients what has brought them to therapy, counselors may also ask it of themselves. What brings us to this work? Is it the clients, the environment, the administrative work, the routine? What do we value most about ourselves? Are the qualities of clarity, humility, comfort, challenge, curiosity, or the satisfaction of deep work with a family involved? As careers progress and caseloads grow, how do we view our professional skills, competence, and resources? These views can be positively or negatively "charged." For example, a family counselor may hold a negative belief about her professional skills after several members storm out of the playroom. She may feel like a failure, believing that she is not smart enough/good enough/capable enough to address her own needs. Alternatively, this same family counselor may have completely different beliefs about herself after a session involving a breakthrough; she may recognize the qualities that make her a good listener, guide, and mediator. C. G. Jung believed that "a good half of every treatment . . . consists in the doctor's examining himself. . . . It is his own hurt that gives the measure of his power to heal" (Jung, 1966, p. 116). Unfortunately, if self-reflection and self-examination practices are not followed, a family play counselor might negate her own needs and fuse with the intense emotional struggles of the families and children with whom she works.

Because of the importance of personal and professional needs, individuals must prepare adequately for their journeys as family play counselors. Just as a vacation requires appropriate packing, counselors need to think about their metaphorical baggage and the restrictions of what they can reasonably carry. Mindfulness practices that include body awareness, awareness of levels of empathic attunement, meditation, yoga, breath work, and stress reduction (Kornfield, 2008) can assist counselors in having the strength to carry these "suitcases." Similarly, Crenshaw (2014), and Counselman and Weber (2004), discuss the benefits of self-reflection through regular supervision and consultation as a way to "distribute the weight" of the suitcases. In these confidential sessions, counselors can share reactions to events in sessions, celebrate personal triumphs, and challenge themselves to think about what is working, what is not, and what they find most taxing among the interactions of family, organizational, or bureaucratic constructs. Through these gatherings (either in person or via phone or Internet), counselors can offer comfort to one another with words and with shared silence. The message is vital: "You are not alone." A "limited disclosure" approach, which includes obtaining permission to discuss a topic from the group, is the most respectful way to ask for help and limits vicarious traumatization. Journal writing (Allan & Bertoia, 1992), dreamwork examination (Bosnak, 1996), ongoing participation in physical activity (Kornfield, 2008; van der Kolk, 2014), and engagement in social and community activities (Norcross & Guy, 2007) also contribute to extending and deepening the process of self-reflection. These activities can be commitments the family counselor makes to himself, so he can be the best therapist possible, as "imperfectly perfect" as an intelligent, well-educated, caring professional can be. The following suggestions for practicing self-care address the biological, physical, emotional, and cognitive needs of family play counselors, and also highlight the importance of mindfulness in daily practice.

Biological Self-Care: Applying the Brakes

Because family counselors are confronted with multiple forms of stress throughout their days, it is important that they pay attention to and understand the impact that their work can have on their physiological well-being. Clinicians can benefit from familiarizing themselves with the theory of autonomic nervous system (ANS) arousal, discussed at length by Rothschild (2006), in an effort to increase self-monitoring and awareness. The ANS consists of two branches, the sympathetic nervous system (the "accelerator") and the parasympathetic nervous system (the "brakes"). These systems are responsible for regulating heart rate, breathing, and other functions during and after stressful experiences (Siegel, 2015).

Rothschild (2003) discusses the framework for "applying the brakes," using the term as a metaphor for helping to manage overstressed clients engaging in trauma therapy. In her later work, Rothschild (2006) made the point that professionals, too, need to recognize their own bodily sensations and affective states and regulate their response to traumatic engagement with clients. She encourages the practice of physical self-care to ensure empathic engagement and regulate physiological arousal states related to stress, and the practice of clear thinking when engaging in challenging therapy situations (p. 3). Employing the term is also a reminder to reduce hyperarousal for the therapist, particularly during challenging family play counseling sessions, in order to protect against " . . . the direct impact of client material. . . . Putting on the brakes will help therapists monitor and manage their own vulnerability to compassion fatigue, vicarious traumatization, and burnout on a day-to-day, session-to-session basis" (Rothschild, 2006, p. 113).

When a counselor regularly uses self-regulation and can "put on the brakes," he can calm his autonomic nervous system and possibly think more clearly. Those readers interested in learning more about Rothschild's suggestions and ANS arousal can find exercises and practice suggestions in the references sections of Rothschild's books (2003, 2006).

Emotional Self-Care: It's Okay to Cry

Families can project and act out dark aspects of emotional expression and experiences in the playroom, such as rage, jealousy, inadequacy, and bitterness (Remen, 2006). Family counselors can easily become overwhelmed in those encounters when there is the feeling of unbearable suffering on the part of family members who demonstrate high levels of disorganization. Furthermore,

> [p]rotecting ourselves from loss rather than grieving and healing our losses is one of the major causes of burnout. Very few of the professionals I have treated for burnout actually came in saying that they were burned out. I don't think most of them knew. The most common thing I've been told is. . . . "Terrible things happen in front of me and I feel nothing." . . . Only people who do care can get to this place of numbness. We burn out not because we don't care but because we don't grieve. We burn out because we have allowed our hearts to become so filled with loss that we have no room left to care. (Remen, 2006, p. 52)

Counselors who permit themselves the opportunity to grieve their families' suffering can ward off burnout. After painful sessions, it is a professional and responsible course of action for family counselors to seek trusted colleagues or personal therapists to help manage the unbearable or residual feelings constellated from within the transference. Moreover, family play counselors' tears in session are sometimes appropriate. Each family counselor has the right to decide what the "best" response is in difficult sessions. Zur (2015) clarifies that it is a boundary *crossing*, not a violation, to express the depth of sorrow and compassion within the therapy session.

Cognitive Self-Care: Reframing Problems with IDEAs

Family counselors who experience approaching clinical burnout may struggle with thoughts that foster feelings of inadequacy and shame (Brown, 2012). Interpreting symbols requires a healthy perspective that can incorporate many layers of meaning and association (Green, 2014). Because of this, the ability to reframe thoughts, consider alternative possibilities, and respect limits is essential for family play counselors, particularly as these skills pertain to therapist self-care. An approach that can quickly guide therapists to more fully appreciate their situations and subsequent choices can be found in the acronym IDEA:

1. *Identify* the problem and related symptoms, such as sleeplessness, ruminating about a client problem or negative event in a therapy session, or "numbing out" after a difficult session.
2. *Define* how the family counselor is experiencing the issue based on both negative and positive beliefs. For example, self-denigrating statements might include thoughts such as, "When I feel trapped in working with this family, I blank out and can't help them find workable solutions," or "I am not up to the task of helping this complicated family work out their problems." Alternatively, the therapist must identify positive self-statements; for example, "I am capable of handling my feelings when I get overwhelmed by a family's conflicting demands," and "I can easily and comfortably find workable solutions to the problems this family faces."
3. *Evaluate* options, such as calling a therapist for personal use, consulting with a colleague, contacting or organizing a peer support group or professional group listserv, reviewing (and possibly revising) a personal care plan, consulting resources (e.g., coursework, books, workshops on clinical burnout), and scheduling time for self-care (e.g., planning a small vacation, building time into daily routine for rest and rejuvenation).
4. *Act* or engage in one or two self-help activities, according to ability and energy level.

Flexibility includes an understanding of appropriate boundaries and limit setting. Going too far in one direction may lead counselors to feel taken advantage of; going too far in the other direction leads to unbounded permissiveness (Zur, 2015). As Henry Ford stated, "Givers have to set limits because takers rarely do." There is an apocryphal story about a family counselor who, in order to set permissive guidelines so that everyone would feel comfortable, allowed a child in the family session to paint the counselor's glasses completely, while the rest of the children swept toys off the shelves. Family counselors have to set limits and guidelines all the time, not only for their clients' well-being, but for their own as well.

Family play counseling is difficult and harsh work at times. It is important to find pathways for humor. Family play counselors can assign families—and themselves—homework in watching humorous television shows, practicing lighthearted banter, singing, and laughing with each other in sessions. These are all ways to remind everyone that life has moments other than dark feelings and distressing actions.

Self-Care through Mindfulness: Be-ing is Good Enough

A yoga teacher asked how much time her students would devote to a home practice. Students mumbled something about 20–30 minutes daily, and then the teacher and class began laughing. The more honest, realistic answer was maybe 5–10 minutes. So, too, must counselors determine what is reasonable for their daily schedules and lives and then adjust for unexpected crises, demands, and schedule changes. Devoting time to mindful self-care activities requires discipline that depends on responsibilities and energy levels at work and in personal life.

Professor Hayao Kawai, a wise teacher, once said, "Learn to do nothing. Well." New and seasoned counselors alike can benefit from reminding themselves that our *presence* with families means, simply, the state of being present to and with them. Counselors do this by sharing time, energy, creativity, focus, teachings, and knowledge, giving each family the fullest and most imperfectly complete attention possible. Family counselors share enthusiasm, questions, heartfelt concern, confusion, and apologies for making mistakes, failing to understand, or neglecting to respect what has been presented in sessions. It doesn't mean silence, although at times silence is required of therapists. It means that family counselors give generously of themselves in and out of the office, to family, friends, health, love, and themselves. That is good enough.

It can be difficult to demonstrate such presence at all times, particularly during a long day of difficult clients and cases. A statement as simple as "I welcome this moment fully. I greet it as a friend" (adapted from Boorstein, 2014) is a simple, daily practice that can be used by counselors to bring themselves back to the present moment. Additionally, counselors may also choose to apply some of the breath work taught to families as a means of grounding themselves in the present.

Breathing in deeply and breathing out very slowly is a beneficial practice that can be employed while glancing out the office window or in synchronization with monitoring a family member's breaths. In addition to grounding, this simple focus on breathing enables the release of energy and affect that is so easy to hold in during each session. Finally, family counselors may delineate and meditate on moments of joy after a meaningful session. Crenshaw (2014) reminds counselors that professional development is a lifetime process and that continuous reflection protects again burnout and facilitates treatment progress for clients.

CONCLUSION

Family counselors who utilize play therapy interventions are encouraged to recognize the need for and participate in self-care and mindfulness practices focused on biological, physical, cognitive, emotional, and social well-being. Family play counselors are confronted regularly with pressures and challenges, and addressing them through the activities presented in this chapter may assist with reducing the feelings of overwhelming stress inherent in the clinical work with families. There is a community of welcoming professionals in peer consultation opportunities, as well as practices that can help with self-regulation and cognitive self-care. Compassionate understanding of the archetypal journey family play counselors travel throughout the professional life cycle—the Fool, the Innocent, the Seeker, the Hero/Warrior, the Caregiver, the Ruler, and the Sage—contributes to overall understanding and competence. In addition to seeking peer and supervisory support, family play counselors should familiarize themselves with strategies to manage vicarious traumatization and other work-related stressors. It is vital that family play counselors remember that they are not alone, and that the very qualities of engagement, dedication, and competence that brought the early stage family play counselor into this career path will help with preventing burnout when regularly used as a self-reflective practice.

It is important for family play counselors to remember that self-care can be quite simple. Considering the answers to questions such as "What am I curious about?" and "How do I feel about the way I am treating my clients?" can ground counselors in the present moment and provide direction. Family play counselors need to take the time to remind themselves that a moment's reflection on each day can serve as a fresh start, and that challenging clinical experiences, while only temporary, can be transformative over a professional lifetime.

Being fully present in each moment is a gift. Therapists need to remind themselves to breathe it in and then let it go. What an amazing invitation: "Be grateful for whatever comes" even if it is "a crowd of sorrows . . . clearing you out for some new delight," as a guide for professional and personal practice.

The Guest House

This being human is a guest house.
Every morning a new arrival.

A joy, a depression, a meanness,
some momentary awareness comes
As an unexpected visitor.

Welcome and entertain them all!
Even if they're a crowd of sorrows,
who violently sweep your house
empty of its furniture,
still treat each guest honorably.
He may be clearing you out
for some new delight.

The dark thought, the shame, the malice,
meet them at the door laughing,
and invite them in.

Be grateful for whoever comes,
because each has been sent
as a guide from beyond.[1]

NOTE

1. Reprinted with permission from Coleman Barks.

REFERENCES

Allan, J., & Bertoia, J. (1992). *Written paths to healing: Education and Jungian child counseling*. Dallas, TX: Spring Publications.

Arrien, A. (2006). *The second half of life: Opening the eight gates of wisdom*. Boulder, CO: Sounds True, Inc.

Bakker, A. B., & Costa, P. L. (2014). Chronic job burnout and daily functioning: A theoretical analysis.*Burnout Research, 1*(3), 112–119.

Boorstein, S. (2014). A bad day at the airport. *Shambala Sun*. Retrieved from http://lionsroar.com/bad-day-airport/.

Bosnak, R. (1996). *Tracks in the wilderness of dreaming*. New York, NY: Delacorte Press.

Brown, B. (2012). *The power of vulnerability: Teachings on authenticity, connection, and courage*. Available from http://www.soundstrue.com/store/the-power-of-vulnerability-2917.html.

Counselman, E. F., & Weber, R. L. . (2004). Organizing and maintaining peer supervision groups.*International Journal of Group Psychotherapy, 54*(2), 125–143.

Crenshaw, D. A. (2014). Reflective practice in play therapy and supervision. In D. A. Crenshaw & A. L. Stewart (Eds.), *Play therapy: A comprehensive guide to theory and practice* (pp. 484–495). New York, NY: Guilford Press.

Green, E. J. (2014). *The handbook of Jungian play therapy with children & adolescents*. Baltimore, MD: Johns Hopkins University Press.
Hollis, J. (2005). *Finding meaning in the second half of life: How to finally, really grow up*. New York, NY: Gotham Books [Kindle DX version]. Retrieved from Amazon.com.
Jung, C. G. (1966). *The collected works of C.G. Jung, Volume 16: Practice of psychotherapy*. G. Adler & R. F. C. Hull (Trans.). Princeton, NJ: Princeton University Press.
Kornfield, J. (2008). *The wise heart: A guide to the universal teachings of Buddhist psychology*. New York, NY: Random House [Kindle DX version]. Retrieved from Amazon.com.
Norcross, J. C. & Guy, J. D., Jr. (2007). *Leaving it at the office: A guide to psychotherapist self-care*. New York, NY: Guilford Press.
Pearson, C. S. (2012). *Awakening the heroes within: Twelve archetypes to help us find ourselves and transform our world*. New York, NY: HarperCollins.
Pirke Avot, Sayings of the Jewish Fathers, Traditional Text. (2005). Public Domain Books [Kindle DX version]. Retrieved from Amazon.com.
Remen, N. R. (2006). Professionals don't cry. In *Kitchen table wisdom: Stories that heal*. New York, NY: Berkeley Publishing Group.
Rothschild, B. (2003). *The body remembers casebook: Unifying methods and models in the treatment of trauma and PTSD*. New York, NY: W. W. Norton & Company, Inc. [Kindle DX version]. Retrieved from Amazon.com.
Rothschild, B. (2006). *Help for the helper: Self-care strategies for managing burnout and stress*. New York, NY: W. W. Norton & Company, Inc.
Siegel, D. J. (2015). *The developing mind: How relationships and the brain interact to shape who we are* (2nd ed.). New York, NY: Guilford Press.
Sorgaard, K. W., Ryan, P., Hill, R., & Dawson, I. (2007). Sources of stress and burnout in acute psychiatric care: Inpatient vs. community staff. *Social Psychiatry and Psychiatric Epidemiology, 42*, 794–802.
van der Kolk, B. (2014). *The body keeps the score: Brain, mind, and body in the healing of trauma*. New York, NY: Viking [Kindle DX version.] Retrieved from Amazon.com.
Zur, O. (2015). *Therapeutic boundaries and dual relationships in psychotherapy and counseling*. Zur Institute. Retrieved from http://www.zurinstitute.com/boundariesbrochure.pdf.

Index

Author Index

About the Editors and Contributors

Jennifer N. Baggerly is professor of counseling at the University of North Texas–Dallas. She is past chair of the Board of Directors of the Association for Play Therapy (APT) and the former chair of the APT research committee. Jennifer is a Licensed Professional Counselor Supervisor, a Registered Play Therapist-Supervisor and a Field Traumatologist. A recipient of the Outstanding Play Therapist Award from the Florida Association for Play Therapy, she has provided child mental health services locally and disaster relief services internationally, including victims of 2013 Oklahoma tornados, Hurricane Katrina, and the tsunami in Sri Lanka. Dr. Baggerly's multiple research projects have led to her being recognized as one of the lead play therapy experts in the world. She has over 50 publications, including two books, numerous peer-refereed journal articles, many book chapters, and several videos. She is also the lead editor of the recently published book *Child-Centered Play Therapy Research: The Evidence Base for Effective Practice* and co-author of *Group Play Therapy: A Dynamic Approach*. Jennifer is a recognized authority on play therapy and has presented internationally in Argentina, Canada, England, Sri Lanka, and Taiwan.

Robert Jason Grant is a Licensed Professional Counselor, National Certified Counselor, Registered Play Therapist-Supervisor, and Certified Autism Specialist. He owns and operates a private practice and training clinic in Missouri, where he specializes in play therapy approaches with children, adolescents, adults, couples, and families. Dr. Grant also specializes in working with Autism Spectrum Disorder, neurodevelopmental disorders, and developmental disabilities and is the creator of AutPlay® Therapy, an autism treatment using play therapy, behavioral therapy, and relationship development approaches. He serves as mentor and is a professional board member for the Southwest Autism Network of Missouri and is a contributing writer for the Missouri Autism Report. Dr. Grant is the author of several books including the best-selling *AutPlay® Therapy Handbook* and *Play-Based Interventions for Autism, ADHD, Neurodevelopmental Disorders, and Developmental Disabilities.*

Eric J. Green, PhD, LPC-S, RPT-S, Jungian Sandplay Practitioner, is an associate professor of school counseling in the College of Education at Purdue University in West Lafayette, Indiana. His previous books include *No Child Forgotten*, *Integrating Expressive Arts and Play Therapy with Children*, and *The Handbook of Jungian Play Therapy*. He's also released psychoeducational films through Alexander Street Press, including *Transformative School Counseling*, *Jungian Play Therapy and Sandplay*, and *Expressive Arts with Adolescents*. He's a regularly invited keynote speaker at mental health conferences across the United States and globally. For more information, visit www.drericgreen.com.

Louise F. Guerney earned a PhD in clinical psychology from the Pennsylvania State University. While her husband, Bernard Guerney, Jr., was director of the psychological clinical program at Rutgers University, Louise joined him in developing Filial Family Therapy. Later, they both returned to Penn State University, where Louise taught Child-Centered Play Therapy (CCPT), and Filial Family Therapy for 24 years. She retired as professor emerita in 1995. Currently, she is associated with the National Institute of Relationship Enhancement (NIRE) in Bethesda, Maryland, where she offers a very occasional workshop on play therapy and working with parents. She also continues to offer limited consulting/supervision in CCPT and Filial Family Therapy.

Rosalind Heiko, PhD, ISST, CST-T, is a psychologist and sandplay teacher who consults internationally and nationally on sandplay and therapeutic storytelling. Her chapter "Spontaneous Storytelling and the Sandplay Journey of an Emotionally Despairing Girl" was published in 2010 in Eliana Gil's edited book *Working With Children to Heal Interpersonal Trauma: The Healing Power of Play* (Guilford Press). She is also published in the *Journal of Sandplay Therapy*. Dr. Heiko is the founder of NC Sandplay Training and a past board member of the Sandplay Therapists of America. She is director of

Pediatric & Family Psychology, P.A., in Cary, North Carolina. She has worked with children, adolescents, and families professionally since 1983. She is an Approved Teaching Consultant in Clinical Hypnosis (ASCH) and is trained in Eye Movement Desensitization and Reprocessing (EMDR), also holding national certification in school psychology (NCSP). She believes wholeheartedly in the power of laughter and the delight that sandplay brings to her clients and trainees. You can reach her through her website: www.drheiko.com.

Linda E. Homeyer, PhD, LPC-S, RPT-S, is a professor at Texas State University. Linda is also director of the faith-based Door of Hope Counseling Center, where she provides play therapy, sand tray therapy, parenting, and supervision. She served two terms as president of the Association for Play Therapy Board of Directors and is the 2013 recipient of their Lifetime Achievement Award. Linda teaches internationally and named an Honorary Professor of International Studies by Texas State University. Dr. Homeyer co-authored *Sandtray Therapy: A Practical Manual*; *The Handbook of Group Play Therapy*; and many other books, chapters, and journal articles. Her work has been translated into Chinese, Russian, Korean, and Spanish.

Sueann Kenney-Noziska, MSW, LISW, LCSW, RPT-S, specializes in using play therapy with abused and traumatized children, adolescents, and families. In addition to maintaining a private practice, she is an instructor in the Play Therapy Certificate Program at the University of California San Diego, a guest lecturer, internationally recognized speaker, & author of *Techniques-Techniques-Techniques: Play-Based Activities for Children, Adolescents, and Families.*

Christine M. Koehler, PhD, is a pediatric diagnostic evaluator and registered play therapist in Dallas, Texas. Her training in both clinical psychology and counseling has led to her integrated approach, which pulls from both medical and holistic models—blending the science with the art of working with parents and their unique children to identify and address emotional, behavioral, and learning challenges in the context of the whole family. She also provides canine-assisted play therapy which can be useful in assessing clinically relevant dynamics within the family while enhancing the fun of therapeutic work for all ages.

Terry Kottman, PhD, NCC, RPT-S, LMHC, founded The Encouragement Zone in Cedar Falls, Iowa, where she provides play therapy training and supervision, life coaching, play therapy, counseling, and "playshops" for women. Terry developed Adlerian play therapy, an approach to counseling children, adolescents, and adults that combines the ideas and techniques of individual psychology and play therapy. She regularly presents workshops and writes about play therapy, activity-based counseling, school counseling, and life coaching. She is the author of *Partners in Play: An Adlerian Approach to Play Therapy*; *Play Therapy: Basics and Beyond*; *Active Interventions for Kids and Teens*; and several other books.

Marshall Lyles, LPC-S, LMFT-S, RPT-S, works as an associate director at the Center for Relational Care in Austin, Texas. Specializing in family therapy for adoptive and trauma-based issues, Marshall provides therapy services, conducts supervision, and frequently presents at workshops and trainings. Additionally, he is pursuing a PhD in marriage and family therapy from St. Mary's University.

Kristin K. Meany-Walen, PhD, LMHC, RPT, NCC, is an assistant professor of counseling at the University of Northern Iowa in Cedar Falls. She has published and presented on topics such as Adlerian play therapy, expressive arts, counseling preadolescents and adolescents, and working with parents as therapeutic agents of change. Her primary research focus is Adlerian play therapy with elementary-aged children.

Catherine Munns, PsyD, recently obtained her graduate degree in clinical and school psychology. She is currently a postdoctoral fellow working toward her state and provincial licensure and registered play therapist certification. Working with children, adolescents, and families has been a demonstrated focus throughout her training, including providing play therapy services in Theraplay and non-directive play therapy. Areas of specialty include pediatric and child clinical psychology, autism spectrum disorders, and integrated primary care with children and adults. She has clinical experience with children, adolescents, and families in a range of settings, including community agencies, schools, hospitals, and medical clinics. She has presented at state, national, and international conferences on Theraplay and research in developmental psychology. As well, she has co-authored a chapter on Theraplay.

Evangeline Munns, PhD, CPsych, RPT-S, is a certified clinical psychologist. She is a registered trainer/supervisor with the Theraplay Institute in Chicago, the Association for Play Therapy in the United States, and the Canadian Association for Child and Play Therapy (on the latter she serves on the education committee). She is a popular presenter and has given numerous workshops on play therapy across Canada, the United States, and internationally. In recent years, much of her time has been spent in training and supervising therapists in Theraplay and/or nondirective and Filial Play Therapy including teaching as a guest lecturer at Western University in London, Ontario, and Sir Wilfred Laurier in Kitchener, Ontario. With over forty years of experience working with children and their families, she offers a rich knowledge in the children's mental health field. She has served as a consultant to many agencies. Dr. Munns has written numerous articles on Theraplay and has edited two books: *Theraplay: Innovations in Attachment-Enhancing Play Therapy* (2000) and *Applications of Family and Group Theraplay* (2009). In the past she received the Monica Herbert award from the Canadian Association for Child and Play Therapy (CACPT) for "an outstanding contribution to the field of play therapy in Canada." Recently, she was the first therapist described in a list of the five top play therapists in Canada, by CACPT.

Amie C. Myrick is a licensed clinical professional counselor (LCPC) whose clinical experience includes work with children, adolescents, adults, and families. She currently treats youth for anxiety, mood, trauma, and self-injurious symptoms as a trauma therapist and general counselor. She completed her graduate training at Johns Hopkins University and completed a post-Master's certificate in play therapy. In addition to her clinical experience, Ms. Myrick has been involved in research for trauma-related disorders for over 10 years, and she is currently a research consultant for a large-scale, longitudinal treatment outcome study of adults with dissociative disorders. She has had articles and book chapters published on a range of issues related to play therapy, trauma, and nontrauma treatment with youth.

Mary Anne Paré, M.Ed., is a child and family therapist whose career began in the field of child care. Recognizing the influence of family on the children with whom she was working, Mary Anne pursued training in family systems theory and practice at Pacific Coast Family Therapy Training Institute, Vancouver, British Columbia, and in the Master's Program of the Counseling Psychology Department at the University of British Columbia, Canada. She received seven years of supervision in Jungian play therapy, concurrent with supervision in multigenerational family therapy. Her work in agencies, treatment centers, and private practice included both family therapy and play therapy. The conclusion that the needs of the two generations are inseparable and both must be addressed in order to effect long-term change for families led Mary Anne to the evolution of an integrated approach that incorporates the theories and practices of Jungian play therapy and family systems. Mary Anne has worked with children and families for 35 years, both in the mental health system and in private practice. She has provided teaching and supervision in both Canada and the United States for play therapists, family therapists, school counselors, and mental health practitioners.

Janine Shelby, PhD, RPT-S, is director of the Child Trauma Clinic at Harbor-UCLA and associate professor in the Geffen School of Medicine at UCLA. Dr. Shelby's supervisorial, clinical, training, consulting, academic, and humanitarian relief work focus on the delivery of evidence-based treatments in developmentally and culturally sensitive ways. Inspired by her clinical experiences in both community settings and international humanitarian work, Dr. Shelby has presented widely in this country as well as in dozens of countries abroad.

Glade L. Topham, PhD, LMFT, is an associate professor of human development and family science at Oklahoma State University, where he serves as the program coordinator for the graduate program in marriage and family therapy. He received his BS and MS at Brigham Young University, and his PhD from Texas Tech University. His research and clinical interests are focused on the treatment of parents and children within the context of the parent-child relationship and the prevention and treatment of child obesity through family-based interventions.

Risë VanFleet, PhD, RPT-S, CDBC is a licensed psychologist, registered play therapist-supervisor, and certified dog behavior consultant with over 40 years of experience in a wide range of mental health positions and settings. She has trained thousands of clinicians in play therapy throughout the world, and especially in Filial Therapy, Animal Assisted Play Therapy, and treatment planning for highly challenging children and families. She has authored dozens of chapters and articles, as well as several acclaimed books in the field. She is the founder and president of the Family Enhancement & Play Therapy Center in Boiling Springs, Pennsylvania, as well as the Playful Pooch Program and the International Institute for Animal Assisted Play Therapy Studies. She is a past president and board chair of the Association for Play Therapy. She has been honored by numerous national and international awards for her training programs and writing, and recently earned the Award for Distinguished Contributions to the Science and Profession of Psychology by the Pennsylvania Psychological Association. She regularly provides in-depth training programs for play therapists and family therapists, as well as online courses. She can be reached at www.risevanfleet.com.

Brittany Wilson, MA, NCC, LPC-Intern, is currently a doctoral candidate at the University of North Texas, where she specializes in play therapy, clinical supervision, and child assessment. Ms. Wilson additionally specializes in work with children exhibiting disruptive behaviors. Ms. Wilson serves as the Assistant Director of Clinical Services at a local counseling clinic at the University of North Texas, where she provides intensive weekly group and individual supervision to master's level internship students and consultation to doctoral level counseling interns. Ms. Wilson has extensive clinical experience working with children, adolescents, and adults. She has advanced training in individual play therapy, group play therapy, activity therapy, and filial therapy and plans to pursue a career in counselor education upon her graduation in May 2016.

www.ingramcontent.com/pod-product-compliance
Ingram Content Group UK Ltd.
Pitfield, Milton Keynes, MK11 3LW, UK
UKHW012039150926
475560UK00001B/80

9 781442 244047